ROBERT KAREN, PH.D

THE
FORGIVING
SELF

Robert Karen, Ph.D., is an award-winning
author and clinical psychologist in private
practice as well as an associate clinical pro-
fessor at the Derner Institute of Advanced
Psychology Studies at Adelphi University. The author of *Becoming Attached*,
he lives in New York City.

THE
FORGIVING
SELF

The Road from
Resentment to Connection

THE
FORGIVING
SELF

ROBERT KAREN

ANCHOR BOOKS

A DIVISION OF RANDOM HOUSE, INC.   NEW YORK

The Library of Congress has cataloged the Doubleday edition as follows:
Karen, Robert.
The forgiving self : the road from resentment to connection / Robert Karen.
p. cm.
Includes bibliographical references and index.
1. Forgiveness. I. Title.
BF637.F67 K37 2001
155.9'222—dc21
00-043004

Anchor ISBN: 978-0-385-48874-7

For my father, Samuel Karen, 1912–1999

"Like a rich jewel on an Ethiop's ear."

And for my mother, Minna, and my sister, Wendy

With more to come.

CONTENTS

PART III

THE LANDSCAPE OF CONNECTION

AUTHOR'S
NOTE

The historical events and the interviews with friends and others in this book are factual, if sometimes disguised. The patient histories, on the other hand, are mostly fictions. I was tempted to say that they had been heavily disguised, but that does not adequately describe the extent of alteration, amalgamation, transmogrification, and invention. I hope I have nonetheless done justice to the emotional truth I am trying to illustrate with them.

THE
FORGIVING
SELF

PSYCHOLOGY
IN FORGIVING AND
NOT FORGIVING

IN ONE OF THE MOST FAMOUS PHOTOS TO COME OUT OF THE VIETnam War, a small girl is running naked down the road, with an expression of unimaginable terror, her clothes burned off and her body scorched by napalm. The man who coordinated the raid on this child's village in June 1972 was a twenty-four-year-old U.S. Army helicopter pilot and operations officer named John Plummer. The day after the raid, conducted by South Vietnamese airplanes, Plummer saw the photo in the military newspaper *Stars and Stripes* and was devastated. Twenty-four years later Plummer told an Associated Press reporter: "It just knocked me to my knees. And that was when I knew I could never talk about this." The guilt over the bombing raid had become a lonely torment. He suffered periodic nightmares that included the scene from the photo accompanied by the sounds of children screaming.

The girl in the photo, Pham Thi Kim Phuc, survived seventeen operations, eventually relocated to Toronto, and became an occasional goodwill ambassador for UNESCO. In 1996 Plummer heard that Kim would be speaking at a Veterans Day observance in Washington, not far from his home.

Kim's speech included the following: "If I could talk face to face with the pilot who dropped the bombs, I would tell him we cannot change history, but we should try to do good things for the present. . . ." Plummer, in the audience, wrote her a note: "I am that man," and asked an officer to take it to her. At the end of the speech, he pushed through the crowd to reach her, and soon they were face-to-face. "She just opened her arms to me," Plummer recounted. "I fell into her arms sobbing. All I could say is, 'I'm so sorry. I'm just so sorry.' "

"It's all right," Kim responded. "I forgive. I forgive." Five months later, still connected by their peculiar history, the two were shown in an AP wirephoto, their heads touching, almost cheek to cheek, his arm around her, both smiling with an almost incongruous delight, as if he had never ordered the raid that left her body scarred and in permanent pain and he did not live with recurrent nightmares. When I called Plummer four years later, Kim had just been to visit.

The need to be forgiven is a profound factor in our lives. The story of the pilot and the girl touches us because that need lives so strongly in us, and it is rare that we see it played out in such direct and dramatic form. And yet in our everyday lives we are touched by forgiveness and haunted by its lack in a myriad of small and often unnoticed ways. Can we be forgiven our insensitivity? Our cruelties? Our betrayals? Can we be forgiven for having critically, damagingly, let someone down? Can we be forgiven the things in us that feel so terrible we dare not speak them? The feelings of others contribute to how we define ourselves to ourselves, and often it is through them, their tolerance, their perspective, their generosity, that we are able to forgive what had seemed unpardonable in us before.

One morning not long ago I was in session with a patient, a woman I had been seeing for several years, for whom revenge was such a powerful force that she had a dark view of herself and her capacity for love. During this session, I suddenly thought I had been making an error in my work with her. She was preoccupied with a superior where she worked, a married man with whom she had had a flirtation going for months but who had no interest in leaving his wife for her or even, it seemed, in having a sexual affair.

She is obsessed with talking about him, trying to figure him out, trying to enlist me in figuring him out. We've been here before with other men. I try to derail her obsessive train of thought. "We're not dealing with *you*," I say, "with your tears, your loneliness." I tell her she's afraid of getting close to this part of her, what I call her lovelornness. This hits her and she cries. I remind her of a central feature of her childhood, the rejection she felt by her father, which had been sudden, brutal, inexplicable. She makes an irritable, disgusted sound. "What are you saying by that?" I ask. "You're too tough!" she screams. I respond, "I haven't been tough enough."

After I say it, it occurs to me that this criticism of my work with her—"I haven't been tough enough"—spoken with concern but without self-recrimination, could gather into something more threatening to me. Right now I can tolerate the possibility that I've made an error without my legitimacy as a therapist being undermined. And yet I'm aware that that could change. Indeed, the change has already begun making little knock-knocks at the door.

"What do you mean you haven't been tough enough?" she says.

"I'm concerned that I may have done you a disservice. You're very stubborn and you need a strong push." She thinks about my self-criticism and seems to be wondering if it's true and whether she should join in. After a moment, she pierces the silence: "What *difference* does it make!" she says with a disgusted fling of her hand, as if to say, "This is irrelevant! Who cares? Why are we bothering with this! Let's get back to business!" The depth of my self-indictment hits me just as I am liberated from it, freed by a forgiving wave of her hand from a bad internal place.

Forgiveness and grudge are at the heart of many human dramas. People are humiliated, jilted, stabbed in the back, robbed of their inheritance, wounded by selfishness and inconsideration, steered wrong by a trusted person. A child finds his father hanging in the closet. A parent leaves home and never returns. A grown child becomes a drug addict who remorselessly drains the family of every emotional and financial resource. The Marlon Brando character in *On the Waterfront,* a promising boxer, is betrayed by his crooked brother in a deal with the mob: "I coulda been a contender!" he cries in a celebrated scene. Two years earlier, the maker of that film, Elia Kazan, committed what many saw as an equally harrowing sellout when he testified before the House Un-American Activities Committee, naming friends and associates who had been with him in the Communist Party, thereby making himself the target of hatreds that last to this day.

In great stories of forgiveness, like *King Lear* or *Pride and Prejudice*, a wronged person finds it within her heart to take back the person who betrayed her. In the Austen novel, Elizabeth is able to overcome the arrogance and class snobbery that caused Mr. Darcy to disparage her family and almost ruin the chances of Elizabeth's sister with the man she loved. In the end, softened by Darcy's contrition and charmed by his wit, she sees the good in him and in doing so she herself grows.

In *King Lear*, Shakespeare takes forgiveness to a still deeper place. The ill-appreciated daughter, Cordelia, is disowned by Lear, her father, an old king on the verge of voluntary retirement, because she refuses his absurd and humiliating request for a public display of her affection. She is banished from the kingdom in favor of her treacherous older sisters who smoothly execute the king's demand and promptly inherit his kingdom. But Cordelia is touched by the tyrant in his ruin. In the course of the play, Lear suffers greatly at the hands of his haughty, ruthless daughters and eventually flees to save his life. Toward the end, aided by the few friends he has left, he is on the run and trapped in a terrible storm. When at last he is deposited safely in Cordelia's tent, pitiful and nearly mad, she gazes at him asleep, her heart wrung by the condition he is in, and says:

> *Mine enemy's dog,*
> *Though he had bit me, should have stood that night*
> *Against my fire . . .*

There is no spite or bitterness in this woman. Cordelia's heart goes out to her father even though she does not know whether his heart has softened toward her. She is different from Elizabeth in this respect. Cordelia will not debase herself, but she remains tender even in pride. Although Elizabeth, too, is an uncommon woman, her pride is of the more common variety: You have crossed me, despicable man, and now you shall never darken my door! But in her, too, love runs strong. She will nurse her resentments only so far. This healthy balance between love and pride, evident in both women, is a cornerstone of the forgiving spirit.

The depth of poignancy that forgiveness can achieve, including its immense potential to uplift, is realized by Shakespeare in the same play when Cordelia and her father finally speak. Lear awakes, realizes he is with the daughter whose love he threw away, and, seeing her expression, manages these words in his semi-addled state:

> *I pray, weep not.*
> *If you have poison for me, I will drink it.*
> *I know you do not love me; for your sisters*
> *Have, as I do remember, done me wrong.*
> *You have some cause, they have not.*

Cordelia, weeping, can only respond:

> *No cause, no cause.*

This is one of the memorable moments in our literature. Whatever anger Cordelia may have harbored evaporates when she sees what has befallen her father; and Lear, who has steadily grown both in self-awareness and in his ability to appreciate the feelings and sufferings of people other than himself, rejoices in the midst of his ruin for he knows and values love in a way he never has before.

FORGIVENESS IS AN ASPECT of the workings of love. It can be a bridge back from hatred and alienation as well as a liberation from two kinds of hell: bitterness and victimhood on one side; guilt, shame, and self-recrimination on the other. The wish to repair a wounded relationship, whether it takes the form of forgiveness, apology, or some other bridging gesture, is a basic human impulse. The need to forgive—which may grow out of understanding, gratitude, sympathy, regret over the hurt one has caused by not forgiving, or simply a wish to reunite—may be as strong as the need to be forgiven, even if it comes upon us more subtly.

All sustained relationships depend to some extent on forgiveness. Successful marriage means an inevitable round of disappointment, anger, withdrawal, repair. People hurt each other no matter how much love they share, and it's a truism that the greatest hurts are meted out by the closest of intimates. No friendship, no marriage, no family connections of any kind would last if the silent reparative force of forgiveness were not working almost constantly to counteract the incessant corrosive effects of resentment and bitterness, which would otherwise tear us apart. Without forgiveness there could be no allowance for human frailty. We would keep moving on, searching for perfect connections with mythical partners who would never hurt or disappoint. In that sense, forgiveness should be thought of not only as a discrete event but also as a way of being.

We come to relationships with certain strengths and liabilities in this respect. One woman can laugh at a man's peccadilloes and forgive even his stupid excuses because she sees through them to a sweetness that touches her. Her attitude gives him a freedom from guilt for which he is deeply grateful. But let her ever feel truly disrespected by him and she goes to a dark place from which she may feel unable to extricate herself. Another woman takes offense at every forgotten anniversary, at every incident of lateness, at every flirtation with a waitress. But there is almost nothing her husband does that will not be mended by a heartfelt display of affection, contrition, or concern. She is quick to bristle and complain, but she is equally quick to melt.

When we think about forgiveness we tend to imagine one person deeply and decidedly wronged by another. But most relationships lack the simplicity of Lear's grotesque misbehavior and Cordelia's innocence. Rather, so much good and bad is going back and forth, and each person is so deeply implicated in everything that happens, that it is not always so clear who needs to apologize and who needs to forgive. Indeed, in such cases, the struggle to forgive and the struggle to apologize are barely distinguishable. I'll cite an example from my practice:

A man, part of a couple I am seeing, complains to me, "My wife has no forgiveness," and he is in agony over it. Six years ago he had an affair, and since then they have reconciled. His wife says she has forgiven him, but she still makes him take an AIDS test every six months, because, she says, she cannot trust him. She won't acknowledge that she is holding a grudge. She can't quite see it. Nor has she been able to grasp how her sexual coldness toward him contributed to his straying. The original blow hit her in such a deep place that all of her thoughts and feelings stay tightly organized around her wound. What is more, his current behavior—barking, raging, denouncing—when combined with her psychology, makes it hard for her to shake feeling like a victim. Unconsciously, she believes that he is much bigger than she and that her grudge is her only source of power: Unless she keeps him in purgatory, constantly begging to be let out, she will get crushed again. It is a sadistic solution, one that satisfies both of their psychologies in ways they cannot see. He reacts to her withheld love like a small, panicked child, pleading and dependent, and then retaliates by bullying her mercilessly. And they've been stuck there, going round and round, each one a victim, trying to live a married life with a bitter, indissoluble wedge between them.

I have heard it expressed that forgiveness is something one can decide upon and give freely at any moment, that it is solely a matter of choice. I believe people are capable of sudden and authentic changes of heart and that they can make important positive choices even when their hearts resist. But the conditions critical to forgiveness, both internal and external, should not be overlooked. If someone told either the husband or wife in this couple, for instance, "You can make the choice here and now to forgive and return to your former love," I would consider that advice shallow and possibly destructive. Each of them is too deeply caught up in a murderous, victimized state that is beyond their capacity to manage. Too many layers of psychology stand in the way. This is not to say they don't have choices. They do, and certain of those choices can move them in a more positive direction, in the direction of forgiveness, assuming that's the way they want to go. They both have inner resources they are unaware of, resources that might surprise them. It is just this zone, where our psychology entraps us and yet also holds the potential to liberate us, that most interests me.

I will not focus in this book on what might be considered acts of evil—like the Nazi extermination of the Jews or the other holocausts of our century in Armenia, Cambodia, Rwanda, or elsewhere. The subject of response to such gross malignant behavior is beyond my scope. Nor will I devote much attention to personal cataclysms—such as the murder of a child, detention and torture for one's political views, or monstrous parental abuse. Although what I write about here is not unrelated to such injuries, they deserve special attention. Most of the hurts and conflicts in this book are of a subtler nature and almost all emerge in the context of standing relationships. They arise out of rage, envy, hatred, selfishness, idealization, false hope, misunderstanding, and all the other frailties to which human psychology is prone. They solidify into the resentments we can't let go of even if we no longer think about them, resentments and silent grudges that comprise the scar tissue of everyday life. Even in good relationships the scar tissue exists, often in the form of things we tiptoe around and don't speak about anymore. How that scar tissue forms and what it takes to dissolve it constitute the core of my concerns. Why do we stop talking to each other about certain things that bother us? Why do we experience ourselves as victims when we've been hurt by someone we love? Why do we needlessly hold on to victim status? Why would we choose to live in resentment rather than let go of it and live in a better place? What is this resistance to forgiveness all about? And is there a forgiving self in each person, a core of security and generosity, that can be located and built upon?

It is tempting to think that some sort of formula could hold the key to becoming a more forgiving person or to simply getting over an impossible grudge state toward someone important in our life. But, given our peculiar needs, deficits, and unrealized strengths, not to mention our immense and wondrous complexities, no book can do any more than throw light on the issues.

The forgiving self can be hard to locate and the grudge state devilishly hard at times to let go of—especially when we feel a bitter right to hold on to it and when being in it gives us a perverse satisfaction. Change, when it comes, emerges, I believe, from determination, inner search, and creativity, not to mention the help of others, including therapists. Ideally, the therapeutic partnership offers something that cannot be found in a book: first, of course, the relationship itself, a relationship in which one is perhaps heard and understood as never before, that can access repressed and disowned parts of ourselves, that can get into the formative machinery and shed light on the forgotten gears and levers of our choices. But it also offers a relationship that may enable us to experience ourselves as cared about in a context where care has been wanting, where we can know our beauty and our ugliness, and where we can know the latter without obsessive self-recrimination but, rather, with a healthy remorse and a desire to grow. The therapeutic experience can—

and should—engender a fresh perspective on what is possible for us in the realm of love and loss. But I do think a book can inspire and at its best reveal a piece of what one has not seen before.

WHEN I FIRST TURNED my attention to forgiveness, it seemed a worthwhile, if unexciting, topic. But as I immersed myself, I realized that forgiveness is as fundamental and important as any topic in psychology. There are few places it can't take you. It embraces the meaning of love and hate, the nature of dependency, the torments of envy, the problems of narcissism and paranoia, as well as the tension between self-hatred and self-acceptance, between striving for maturity and refusing to grow up.

In *The Sexual Self,* Avodah Offit writes: "Sexual attitudes, activities, and fantasies constitute the most graphic measure we have of character. In our sexual lives, we express our basic relations to others." A similar statement could be made about forgiveness. In our capacity or failure to forgive we reveal our ability to recognize the humanity in someone who has hurt or disappointed us, as well as to see our own limitations and complicity. It represents an ability to imagine what life is like on the other side of the fence, where another human being is engaged in his own struggle, to let go of the expectation that people exist to be just what we need them to be. And this sensibility applies to our view of ourselves, too: for forgiving others is nothing but the mirror image of forgiving oneself. Significant acts of forgiveness also entail letting go of a precious story we tell about ourselves, risking the awareness of a larger, less self-justifying truth.

What we do in the realm of forgiveness says a great deal about both how we mourn our losses and how well we have separated psychologically from our parents, two fundamental issues in emotional health and development. It speaks to the magnitude of our self-centeredness and the extent to which we organize the world into a simple pattern of good versus bad, as opposed to a more mature ability to tolerate ambiguity and ambivalence. In the capacity to forgive we see our largeness of heart. And, in struggling to forgive what is most difficult for us to forgive, we reveal our courage, imagination, and potential for growth. The development of forgivingness is, I now think, as clear a marker of general psychological development as there is.

Coming to terms with a parent often captures this braiding of forgiveness and growth. Allison, an acquaintance of mine in her early fifties, describes how she reconciled with a father by whom she had felt deeply hurt:

> When I was sixteen, my father left my mother. I was furious with my dad and felt abandoned. He went to Mexico and got a divorce, and then he married his secretary. He didn't tell us kids about the wedding, but several of my siblings happened upon my father and his new wife when they were leaving the church. People were standing around throwing rice on them, and my sister and two brothers walked into this, just came on the scene. So it was awful, it was just awful. And this was back in 1967, when not many couples, at least in the town where I grew up, were getting divorced. So there was the stigma of it, and I carried all that pain around for a long time. When I was in my twenties, I did have conversations with my father where I confronted him with what he had done and told him how terrible it had made me feel, and he apologized. At one point he actually broke down and cried, and I felt sad for him at that time. But I don't think I understood what forgiveness was. So if we were talking about my dad and my feelings about him back then, I could have said, Oh yeah, I forgave him for what he did to me and the family when he left my mother. But I don't think it really would have been honest. I still carried around this sort of hard nut of anger and resentment.

Her father's leaving home the way he did was really the second abandonment for Allison. The first was Allison's sense that her oldest sister had cornered her father's affections. Allison felt that her father never really saw her. In her teens, she says, "I felt that he was focusing on outside things, complimenting me for being pretty as if I was just an extension of him; and the ways in which I reflected well on who he was were the things that made him feel proud. I thought, He has no idea who I am." She believes this contributed to a perfectionism that dominated much of her life. If she were the very best at everything, then Dad would notice her.

When Allison was in her forties, her father became seriously ill, and she was the only child nearby. She was knowledgeable about medical matters and spent a lot of time advising him, helping him find doctors, and just being alone with her father, which was new.

> We had some really special times together. Ordinary things. I went with him to talk to a doctor and I saw my father in a vulnerable situation where he had a serious illness and I learned things about him that I had never known. I was able to see how he, in a very subtle way, insisted that the doctors treat him as a human being, as an individual. When we would meet with them, he would start talking about the house that he built with his own hands and other things about his life, to communicate who he was. He wasn't just sitting there silently accepting whatever treatment was being offered. He was engaging the doctors in seeing him as a human being, and it allowed me to see him as a human being and I started noticing qualities that I admired and I liked.

Allison's bitterness toward her father was abated by her concern, her caring, and the gradual erosion of the perfectionism that had been disabling her in many ways. She had to be perfect; Dad had to be perfect; anyone she loved had to be perfect, which had made it hard to form a bond with a man. Her perfectionism, her intolerance, represented an anti-forgiving quality that was directed most severely toward herself. Indeed, she had begun our conversation by saying, "I don't think I really knew how to forgive people in a meaningful way until I learned to forgive myself." Her father, too, meanwhile, was taking steps toward repair.

> There was a weekend when my stepmother had to be abroad, and my father and I had this time at breakfast where my father said to me—and it was the only time that he has ever said anything like this—he said, "You know, I really love you, and

what I love about you is what a sweet nature you have and what a sweet person you are." And my heart just melted, and whatever resentment I carried over all those years evaporated and healed. And over the next year and a half, until his death, my husband and I spent as much time as we could up in the country with him and with my stepmother.

The other ingredient that spurred us on was that my father loved my husband and saw what a wonderful choice I had made. He was the only person in my family who wholeheartedly supported my choice and loved having him around. That also helped soften whatever grudge I had been carrying.

Reflecting on her experiences with her father, Allison came to recognize certain things about herself:

I learned that I had closed my heart and that opening it up to him and to who he was allowed the transformation to happen. And I think the other thing I learned was that I was judging my father, judging him on my terms, and I came to realize that my father was the man that he was. There were things that I liked about him and things that I didn't like about him, but I didn't judge him anymore.

I think forgiving my father changed me as a person. I think it made me feel less fearful and more open generally, less sensitive, less thin-skinned, less paranoid. I think it softened me and made me more generous.

She also saw that blaming her father had been a crutch of sorts. It enabled her, as she puts it, to

blame him for whatever was not working in my life. Well, I had a bad relationship with my father and so, you know, how can I get married—how can I have a good relationship with a man? I have this bad history—a father who abandoned me and the rest of the family. I think it was a way for me not to take responsibility for myself and really grow up, really become the person I am.

All sorts of awful things happened in my family after my father died, but my being able to forgive him and the connection that we made in those last two years of his life will never go away. No matter what happens to me, I carry around the knowledge of his love for me and that's very powerful.

THE CAPACITY TO FORGIVE is an important measure of emotional development, as Alison's story convincingly shows, but I am wary of making forgiveness a yardstick by which we can simplistically judge ourselves and others. For one thing forgiveness is so many different things. It comes about in an endless variety of ways. It can happen in an instant or it can take a lifetime. It is a different struggle if there is an apology than if there isn't. It varies greatly according to the depth or absence of a relationship that preceded the offense. People's processes and creativity in this regard need to be respected. Even nursing a grudge, which is clearly anti-forgiveness and anti-self in most instances, may serve a vital purpose at certain times in certain lives. In short, I don't want to tell anybody, especially somebody I don't know, that forgiveness is the right path for him. Life is too complex for that. There are too many reasons why forgiveness may be difficult, impossible, or wrong. Besides, you never know what's within a person's reach and what might be years down the road.

A central concern here is what psychologists call *agency*—whether we are truly the authors of our own actions, whether we are able to attend deeply to our feelings and needs and act on our own behalf; or whether we are driven and controlled by others, by the internalized voices of our parents or other authority figures, or by compulsions that are automatic and thus bypass the self. If the wish to forgive is unthinking, is lacking in agency, it can be as much a self-betrayal as seeking revenge. The forgiving self is in possession of itself.

The question of forgiveness and repair is, therefore, quite complex, as complex as love and hate themselves. Any effort to simplify it by turning forgiveness into a commandment that compels immediate obedience rather than something to be striven for—or, at times, reasonably rejected—does not do justice to the intricacy of human psychology and human relations. When forgiveness becomes the battle cry of moral and emotional health, we are no longer respectful of people's wounds and people's struggles.

A totally forgiving posture is neither possible nor desirable. Hatred, revenge, and striving for justice, not to mention the need to protest and to feel we are heard, are as much a part of us as love and the wish to make amends. They need to be attended to. How often do we forgive mistreatment in order to avoid conflict? Or welcome the renewed warmth of someone who was just abusing us, happy to forgo any protest, not to mention hope of better treatment in the future, in exchange for a smile? Is this a forgiveness worth having? So the questions become, How can we make a place for all the parts of ourselves? How can we not sacrifice, deny, or dissociate from authentic aspects of our being? How can we have our anger, even our murderousness, without its getting in the way of repair or spoiling the goodness of our connections with ourselves and others? These are the questions that one can struggle over for a lifetime, and they need to be kept in focus, even if they can't be answered; they are more important than a blind obedience to forgiveness.

In the best relationships there are islands of resentment that expand or contract with circumstances. Acceptance and rejection swim in and out of and around each other in complex ways. True, we may want to keep someone in the doghouse forever—which means, although we don't necessarily look at it that way, that we are forever in the doghouse as well. But we are also capable of keeping someone in the doghouse for a limited amount of time, only to make sure he suffers. Just as we have the capacity to embed anger within a framework of love, we have the capacity to build a doghouse within that love. I am angry at you, I will not drop it, no way am I letting you off the hook, you're not sneaking out of this without owning up; and yet, as serious as it is and as furious as I am, we both know that this is a play within a play and that on the bigger stage my love for you and my knowledge of your love for me has never truly wavered.

Even engaging in what looks like mean or anti-forgiving behavior can be a step in the right direction. Someone who has spent his life having to be "good," as an autocratic parent defined it, will be harboring negative passions of all sorts, from greed to ragefulness, and will need to get on better terms with them before he can begin to temper them. Allowing himself to be greedy, allowing himself to be judgmental, allowing himself to keep someone in the doghouse may, therefore, be important aspects of his growth.

The need to forgive, like the need to apologize, is an authentic aspect of our being. These are visceral needs that rise up within us and are for us. But we are not always willing to act on such needs. Because to do so is to feel things—losses, self-hatreds, cracks in the soothing stories we tell ourselves about who we are—that we are not willing to face. For this reason, we may at times need to be reminded of the importance of forgiveness or apology and to be helped, even pushed, in that direction: forced, as it were, to grow. But in such cases the reminder will be at least as much for our own benefit as anyone else's. It's like being reminded to eat.

UNTIL RECENTLY, forgiveness has not tended to be a big topic in psychology, except among Christian psychologists. In recent years, for the first time, a number of academic psychologists, most prominently Charles Enright and his colleagues at the University of Wisconsin, have been investigating the topic. But in psychoanalysis, and clinical psychology in general, where you might expect an in-depth examination of the dynamics of forgiveness and how they relate to individual psychology, the subject has been barely addressed. It's one of those topics that, by its very nature—it's about what people do rather than what they are—escapes focus and falls between the cracks. Melanie Klein and her followers have been something of an exception. Klein, an Austrian analyst who settled in England where she became very influential, did not write about forgiveness per se, but in her efforts to understand infant psychology she circled near it, perhaps especially in her insistence that the need to repair what we have destroyed, including the image of the other person that dwells within us, is an early and powerful force in our development. In the theoretical work of others, if forgiveness was considered at all, it was assumed that it would emerge naturally from improved psychological functioning and was therefore not needful of special focus of its own.

Forgiveness also presents a problem for clinicians because it comes festooned with images of virtue and moral rectitude, and psychoanalysis, officially, at least, abhors preaching. People need to be allowed to experience themselves fully—the good, the bad, and the bad that's not really bad but rather shame-encrusted—and it is only through an openness to themselves that they will find their inner path and their own motivation to do the right thing. Their values cannot be imposed by the therapist. So on the one hand, psychoanalysis is by its nature forgiving—in the sense of being tolerant—because it is built on the theme that people need to be free to be who they are. On the other hand, it would be naturally reluctant to embrace forgiveness as a goal, because it is put off by the moral rigidity that would force people into almost any position that did not take circumstance or psychology into account, that did not emerge from their own evolution.

Finally, there is the question of the will. The importance of choice and responsibility, although emphasized from the time of Freud, has often taken a backseat to the power of conditioning. Although I don't think psychoanalytic practice typically overlooks matters of the will, there has probably been a tendency in psychoanalytic writing to favor unfolding and exploration over pointing to the choices made, as well as those that could have or should have been made.

For all these reasons the idea that forgiveness is not just a by-product of growth but rather that the struggle to forgive can *promote* growth has perhaps been overlooked. And yet that premise strikes me now as both valid and imperative and lies at the core of this book.

As it turns out, doing psychoanalysis, indeed any depth psychotherapy, is a good training ground for dealing with problems in forgiveness. Holding a grudge against someone and being his therapist are antithetical. Therapists are subject to all the emotions that emerge in intense relationships: love, gratitude, pity, admiration, anger, resentment, envy, murderousness. Psychoanalysts, especially, are trained to be attuned to their own responses to the patient no matter what they might be, and to find some way to use them creatively, rather than be mindlessly controlled by them. There is no walking away from your feelings. There is no annihilating him. Of course such things do happen, but the presumption is that somehow you have to find a way to stay connected with yourself and the patient and to deal.

There is a fourfold assumption when you're doing treatment and you want to murder your patient: one, that he is probably doing something hostile and infuriating; two, that you are experiencing some vulnerability that magnifies his affront and makes it hard for you to respond in a straightforward, confident, nondestructive way; three, that the two of you are reenacting some drama from the patient's past and also from your own of which neither is conscious; and four, that the responsibility for whatever murderousness you feel is still, in the end, all yours. I think it is a good model for relationships in general.

WHILE FORGIVENESS may have been underplayed in psychology, the counsel to forgive is nevertheless ubiquitous. It flows from the TV, the radio, and the pulpit endlessly. It is a staple of Alcoholics Anonymous and other twelve-step programs. It is a cornerstone of Christianity and important in the Jewish tradition, too, especially in relation to the highest of holy days, Yom Kippur, the day of atonement. Its modern advocates tempt us by promising that forgiveness will lower blood pressure and provide other health benefits. And yet, in certain respects, ours is an era that militates against forgiveness. People are concerned about their rights, they are quick to feel wronged or abused, they want freedom, selfhood, independence, and, when necessary, revenge. The cry, "Never again!," the *idée fixe* of many a colonized, brutalized, or otherwise wronged people, is echoed in our individual hearts as we nurse grudges against our parents, siblings, spouses, ex-mates, former friends, the gods who dealt us a rotten hand. A strange national dissociation is at work here. Nurse your killer instinct in the service of the self and then throw it away in the service of misty virtue (and better health).

For centuries the discussion of forgiveness has been mainly in the realm of religion and values and often accompanied by commandments that took inadequate account of our inner processes. In feudal Christianity, forgiveness was but one note in a complex chord that included acceptance of one's station, not responding in kind to abuse, unquestioning obedience to elders and authority figures (including husbands, fathers, priests, and nobles), and passivity in the face of privilege. We have been rebelling against that order for five centuries, from the Renaissance to the counterculture, with, in the West at least, ever greater conquests for individual rights. But greater freedom for the individual has been accompanied by a weakening of social bonds.

Perhaps we need to be reacquainted with the value of forgiveness, even if it is not always achievable; with the spiritual and psychological struggle it often requires; with the obstacles we may have to contend with along the way; and, not least of all, with its power to transform. But any reacquaintance needs a fresh perspective, one that frees forgiveness from its moralistic moorings, that takes into account the subtleties of what is psychologically and emotionally possible, and that respects our capacities for both goodness and murderousness, as well as the surprising creativity, which is also ours and which can pop out from unexpected places.

PART I

THE
LANDSCAPE
OF
LOSS

ONE

If I am not for myself, who will be for me?
If I am for myself only, what am I?
If not now, when?

HILLEL   (30 B.C.–10 A.D.)

SAINTS
AND
MONSTERS

IN TALKING TO PEOPLE ABOUT FORGIVENESS I'VE BEEN SURPRISED
at the resistance that some smart, sensitive people feel to this subject.
They believe that to forgive is to condone somehow the harmful things
people have done; that it's not only a pardon for past crimes but a vir-
tual license to commit them again; that to forgive is to lack the guts to
call a spade a spade and to condemn what deserves condemnation. They
feel that the admonition to forgive is a kind of coercion that takes no account of the offense, the presence, absence, or degree of contrition in the
offender, or the emotional readiness of the victim to let go. I have a
friend who told me point-blank, and with some passion, "I don't believe
in forgiveness," largely for these reasons. But she admitted, "Once I understand, I can't hold a grudge any more. That's the big thing for me.
Understanding."

"So you do believe in forgiveness then," I said.

"How do you define forgiveness?"

"Allowing someone back into your heart."

She thought a moment. "Yes, if that's how you define it."

What tarnishes forgiveness for some people is a churchy moralism
that ignores ordinary human feeling. An extreme example was reported
in the press when high school students in a Christian prayer group in
West Paducah, Kentucky, responded to the shooting deaths of three of

their classmates on December 1, 1997, by announcing with large plac-
ards, "We forgive you, Mike," to the disturbed boy who committed the
murders. Ordinary sensibility is struck dumb. Leaving aside the question, Who are they to forgive this, and in such a public manner?, one
wonders if they allowed themselves to experience the terrible losses involved, let alone to deal with them. Such fanatical piety feels shallow and
misguided, even repugnant, especially to those most immersed in the
hurt, including the boy and his family. There is always something deadly
about inauthentic forgiveness. Often it is little more than a cover for
contempt.

In a famous dilemma, created by psychologist Lawrence Kohlberg as
part of a study of the psychology of morality, a man named Heinz has a
wife who is near death from a rare form of cancer. One drug might save
her, which has been discovered and produced by a local druggist. The
drug is expensive, costing the pharmacist $200 per dose to make, and he
sells it for $2,000. Heinz, a poor man, goes to everyone he knows but
can only borrow $1,000. The druggist, insisting on his right to a profit,
refuses to sell it at that price or to let Heinz pay the balance later. So
Heinz, in desperation, breaks into the pharmacy and steals the drug.
Kohlberg asked his child subjects whether Heinz was right to do so.

Years later the same fable was revived by Charles Enright for the
study of forgiveness. A psychologist asked adult subjects if they thought
Heinz could ever forgive the pharmacist if he were unable to get the drug
and his wife died, especially if the pharmacist showed no remorse or
change in behavior. "Yes," one subject responded, "despite his anger toward the druggist, he'd still love him because he is a human being worthy of respect and love. Heinz would be angry at the druggist's actions,
but not at the druggist himself." This answer was taken to reflect advanced moral development.

It does sound enlightened. Stigmatize the behavior, not the person.
This is the way we often try to train children. But there are two realities
here. One is the reality of who the pharmacist is, which is probably quite
complex, including admirable and lovable aspects, wounds that might
cause us to sympathize with him, and perhaps some feeling of bitterness
on his part toward a community that he may feel has cheated him in the

past. The other is the reality of how the bereaved husband feels in the wake of his monstrous behavior—he is unlikely to take that complexity into account and can't be expected to. So, for me, this is not a human response. In fact, I suspect that most people who report such responses are voicing what they believe they should feel, rather than what they do feel. I would be more encouraged about the possibilities of eventual, authentic forgiveness in the subject who says he wants to "kill the fiend" or "string him up for eternity." The overly humane response—"I would be angry at the druggist's actions but not at the druggist himself"—just doesn't ring true, not among non-saints anyway. I think people who speak this way tend to be afraid of their own aggression—afraid of what will happen to themselves or others if they express it—and so they straitjacket themselves into a strict, unnatural goodness. In such a rigid state, where you are not allowed to be bad, where, in fact, you are determined to be so pure that you dare not indulge any wish to hurt, to be mean, or to hold a grudge, hatred—denied, hidden, disfiguring—hardens into rock.

Saintliness attaches itself to the idea of forgiveness like a cat to a warm pillow. Philosophers and theologians have traditionally argued that forgiveness is a gift that the victim bestows on the wrongdoer and that this gift must be unconditional. No strings should be attached, no demand for apology or atonement, no promises of better behavior in the future. This is the Christian ideal. It emphasizes that forgiveness is an internal process, a choice that we make, and that we choose it as much for our own spiritual well-being as for the wrongdoer's. It should not be held hostage to the recipient's state of mind.

Each of these tenets of the forgiveness ideal makes good sense. But we get caught in some impossible binds when we turn them into requirements. Forgiveness has many faces and proceeds by degrees. Each opening toward the other person, however minuscule, however incomplete when measured against the ideal, is important and may even be immense in its own way. To spare the druggist's life, if it were in one's hands to do so; to gradually let go of one's rage and bitterness; to be willing at some point to entertain the thought of him as human; to allow him his wish to apologize or atone—each of these are steps in a process that can legitimately be linked to forgiveness, even if they take a lifetime. And each step represents growth for the person who takes it, so that he is not quite the same as before.

The process of forgiving can be complicated, both internally and interpersonally. It can be premature, such that one's legitimate protest gets lost. It can be more related to submissiveness or compliance than a genuine act of strength, of giving. It can be real and yet coexist with hatred or resentment. It can come piecemeal (as is often the case with parents or ex-spouses) because there is so much to deal with and because you open up gradually as you grow, as you recognize your own complicity, as you accept the humanity of others and therefore allow them their flaws, as you see their suffering or contrition, as you understand their struggles. We are so complex and capable of such creative means of parsing reality and dealing with it that forgiveness can take an infinite number of shapes. Anger, protest, and the wish to hurt back may all play a vital part. Even the style of anger, its murderousness or warmth, will indicate subtle movements in the forgiveness continuum. Contrary to the saintly view, anger is not anathema to forgiveness. It can coexist with it. It can be its harbinger.

DOSTOEVSKY'S SAINT

Like many people, I have at times been enthralled by saints. As an undergraduate, I was riveted two nights in a row by successive screenings of Buñuel's film *Nazarin,* the story of a village priest imbued with the wish to emulate Jesus, and I was completely unaware that Buñuel, who admired his protagonist, was also commenting on the folly of such an effort. But the saintlike man who most captured my imagination is Dostoevsky's Prince Myshkin, the title character in his novel *The Idiot.*

Dostoevsky was passionate about Christianity and the person of Christ. In his story "The Grand Inquisitor," embedded in *The Brothers Karamazov,* Jesus appears during the Spanish Inquisition, which is being carried out in his name. He is taken into custody and sentenced to death. The Grand Inquisitor visits him in his cell and explains to him why mankind is better off without him: People do not want to be free in the way that Jesus wants them to be free. They want to be fed and told what to do by authorities who speak in his name. Jesus, who sees all the way through to the core of this man, past his imposing power, his authoritarianism, and his defenses, right to the soul and all its buried suffering, plants a loving (and deeply rattling) kiss on the old tyrant's forehead before being led to execution.

In *The Idiot,* Dostoevsky tried to create a convincing representative of such a divine nature in a living human being. He built into Prince Myshkin an extraordinarily loving and empathic nature and the capacity to stay focused on the deepest, most important things. Myshkin comes to Moscow after having spent much of his youth in the care of a Swiss doctor who treated him for epilepsy. There he is soon surrounded by a swarm of characters from all strata of Russian society, each one compelled by this intense, earnest, startlingly direct, compassionate, and childlike man with little sense of social proprieties—an "idiot" according to some.

A young man named Ipolit, who is suffering from tuberculosis and will not live long, is not sure whether to embrace or detest Myshkin. Ipolit is one of Dostoevsky's brilliantly dark figures, bitterly cynical, a snarl almost permanently attached to his lips, tormented but unable to accept anyone's caring. Late in the book, he and Myshkin have a climactic encounter. They speak awkwardly of Ipolit's impending death and of the way certain famous Russians of the past have faced death. Ipolit is torn between seeing the prince as absurdly naïve, warmly sincere and deeply spiritual, or cunning and wanting to trip him up. As they speak, Ipolit keeps finding reasons to take offense. "Well, all right, then," he says half-tauntingly, "tell me what in your opinion would be the best way for me to die? I mean so that it would be as . . . virtuous as possible. Tell me!" Myshkin responds in a low voice: "Pass on by us and forgive us our happiness." It is a stunning moment in which the prince, with uncanny simplicity, addresses the agonizing envy that eats away at this young man. Ipolit's cynical laughter breaks the silence: "I knew you'd say that," he says.

Myshkin also becomes entwined with Lebedev, a degraded and self-degrading individual who is a compulsive and shameless conniver. He repeatedly betrays the prince only to confess and wheedle, plead weakness and poor moral fiber, and beg for forgiveness. Myshkin is exasperated but always forgives. If you are the average person (that is, not a saint) and you are confronted with someone who is repeatedly late, even if it is just ten minutes, after a while an apology won't satisfy you, no matter how heartfelt it is. It will simply not be enough. You are going to want to know *why*, and you will want the lateness to stop. If he repeatedly steals from you or undercuts you, or leaves you in the lurch, the situation will be that much worse, and he may, after a while, never be able to get back in your good graces. But Myshkin is not like you or me in this respect. He does not need an apology, let alone an explanation, let alone cessation of the offense, for there seems to be no response that is beyond his capacity to tolerate or forgive. He experiences Lebedev's humanity in all its abject corruption, experiences *himself* in Lebedev, and loves him, as if he were his own errant child.

When Myshkin first arrives in town he finds lodgings with a young civil servant, Ganya, who lives with his father, mother, and two younger siblings. As a result, Myshkin, along with a number of family friends, witnesses a feverish conflict in which Ganya behaves viciously and is on the verge of striking his sister, Varia. The prince intrudes, catching his arm and exclaiming, "Enough—enough!" Ganya is infuriated:

> "Are you going to cross my path forever, damn you!" cried Ganya; and loosening his hold on Varia, he slapped the prince's face with all his force.
>
> Exclamations of horror arose on all sides. The prince grew pale as death; he gazed into Ganya's eyes with a strange, wild, reproachful look; his lips trembled and vainly endeavored to form some words; then his mouth twisted into an incongruous smile.
>
> "Very well—never mind about me; but I shall not allow you to strike her!" he said, at last, quietly. Then, suddenly he could bear it no longer, turned to the wall and murmured in a faltering voice: "Oh! how ashamed you will be of this afterwards!"

The prince's words were not a retaliation but an act of tormented compassion and warning. It is as if Myshkin had said, "Oh, my God, what have you done to yourself!" Seeing this scene in a Russian film version of *The Idiot* when I was twenty-one compelled me to read the book. Its majesty suggests the pettiness that normally consumes us and sheds light on the unexpected possibilities of love.

But this, of course, does not change the fact that you and I are not like Myshkin. We take the slap personally; we feel, at least initially, and often for a long while after, "Oh, my God, what you have done to *me!*" This reaction is natural, deeply rooted, and not to be sloughed off, even with Myshkin's example staring us in the face. And yet we are prone to expect such heroism from ourselves. I think, for me, the appeal of saintliness was, in part, that it offered me a way around my own aggression. I was terrified of my own aggression, convinced it made me a monster, unfit to live among other human beings, who would cast me out when they saw it. Saintliness offered a new kind of power, if I could only rise to that level.

I now believe that forgiveness, to be a realistic option, has to take into account the full reality of human psychology, including the strength of our negative passions. Any effort to promote forgiveness by encouraging people to be saintly or Christ-like strikes me, as it once struck Buñuel, as folly. We are not saints and we are not meant to be. We get hurt, we get angry, sometimes murderously so, and, from there, growth or reconciliation either proceeds or doesn't.

It is interesting, in light of this, that Dostoevsky built a critical flaw into his hero, whose uncanny empathy operates at times in the service of a tormented martyrdom. Much of *The Idiot* revolves around Myshkin's pursuit of a beautiful, poignant, captivating woman who is at once self-hating and impossible. He sees through her devil-may-care flamboyance to her hidden pain and believes with great passion that she is essentially good, that there is an innocent, unfairly persecuted child inside her, and that his love, if only given a chance, can heal her. But there is an obsessed quality to his love, like that of a child who needs to heal a hurtful mother; and he follows her self-destructive path directly to his own doom, casting aside another passionate, beautiful woman (this one more emotionally sound) along the way.

"If I am not for myself," asked the great Jewish thinker, "who will be for me?" The prince's disability in this regard, his tendency to forsake his own best interests, is reflected in his almost total failure to locate his aggression, his sexuality, his natural selfishness. He cannot act forcefully in his own behalf. It is as if he is impelled by an unconscious inner drama that says to him, "This is most real, this is the core, saving this desperate and destructive person is what life must be about for me," even as he is consumed.

Playing opposite Myshkin in *The Idiot*, however, is Rogozhin, who incorporates much of what the prince lacks. Rogozhin is a shadowy figure, wealthy and brutish, who slices his way through the novel, primitive, impulsive, desperate, bragging, paranoid, vindictive, with a band of ruffians and opportunists following in his wake. Aggression pours forth from him untamed. He is a raging dynamo, poignant and beautiful in his way. He can be selfish, violent, cruel, and ends with blood on his hands, but one senses the desperate need for love that underlies his wild intensity. But Rogozhin does not see this in himself. He can no more acknowledge his goodness than Myshkin can his anger. The two men seem to represent the extremes to which the human psyche is prone; and I think their side-by-side presence in this novel suggests the perils that face us when these extremes are not integrated.

THE KILLER INSIDE US

Settling scores is basic to our nature. It's tribal, it's biblical, it's Freudian. An eye for an eye is one of the ancient fundamentals of justice, and many societies allow victims to exact a terrible price from those who have wronged them. We expect such passions when trust is violated:

> *Heaven has no rage like love to hatred turned,*
> *Nor hell a fury like a woman scorned.* *

And yet we are divided on the subject of revenge. We love it, we root for it, we disapprove of it. To punish too severely or too long can be a disease. We see it in people for whom anger, hatred, envy, or resentment has become too good a friend. They want to cut off the hands of the

---

*William Congreve, *The Mourning Bride* (1697).

thief, scorch the fields of the enemy, ruin the former spouse, respond to any and all hurts with annihilating fury. The impulse toward murderous retaliation emerges from the most primitive and unconscious places inside us. We all have it, the wish to rip apart and obliterate. At this level, revenge doesn't think about consequences, about relationships, about the fact that the hands of the thief might be good to shake again one day.

Our murderousness is not just reserved for the guy who raped our sister. This is how we may feel when someone we love criticizes us (fairly or otherwise) or raises an eyebrow at the wrong time or acts as if he doesn't know what we're talking about when he damn well does. A woman tells me she wants to write her brother a denunciatory letter because he hasn't called once since the flood that destroyed a large portion of her home. I ask, Do you want his love or do you want him to feel horrible about himself? She hesitates. She wants the latter. The impulse to kill may not look like love turned to hate, especially when it develops into the habitual response. But it often is just the same.

Children, as we know, can feel murderous toward parents they love. A preadolescent boy, written up some years ago in the psychoanalytic literature, killed the mother who repeatedly threatened to abandon him, "because I couldn't stand to be without her." A six-year-old child in a study of early attachment imagined killing his parents with his bow and arrow were they to leave him for an imaginary weekend away. Parents, too, have murderous fantasies toward their children. They want to kill their kids when they defy them, when they don't live up to their expectations, when they sulk and act wounded. And they do kill—with their rage, their guilt trips, their condemnations. But the impulse to kill is not just an aspect of psychology gone wrong. It is universal. After a difficult day with her three-year-old daughter, who had been acting savagely toward her, a loving, responsive mother has a dream of bashing the girl to death with a telephone receiver. On waking, she is nearly crushed by mortification: How could she dream such a thing?

But we all dream such things. The problem is not the impulses or the wishes, it's what we do with them. A young man eyes a red Corvette parked near his school and salivates at the thought of stealing it and driving it to California with his girlfriend. Is he a thief? If he has a longing to sleep with his friend's girl, is he a traitor?

It's unfortunate that we tend to stigmatize thoughts, feelings, and wishes, almost as if we cannot distinguish between what we think and what we do. It's not only harsh, but we lose a lot in the process. We lose, most prominently, a vital part of ourselves, in that we are not on good terms with our own passions and force ourselves to disown them. There is power in these feelings, power that could be harnessed in constructive ways. It's part of the juice of being. It's good for the young man to know what he wants and to feel the strength of it, even if its raw expression might be disastrous. To allow yourself to know you want to smash your daughter, or steal a car, or sleep with your friend's wife, or even blow up the world is not only to be more fully alive but to be in a better position to understand and sympathize with yourself—and to restrain yourself. Sometimes, just the experience of being on our own side ("Of course I wanted to smash the kid!") releases us from the tight grip of violent emotion and frees us to experience other parts of ourselves ("Poor kid!").

By disowning our negative passions, on the other hand, we let them control us. There is no self-knowledge, no self-forgiveness, no growth. But when we divide the world so starkly into good and evil, into acceptable and sinful feelings, we dare not know anything about ourselves that seems bad.

Lucy, a young woman I am seeing in treatment, grew up with a very disturbed older sister who wreaked havoc in the family. Lucy was supposed to be the good child—"the only role that was being auditioned for by the time I came on the scene"—which meant being quiet, appreciative, uncomplaining, undemanding. Her mother was too burdened already, with doctors, disasters, disciplinary actions, to deal with Lucy's feelings of neglect and misery. Even now, Lucy feels, "How can I be angry at her given how good she was and given all that she had on her plate?" But she *is* angry, furious that her mother was oblivious to her plight, furious for feeling unheard, unseen, unhelped. But her murderousness is rigidly suppressed, so much so that she suffers a lack of vitality. Even as a small child, she had low energy and wasn't much good at anything that took exertion. This served her unconscious strategy of finding a disability to rival her sister's (a *good* disability, a well-behaved disability) that would bring her attention. But the suppression of her rage, a suppression that was reinforced by the expectations and psychology of her parents, has played a part in her depletion. At twenty-two, she feels like an old woman who can barely make it up the hill. Her untapped anger, however, could light up the Empire State Building, if she could only plug into it. But she is understandably afraid of what this might lead her to.

Lucy is the good daughter still, but her mother might well ask, With a good child like this, who needs bad ones? Lucy loves her mother, she defends her mother, she suffocates her mother with her clinging attachment, and she abuses her with her listlessness, her fuck-ups, her inexplicable and endless ennui. She has a kamikaze depression and her mother is the boat. Meanwhile, she has constant obsessive fantasies about her mother dying if Lucy steps on a line on the sidewalk or utters the wrong magical word, and she treats her mother's presents—including a twenty-first birthday gift of a much-longed-for necklace that had belonged to her great-grandmother—as if they were nothing. I say, "Better to want to kill her and to know it, than to act it out by having no energy, taking no pleasure in her gifts, and suffering endless anxieties about her dying."

Ironically, in reowning her anger toward her mother, Lucy would also be closer to having a real connection with her, one that would nourish her and allow her to grow up, rather than one that is neurotic and loaded on one side with guilt, on the other with covert revenge. Lucy's fury does, after all, come from love: I love you so much, Mom, how could you have let me down? I'm so wounded in my love for you that I could kill you. From that place and that knowledge new things become possible, including apology, sorrow, forgiveness, and the freedom to move on.

The disavowal of our murderousness gets played out socially in many ways. In his televised debate with Republican nominee George Bush in 1988, the Democratic presidential candidate, Massachusetts governor Michael Dukakis, could not respond with any passion to the question "If Kitty Dukakis were raped and murdered, would you favor an irrevocable death penalty for the killer?" The whole nation seemed to gasp at the effrontery of the question, only to be disappointed by Dukakis's bland recitation of his opposition to capital punishment.

Such a question, under such circumstances, demands a response of controlled rage: "The first thing I would do as President, if I had the power, would be to outlaw the sort of intrusive and profane question you just asked. But since it is on the table, I will say this: If anyone physically harmed my wife or anyone in my family, I wouldn't want to wait for the legal system to act. I'd want to rip him to shreds myself. Public policy, as I hope you well know, is another issue entirely. Ideally, it is not made by people who are feeling the kind of fury I am experiencing right now."

But such an angry response did not seem to fit the values Dukakis wanted to uphold. That personal response and public policy could be two different things seems to have been lost on him, at least at that moment. That he could want to kill (both the rapist and the questioner), that he could have that impulse within him, even though he would hope in most cases not to follow through on it, also seemed to elude him. His response was horrifyingly bloodless; in his denial of his negative passions, he completely lost his way (and possibly the election).

Many people find it easy to accept that they harbor a rageful self, but only in the context of justifiable retaliation. Then they are merely, to quote the title of a Steven Seagal cinematic bone-cruncher, "out for justice." But there is a similar kind of denial at work here: My revenge is good revenge, my rage is not truly an aspect of my being. It only exists in response to abuse, it only attacks deserving targets.

When cases of true monstrousness come to our attention, like Theodore Kaczynski's series of lethal letter bombs to academicians, or the bombing of the Federal Building in Oklahoma City by Timothy McVeigh and Terry Nichols in 1995, or the massacre committed by two students at Columbine High School in the spring of 1999, still fresh in the nation's mind as I write this, there is a tendency on our part to shrink back and think of the perpetrators of such acts as untouchably *other,* freaks who exist outside the human family. But these are the extremes that exist in all of us, and their behavior is not unlike the annihilating way in which more balanced people act out their grievances, even if their violence is limited to the verbal realm.

That we don't know how to make good use of our anger and that we respond so poorly to the anger of others are part of what makes our lives with one another so hard. The inhibition of anger, the abuse of anger, and the unconscious acting out of disavowed anger are pervasive aspects of our everyday reality, greatly complicating and confusing the issue of forgiveness. What is not asserted cannot be resolved. What is asserted brutally generates a new level of grievance.

Although I believe that in most cases it is only through a working out of our anger that we can come to a genuine forgiving position, I don't want to dismiss the idea of saintly empathy. It does seem to exist, even if not in one person all the time. Witnessing it can remind us that there is a human core even in the worst wrongdoer, even if we ourselves cannot always perceive it. It can temper us—in our unforgiving rage at ourselves and others. It may suggest at times that forgiveness is, after all, an option, even if it seems remote. By its example, heroic empathy reaffirms that there is nothing human that cannot be forgiven, even the behavior of someone who is unrepentant. But it is only a small part of the large world of forgiveness.

A respect for our own inner process may lead us down surprising paths that are legitimate even if they don't take us straight to forgiveness. Forcing ourselves to emulate a more saintly response takes us away from who we really are and thwarts a healthy working through of our negative passions. It risks that rage, vindictiveness, envy, depletion, papered over with a compelled smile, will remain within us in undiluted, unevolved form, only to emerge later in destructive fashion. In some people it can lead to an unhealthy martyrdom, in others to a false or premature forgiveness that is worse than no forgiveness at all.

Disavowed murderousness is the ground from which little murders crop up. The grudge itself is a kind of endless little murder. Born in hurt, it is often nurtured by relentless self-righteousness and a refusal to see oneself and one's own complicity, to budge from a psychologically safe place. At times, the grudge is quite open in its murderousness—"I could still kill him"—indicating an obsessive involvement with the one who caused the hurt. At other times the murderousness is concealed, dressed up as saintliness, a wolf declaring its wounded sheepdom.

THE UNFORGIVABLE ACT

On May 15, 1997, a column appeared in the *Jerusalem Report* attacking Natan Sharansky, a Jewish hero and an Israeli national icon. Sharansky had been a leader of the human rights movement in Moscow. He had spent nine years in Soviet prisons, at last emerging in 1986 unbent and uncompromised, after his wife and thousands of others had campaigned for his release. In Israel he formed a new political party in the cause of the thousands of new Russian émigrés and won seven seats in the Knesset, joining the right-wing government of Benjamin Netanyahu as minister of trade and industry in 1996.

Sharansky was not in office long when a mildly critical profile appeared, angering him. "Natan has a hard time with criticism," the author, who had been a friend of Sharansky's, later said. "I get the impression that criticism is seen as betrayal, and it's not."

In 1997 Netanyahu came close to losing his office in one of the worst corruption scandals in Israeli history. Sharansky was quoted as saying, "If there is even ten percent of truth in Israeli TV's story, this government has no place in continuing to govern." An official investigation suggested there was much more, finding that Netanyahu's behavior had posed "a real threat to the rule of law." Netanyahu had felt betrayed by Sharansky's "ten-percent" remark. But he needed Sharansky and his seven votes. The two men cut a deal. The government did not fall.

One of Sharansky's closest friends was the journalist Hirsch Goodman. He was outraged at Sharansky's decision to support Netanyahu and angry, too, that Sharansky had endorsed a new law that would give Orthodox rabbis the right to control all conversions to Judaism within Israel, a law that had unnerved non-Orthodox Jews all over the world. Goodman now attacked Sharansky in the *Jerusalem Report*.

In his column, entitled "Mr. Ten Percent," Goodman accused Sharansky of selling out half of world Jewry because "his political survival depended on his caving in to ultra-Orthodox ultimatums." He argued that Sharansky supported the prime minister because he feared new elections would diminish his own power in parliament. He said that Sharansky had become "just another cheap politician." Goodman must have underestimated the pain this column would cause Sharansky. He certainly did not expect it to end their friendship. Rather, I think, he saw it as a legitimate political statement, the sort of thing that people in politics must be prepared to endure, even from friends. He may have felt, too, that professional pride required him to treat Sharansky, a friend, as he would any other politician. As a courtesy, he sent Sharansky an advance copy so Sharansky would not be taken by surprise. As of this writing, the two have not spoken again.

In a story on Sharansky in the *New Yorker* that year, journalist David Remnick asked Goodman about the incident. "The whole thing pains me," Goodman said. It was evident that he felt guilty, that he still loved Sharansky, that he regretted turning people against him. "Recently, I gave a lecture to a Jewish group in Los Angeles, and there were six hundred people there. At the mention of Sharansky's name, they booed! It was like a knife through my heart."

From Sharansky's point of view, Goodman's column revealed an unforgivable misinterpretation of Sharansky the man. "He was saying, 'You are a guy who once had principles and now you have no principles at all.' " Sharansky now seemed to see a truth about Hirsch Goodman that he had not seen before. It was as if this one act, committed in heat and later regretted, revealed the true enemy, always there, beneath Goodman's benign exterior. It's a strange way of viewing things—the one defining act. But it is part of the black-and-white, saint-versus-sinner mentality to which we are prone in our most aggrieved moments. "There's nothing to talk about," Sharansky told Remnick. "It's as if six years together were nothing. . . . Why reconcile if that's the situation?" At this point Sharansky could probably have forgiven his Russian jailers more easily.

Sharansky felt stabbed in the back, and that is hard for anyone to endure. Besides, he is a tough man, he survived the Soviet prison system, and the very qualities that made him a hero may also make him implacable at times when flexibility might serve him better. In any case, Sharansky could neither reconcile nor forgive.

Carrying a Torch

In many grudge states, there is no clear victim, even if all concerned eagerly claim the mantle. But the experience of being a victim, valid or not, is perhaps the thing that most feeds the grudge and activates the grudging self. April and Roseanne, women in their early thirties, who had been very close, stopped speaking when Roseanne found a boyfriend to whom she was soon engaged. Both women hurt each other and soon found themselves with their backs against the wall.

Roseanne wished to cast off the memory of her single years and her sidekick relationship with April. She felt guilty for moving away from April, didn't quite understand it, couldn't explain it, didn't feel she had a right to do it, and so just moved ahead denying everything. Meanwhile, she became annoyed by April's panicky accusations of abandonment and infuriated by an implied attitude that she somehow had a right to Roseanne's time and her life.

On April's side jealousy, envy, and feelings of rejection resonated painfully with aspects of her past. April's mother had been the mayor of the small town where April grew up. She was a star in the community, a doer of good deeds, who never had time for her family. April worshiped her but felt like a supplicant who could never get an audience. When she began turning toward her father, her mother could not tolerate their connection, turned cold and disapproving, and further shut April out. And now here was Roseanne, not only shutting her out, but circling the wagons around herself and her man. The similarity registered unconsciously, and April found herself, without knowing it or understanding, re-engulfed in the traumatic feelings of her childhood. April had the added problem of feeling humiliated by the status shift she perceived. In her mind, Roseanne's engagement had decreed Roseanne a desirable woman, while April descended into inferiority and shame.

To forestall this descent, April stoked her rage at Roseanne. There's nothing wrong with me; it's *her!* She's a bad friend and a bad person, and, besides, that's a weird marriage she's in, the two of them are sickeningly co-dependent, and when they break up and she's miserable, which I hope will happen soon, I will have moved on, although her pleas and apologies will be music to my ears.

Blame is a way we lie to ourselves. It is not just a way of refusing to look at who we are or avoiding responsibility. It is also a defense against knowing our pain. To face that pain is to begin to mourn what was too overwhelming to be mourned before. To face it and not blame it on the person who happened to stir it up is certainly the road less taken.

Understanding has long been recognized as a cornerstone of forgiveness, and it is certainly a way out of blaming. But as April experienced the situation, understanding Roseanne's position—what it's like to fall in love, especially when you've waited for it for a very long time, why you might be neglectful of an old friend at such a time and maybe even for some time thereafter, why you might even want to put some space between yourself and that friend, how April herself may have acted in a way that contributed to Roseanne's behavior and made it worse afterwards—was to risk the floor collapsing from under her. She needed Roseanne to be Bad in order to sustain her defenses, to keep herself from knowing what she could not afford to know and from feeling what she could not afford to feel. So instead she focused obsessively on Roseanne's bitchiness and impatience. As she hit full throttle, April concluded that her once great companion had never valued her but had merely used her as a way station on the road to a man. "What happened to you and Roseanne?" friends would ask. "I realized something about her," April would say. "She's the kind of woman who will walk over you for a man. I can't have people like that in my life."

Two years later, when Roseanne was pregnant with her first child, she called April, expressing a wish that they reconcile. April said, "I'm sorry, but it's dead." Roseanne pursued April in various ways after that. She let her know that she felt sorry about some of the things she'd said and done. But April would not budge.

IF NOT NOW, WHEN?

We are sensitive beings. We are vulnerable. We are defended and stuck in our defenses in ways we do not see. Sparks fly in every relationship. Hurt is inevitable. So is estrangement. But for how long?

We make choices about where we want to live emotionally. A woman comes into therapy relating an uplifting incident—her son has behaved lovingly toward her after a long period of rejection. But without pause she moves quickly away from this good thing to some minor effrontery on the part of her daughter-in-law, which she now speaks of at length. A man talks about an experience with his wife, emphasizing how terribly she behaved to him and overlooking the fact that she came around very sweetly after he protested. They are each making a choice about who they want to live with and who they want to be. This is the kind of choice that April made with Roseanne, even though she experienced herself as having no choice.

Within her woundedness, self-hatred, envy, paranoia, and contempt, April had found a familiar if disturbing home. Such familiarity has the power to draw us in and embroil us, like a sickening, addictive drug. April, like almost anyone at one time or another, had the capacity to wrap herself around a kernel of rejection such that her entire life existed solely in relation to that bit of toxin. Some aspect of her inner life, which first came into being in the cauldron of childhood suffering, had developed a taste for The Wound, and for being The Wounded Party, and became morbidly absorbed in the suffering, rancor, and opportunities for revenge that go along with it. Her grudge was, in fact, a debilitating form of self-victimization, almost like carrying a torch for the lover who got away.

Is there free will in any of this? Or is it like being seized by a rapids over which one has no control? A reasonable case could be made for both, and in a sense both are true. The task for someone who wants to change is to see the element of will, to find the place where he has some leverage, where change is possible for him. April's was not an easy position, especially given her psychology. But psychology is not destiny, although it often seems that way.

To become a more forgiving person, to decrease the hold of powerful and ingrained psychological factors, requires a confrontation with oneself. Perhaps, especially if she had had the right sort of help, April could have said to herself: "I am going blindly in a familiar direction; I have been there before with other close friends and I don't want to go there again; I am reexperiencing the crushing despair I felt as a child and I am blaming it all on Roseanne." But, given where she was and what she had to work with, such clarity was as likely to emerge as a smile from a splitting headache.

"I couldn't admit that I was wrong." "I couldn't stand the thought that I had been betrayed in some way." "I felt humiliated"—or abandoned, cheated, deprived, made a fool of, put down, or taken advantage of—"and that's one thing I can never forgive." These are some of the primitive trigger issues that bring us back to the worst experiences of childhood, of feeling deprived, unwanted, or expelled from the loving circle, and of having deserved whatever we got because of our own innate rottenness. And from this place we sleepwalk into sullen rejection and revenge.

And yet the need to forgive remains a part of us, even if repudiated for a very long time. Things happen that change our perspective, giving us a different kind of ache than existed before. Sharansky may feel it with Goodman—the cold space between them and the yearning to reconnect. April may feel it, too. She may also feel remorse because of the pain she sees in Roseanne. And she may want to emerge from, may no longer be able to bear, her own imprisonment.

Routine, superficial forgiveness is easy enough, but to become more forgiving, to forgive where it is hard to forgive, is to will oneself to grow. Some people live isolated, or nonintimate, lives in order not to have to revisit their pain and resentment. And it is not only for the sake of self-preservation. They may be as afraid of what they will become and what damage they will do to others as they are of what harm may befall themselves if they open themselves to their feelings. So to forgive, which requires that exploration, is to ask a lot of oneself. On the other hand, to not ask it is to forgo a lot.

There are many barriers to forgiveness—pride, fear, resentment, hopelessness among them. I've tried to apply Hillel's aphorism: If forgiveness is a process, if the process is different for each person, if each one needs to go through his own particular journey at his own speed, how does Hillel's last line, "If not now, when?," apply?

Within the emotional labyrinth, with all its stop signs and barriers, including options that our emotional growth has not yet prepared us to take, there is usually at least one open pathway. It may be something as big as Roseanne's invitation before the birth of her daughter or as small as a willingness on April's part to acknowledge to herself, and to herself alone, that she has never stopped wanting to hurt Roseanne, to hurt her very badly, and while there is something legitimate in this—in the sense of being understandable, human—there is also something amiss in it and in the way she holds on to it. A positive step may be something that on the surface does not look at all positive, such as the hurt eruption of anger where there had been a cold distance before. But if forgiveness makes sense at all, some such step, some venture into new territory, must be taken. "If not now, when?" applies there.

THE FLIGHT
FROM
MOURNING

A MAN IS DRIVING PAST A ROW OF PARKED CARS. A WOMAN STEPS out from the cover of the cars without looking. He sees her form appear suddenly in front of him just before he hits her full force without having swerved or applied the brakes. She is dead on arrival at the hospital.

There's an inquest. The woman's family is there. The driver of the car, miserable over what he's done, looks toward them pleadingly. The dead woman's husband takes the stand. He seems crushed. "Everything was going right for us," he testifies. He looks at the driver coldly.

The inquest absolves the driver of all guilt. But his guilt does not end. In fact, he is eaten up by guilt. Outside the courthouse afterwards, he tries to approach the widower, but the bereaved man brushes him off.

After some months the guilt-ridden driver, whose name is Corby, gathers the courage to go to the dead woman's home. The husband, Nigel, is incredulous and bars his entry. Corby pleads to no avail. After sitting dejectedly on the stoop for a few moments, he looks up to see Nigel, still hostile, opening the door and allowing him in.

"I tried to write to you," Corby says. "After . . . you know. Tell you how sorry I was."

NIGEL, icily: "Thanks."

CORBY: "I was going to phone, do something but . . . I couldn't. I didn't know what to say. I still don't."

NIGEL: "Well, why don't you think about it on the way home."

CORBY: "Mr. Bates, please, I'm sorry."

NIGEL: "Yeah, you said that."

CORBY: "It wasn't my fault."

NIGEL : "Fine. That it?"

CORBY: "You've got to believe me."

NIGEL: "Why?"

CORBY, desperately: "Because it's the truth! You heard the coroner. He said no blame could be attached to me."

NIGEL: "I know."

CORBY: "And the witnesses, the police—they all said the same thing."

NIGEL: "Well, there you are then."

CORBY: "It wasn't my fault!"

NIGEL: "Then why are you here?"

Corby's face is cracking: "I need *you* to tell me that you don't blame me for what happened." He stares at Nigel imploringly: "Please."

Nigel's wall is softening, but he's not ready to abandon his position. "I do blame you. I blame you for everything—you've ruined my life, Mr. Corby, d'you know that?"

This is what Corby feared. He nods pathetically. "Yes," he says. "And mine."

"Yours?"

"I can't sleep," Corby says. "I don't eat, see my friends. I can't even touch my wife—knowing I've got something you haven't. I keep seeing it again and again, over and over in my mind. She didn't look, but so what? I should've swerved. Or braked. Done something, but I didn't . . . I didn't." He's quiet. "I can't forgive myself—why should I expect you to even try?"

Corby stares at Nigel, his eyes beginning to tear. Nigel offers him some tea.

As they sit sipping their tea, Nigel says, "Look. What I said earlier—about blaming you—it's not true."

"Isn't it?" Corby says.

"I was angry." Nigel points to some packages: "These are some of my wife's, Debbie's, things. I've been clearing them out—remembering. You, you just came at a bad time, that's all."

Corby is not satisfied. " 'Everything was going right for us'—that's what you said in court. I've ruined your life. . . ."

Nigel won't permit this any longer. "It was an accident. She didn't look. You've got to hold on to that. There was nothing you could do."

CORBY: "You don't think that."

NIGEL: "I do."

"No."

"It wasn't your fault, Mr. Corby," Nigel says, kindly, emphatically. "I know that. I've always known it. Blaming you helped for a while. But I don't need to do that anymore. Nor should you."

Corby looks at him tearfully and with immense gratitude.

The story, written by Richard Zajdlic, from an episode of *East-Enders,* a high-quality melodrama from the BBC, could be considered a sophisticated and secular morality play on the power of faith: on Corby's side, faith in forgiveness and his own right to it; on Nigel's, faith in the process of mourning—in letting go of bitterness and submitting to his core experience. But, as heartwarming as it is, it does veer considerably from life as most people know it. We understand how Corby feels when he says, "I need *you* to tell me that you don't blame me for what happened," and we root for him to get what he came for. We know it's going to be difficult for him to get out from under the thumb of his self-recriminations as long as Nigel's hatred is hanging over him. But it is hard to see ourselves making such a pilgrimage. It is easier to imagine shrinking away, not daring to think ourselves worthy of redemption or too convinced of a persecutory response to lay ourselves bare.

Nigel's behavior also seems one or two standard deviations beyond the norm. Even if we know that the person whose actions have destroyed our happiness didn't mean to do it, do we embrace him? Do we reassure him? How soon? If we are determined to have a target for our hate, we are bound to find some aspect of what he did or of his manner since to fit the bill. And so we might continue to torture him—as Nigel did for a while—until we get our full measure of resentment's perverse reward. And yet, despite a degree of courage in these two men that we ourselves might not easily muster, we do identify with them, in what they suffer, and in the positive impulses that motivate them.

Corby is enveloped in guilt. Guilt of this magnitude is a hell built for one. There is no eluding it. Although he meant no wrong, he is in a state akin to that of murderers who turn themselves in because they can no longer endure the endless nightmare of remorse and isolation. The feeling of guilt, deserved or not, is not easily erased, and even if we manage to squeeze it out of awareness, it does haunt us.

Corby may have tried to convince himself that legal exoneration settled the question, but such convincing takes a sustained unconscious effort that continually colonizes a piece of one's mind: "It was not my fault! It was not my fault!" is a pernicious labor. Were he another man, he might bolster this mantra with rationalizations in which he subtly alters the story such that all blame is transferred elsewhere. The dead woman now becomes an unbalanced lunatic with suicidal wishes and her family rageful neurotics who are using him as a scapegoat. Such unconscious mental work, the obsessive enslavement to creating and sustaining excuses and blame, is like a monument to one's guilt. It saps one's vitality. It adds weight to one's self-hatred. It radically narrows who one is as a person, and it limits one's ability to be close to others, because they can threaten one's story.

Corby is not exactly consumed by the need to apologize. He doesn't come to atone. He is in that ambiguous zone where he feels responsible, senses he could have done better despite his official exoneration, feels bad about himself, is still on trial internally, but his is the guilt of an essentially innocent man. He's come because he is in a frenzy about having caused this death, was devastated by the family's hostile response to him, is perhaps panicked that he will never be able to forgive himself as long as they blame him, and desperately needs to be let off the hook. What's special about Corby is the directness with which he pursues Nigel's forgiveness.

In Nigel, too, we recognize ourselves, even if we are not usually as splendid in our generosity or our faith. We understand his sense that he is committing an injustice by holding onto his self-righteous, condemnatory fury toward Corby. It is an abuse of power, the power that the victim has over the offender. We know what he means when he says, "It was easier to blame you." Blame distracts, blame walls off the loss. Through blame we hold someone hostage to our own dread of facing loss. Nigel's forgiveness of Corby suggests something about the powerful connection between mourning and forgiveness. The connection is a deep one and cuts across almost every situation in which forgiveness is a factor.

IN THE REALM OF DEPRESSION AND TERRIBLE TRUTH

In the psychoanalytic literature mourning first arises as a problem for the child who has lost a parent. Such profound loss tends to overwhelm the child, striking deeply at his still forming, still fragile identity. The child feels abandoned. He feels emptied of goodness. He feels an unbearable need to have the parent back. He also feels persecuted. Why did Mom or Dad leave me this way? Why didn't he love me more? What is so terribly bad about me? Why does the world hate me? To such questions, the child makes answers. If he had been a better son, he would not have lost his father. If he had not hated his father and wished bad things on him, if he had not been angry at him and refused to kiss him good-bye on the day he died, he would not have lost his father. Every child has a natural ambivalence about his parents—including perhaps an ongoing, bottled-up fury at daddy for his meanness, the occasional wish that he would die, or the oedipal desire that he would disappear so that the little boy can have his mommy to himself. All this is a struggle to manage under any conditions, but with his parent's death, he now uses it against himself more fiercely. He gets stuck in his guilt.

Without enormous support and encouragement, the child's grief is too much to bear (and even with such support, he may only deal with it slowly, incompletely, over a long period of time). His only means of emotional survival is to cut himself off from the self-indicting thoughts and feelings, building rigid defenses to protect himself from them, some more adaptive than others. He is left with an unprocessed pool of trauma that he fights desperately to stay out of and yet is always somehow in. He may engage in disturbed and disturbing behavior, which infuriates those around him and gets him into more trouble. Later in life he may suffer from emotional flatness, lack of motivation, deflated self-worth, a sense of pointlessness, and other signs of depression, the loss weighing on him in ways he does not understand. And whenever he experiences a new loss, it may hit him with the depressive force of the original. This is common for people who have suffered the loss of a parent in childhood. Often we find that certain aspects of their development stopped short at the age when the death took place.

It is not this way in every case. If the child has a loving connection with another adult, ideally the remaining parent, who is committed to helping him experience, express, live through the grieving for however long it takes and to cough up all the feelings associated with it (including anger at the surviving parent), his chance of being able to digest the loss, in all its complexity, well enough to move on is much improved. He is bathed in the caring of the person who stays and supports him; and, gradually, he can be bathed in his own caring as a result of his identification with that person. Successful mourning can thus be understood as an aspect of self-love, and like all self-love, it is learned in relation to a loving other. In the process, the child can get beyond his sense of being broken and diminished, get beyond the guilt he naturally feels about having ill thoughts of the dead, understand that his anger or hatred was and is okay, that it does not invalidate his love. He is able to reconnect in a good way with the full range of his feelings, and, in the end, retrieve the loving connection with the lost parent. Daddy left me, but Daddy loved me, and I still love Daddy.

Why such an emphasis on loss and mourning? Because loss is what we've been talking about all along—the Vietnamese girl, her life shattered by a napalm bomb; Cordelia and King Lear; Ipolit facing his own death from consumption; April abandoned; Sharansky betrayed; the orphaned prince. These stories are all in some way about loss, loss and how we manage it. Our history with loss provides an important part of the picture of who we are as forgiving beings.

Obviously, we don't all lose a parent at a tender age, but all lives are rent with losses from the very beginning. We lose the paradise of mother's breast, the status of fussed-over baby, the privileged position of only child, the fantasy that we will marry Mom or Dad when we grow up. A divorce, even if handled sensitively, even if it comes in later childhood, will likely leave the child feeling somewhat damaged because of the loss of his intact family. The shattering of his external world is reflected in his sense of self—smaller, lacking, less good. There's no escaping such traumas.

If we get into destructive power struggles with a parent, we may feel that we have lost him even though he is still alive. Often the loss is self-created—in the sense that the child shuts off from the parent whose behavior he cannot endure. Children blame themselves for everything, even if they are not being blamed outright by others, so such a shutting off is inevitably tinged with guilt and shame. He thinks, I am hateful and unloving and finds himself to be at fault no matter how destructive the parent's behavior. Many of us have been gently helped through these expectable traumas—reassured, encouraged, apologized to, allowed regressions, held—so that even if some scar tissue is left, as it inevitably must be, it is manageable and doesn't get in the way of essentially healthy development.

In much the way childhood colds and diseases help the body to fight future assaults, the emotional losses of childhood provide a training in how to mourn. Successful mourning confers considerable emotional resilience upon the child. Future losses can thus be dealt with creatively, so that one does not keep replicating the original trauma and shutting down more and more (I couldn't bear Mom's coldness and temper and had to shut off my love and longing and now I must do the same with you). Instead, one has the capacity to suffer. But not only to suffer. To suffer and to move on, to discover oneself anew, to hold on to the positive in those who hurt us—and, where applicable, to maintain a connection that might otherwise be lost to resentment and grudge. In all this, we see the characterological basis of the capacity to forgive.

But, from the very beginning, we are often not helped to mourn our losses—quite the contrary; with the result that we get stuck in various ways that compromise our psychological well-being. We are told that things aren't so bad, that what we have seen or experienced did not really happen, that we ourselves are being a problem. What's wrong with you that you hate your baby sister? What's wrong with you that you are so angry at your dear, departed father? He was a saint who sacrificed everything for you. Extreme efforts are made at times to undo a child's reality. In a 1972 study by Cain and Fast of psychiatrically disturbed children who had lost a parent to suicide, it was found that many of the children had been pressured to believe that they had not seen what they had seen, did not know what they knew. "A boy who watched his father kill himself with a shotgun . . . was told later that night by his mother that his father died of a heart attack; a girl who discovered her father's body hanging in a closet was told he had died in a car accident; and two brothers who had found their mother with her wrists slit were told she had drowned while swimming." If the children persisted in their beliefs, they were in some cases ridiculed, in others told that they were confused by something they had seen on TV.[*]

A similar disconfirmation campaign is often waged to discredit the child's perceptions of the parent himself, especially when the parent is acting cruelly or negligently, with the effect that the child feels the par-

---

[*] A. C. Cain and I. Fast, "Children's Disturbed Reaction to Parent Suicide," in A. C. Cain, ed., *Survivors of Suicide*.

ent's love is being withdrawn and, despite his pleas and protests, he cannot find a way back to it. Mom has a cold, angry, critical, rejecting streak, Dad is distant and unavailable, and I am told by both of them that I am a whiner and an ingrate: "How dare you talk about your mother like that?" There is no one to express myself to, to help me feel the pain and know I am being hurt, to help me make sense of it, to tell me that my anger and feelings of hatred are okay. So I am left with my parent's depiction of me and may even act in such a way as to certify it. What child is able to step outside the orbit of these two beloved and idealized figures and say: "This is not about me. My mother is simply a disturbed person. She is too depressed"—or too angry or too embittered by envy—"to love me properly"? What child has the intellectual or emotional resources to say: "My mother is nuts, she accuses me of the most ridiculous things and Dad is too deadened or too enthralled by her to help me; I just have to manage the best I can"? Or, "My parents never should have had children; they don't know how to love and enjoy a child; but I'm okay"?

Because of the tremendous need children have to idealize their parents, to see them as figures of magnificent ability and goodness, they would rather blame themselves than believe something is wrong with even an abusive mom or dad. (Indeed, the more abusive, the more they may cling to a crippling idealization; it's their defense against despair.) Unless there is another loving presence—a sibling, a grandparent, or some other close person—who can provide the child with the perspective of a different type of relationship, he has nowhere to go. He is left with a chronic sense of badness and resentment and a total absence of clarity about his loss: Do I feel loved by Mom and Dad? I guess so.

What cannot be successfully mourned remains like an indigestible lump in the psyche, a place of unbearable, irreparable loss that mars the self. Words don't do justice to this crushing sense of being cast out, unloved and unlovable. It becomes an area of shame and dread, a realm of experience we must not visit—must not know, must not feel—because it is too devastating. This is the realm of Depression and Terrible Truth. It is as if the original wound is surrounded by electrified barbed wire and warning signals that blare, "Do Not Come Near!" If the shutdown has been pervasive enough, any sort of mourning becomes impossible because any pain threatens to bring us back to our deepest un-mourned losses. We can cry for the whales or the actress on the screen but feel nothing for ourselves. This undigested, unprocessed pain repre-sents (among many other things) the raw material for resentment and grudge.

In adult life, the inability to work through and move beyond hurts and losses may apply to the smallest of setbacks: a child's anger, a boss's grimace, the failure of a relatively unimportant person to return a call—the list is endless because of the unique associations that the minutest events can trigger in us. These associations threaten to return us to that hopeless place of childhood despair, just a whiff of which is enough to bring on depressive symptoms or panicked flight. For example:

- You and a co-worker, traveling together, leave an important piece of work on the train and can't get it back. Are you able to move on and redo the work? Do you get defeated and fear you will never duplicate it? Do you become obsessively focused on retrieving it? Do you and your partner lock horns over who was to blame?

- A person you've dated for several months and have been infatuated with tells you she's going back to her former lover. Can you have your cry and let go? Do you become despondent, ruminating over your hatefulness, weakness, or stupidity, as you replay what you did and should have done? Do you seal your sorrow over, dive into some addiction, and soldier on, more rigid and secretly depressed than before? Or do you, perhaps, become obsessed and retaliatory and plead to be taken back?

- You realize one day, as if out of the blue it seems, that your son, whose timidity bothers you, is terrified of your judgments. He glances at you repeatedly, especially at times when others are around and he is interacting with them, as if he were a sparrow and you a hawk of propriety and correctness circling overhead. The image heats you up with a burning sense of guilt, shame, and regret. Can you let in the tragic

sadness about you as person and parent which is implicit
in this insight? Can you allow yourself the suffering and
the loving changes that may emanate from it? Do you flee,
panicked by the implications of your own badness? Or do
you become more covert and more controlling, try even
harder to erase your son's timidity so you won't have to be
haunted by it anymore?

I doubt there is a person alive for whom the flight from mourning
implicit in these questions is not relevant. A great deal of work in psychotherapy has to do with interrupting the depressive plunges or obsessive escapes associated with the flight from mourning to which people
are prone.

I think we have all marveled at people who cope with physical dis-
abilities creatively, who can lose their sight or become wheelchair-bound
and still hold onto a good feeling about themselves and their lives, even
to the point in some cases of turning dross to gold. They manage to
mourn their loss fully enough to hold on to a positive relationship with
the body that betrayed them and to reopen themselves to the ways in
which it is still possible for them to be alive. In the process they recruit
the love and help of those they are meaningfully connected with and
perhaps reach out to new people as well. Others, with the same disability, succumb to defeat and embitterment. They cannot find a way out of
the feeling that the gods have turned against them, and they may feel
that the people they love have done so as well. Without realizing it, they
may act in ways that promote their isolation. In both of these responses
to tragic loss, we hear the echoes of early experience—early love and encouragement or neglect and oppression, as well as early losses and how
they were managed.

Psychoanalysts, indeed psychotherapists in general, are often accused of encouraging people to blame their parents and to dwell in the
past. But the purpose of mourning is not to blame even if it does include
a period of anger. Its purpose is to reexperience and process a pain that
could not be processed before, a pain that dwells within us in bitter,
undigested form, along with a set of largely unconscious beliefs about
ourselves and others that comprise our grudging self. But whether we

engage in this struggle or not, we are all affected by the past. The more we try to push it away and believe that it can't touch us, the more we are controlled by it.

IF UNMOURNED LOSSES are like wounds waiting to be reopened, then the hurts and disappointments we mete out to each other in the normal course of life are the arrows that repierce those wounds, causing what often feels like unforgivable pain. To return to April and Roseanne for a moment: These two women were more than best friends. Theirs was a platonic love affair. The feelings of envy, jealousy, and loss as Roseanne withdrew were devastating to April, recalling the buried wounds of childhood. Then came the blaming, the denial, the retaliation, all designed in part to keep the devastating feelings at bay.

In loss dependency issues arise. We've been talking about this indirectly all along. We need the person we love and we are unprepared to lose him, especially in childhood, but at any time in life. There is often a period of morbid holding on—crawling into the grave, retasting the delicious love. In disturbed mourning this never ends, so that the tears shed ten years afterwards are as drenching as those shed at the funeral.

April feels as if she has lost Roseanne. She feels betrayed by her and cannot imagine how she herself could make things better. She sees the problem emanating from Roseanne, and only Roseanne can fix it. This is just as she felt as a little girl when her mother was being self-centered and rejecting. A depression comes over her that replicates her childhood depression, when Mom was omnipotent and irreplaceable and April was powerless and crushed. Her only way of reclaiming her sense of self, her sense of power, her sense of goodness, was for Mom to be good again, to say she's sorry and scoop April up in her loving, reparative embrace. Developmentally, she is still in that same place with anyone she loves this deeply and gets hurt by. She becomes like a child without the capacity for creativity, with no sense that she could contribute to a repair, or perhaps more accurately, with the child's stubborn refusal to give until Mom becomes good again.

So this is where April ends up with Roseanne. April does not feel she has the power to be alive on her own, that she can be different even if

Roseanne is stuck. April can't find those resources within herself because of the powerful unmourned material in her relationship with her mother that still lives within her and gets played out through her dependent feelings with Roseanne. And this is what we all do at times. It is the paradigm for how unmourned, unprocessed losses, and the dissociated agonies that go with them, come back to haunt us and the people we will not forgive.

To be able to say without resentment, "I feel sad that our old chumship can't be what it was, it hurts not to have you that way," or—in a slightly different context—"I feel sad that we're breaking up, I'm going to miss you," is not only to hold on to the goodness of what was and what remains, but to hold on to a strong, loving aspect of ourselves. It is the part that is able to let go, to rebuild, to make something positive out of the crisis of change. Years ago I read a column in the *New York Times* by a rabbi whose wife had gone back to work after having been a homemaker all their married life. He described how awful it was to come home to an empty house, to have to turn the lights on, to feel the coldness and the absence of her loving presence. She used to be there. She'd been welcoming and warm. Now she's working. She's giving her warmth to other people when he wants it. You could feel what a painful thing he went through and was perhaps continuing to go through. You could feel, too, that he could forgive his wife this hurtful change that so altered their longtime contract, one on which he had come to depend, and that his ability to forgive was built at least in part on his ability to face the loss, to let go of what was, to tolerate sadness and pain, and hold on to his love. I think I remembered his story all these years because of how uncommon I found it. More typically, the legitimate changes of the people we love, like a grown child's moving away or falling in love with someone else, become not just hurts to be dealt with but the beginnings of grudges.

Mourning and the need to tolerate sadness and pain are lifelong challenges. There is so much we have to face that dashes our dreams, that makes us feel small and rejected, that brings us back to the dissociated agonies of the past. We don't want to see a child's pain because the suffering of children has a way of evoking our own unmourned losses. We don't want to deal with a friend's pain, to really hear him out about his loss, or his guilt, or his feeling of worthlessness, for the same reason. We offer some useless encouragement to ward off the sadness we don't want to feel. Cultural trends that favor diversions, obsessions, and quick fixes support this flight from feeling. Medicine colludes when people who don't need it are routinely prescribed psychiatric medication. No one should feel any sadness. In exchange for the sadness, however, if we are willing to experience it, may be an opportunity to locate our own self-caring, the opportunity to become more whole, a deeper capacity for connection, and some restraint on depression.

TO RETURN ONCE MORE to the *EastEnders* episode we began with: We do not learn much about Nigel's inner process, but it helps—and this is another Utopian aspect of the story—that his feelings toward his wife, Debbie, seem to be so lacking in ambivalence. He is not tormented by nagging disappointments or resentments about her—that she never lived up to his hopes sexually, for instance, or that she failed to encourage him—and he is not tormented by guilt for harboring such feelings or for not having loved her enough. There is no sense that Nigel was either clingy or rejecting or has anything to work out on that score. There is no suggestion that he is enraged with Debbie for being careless—that he feels abandoned and angry, for example, because of her dumb indifference to danger. Nor does he feel guilty about moving on and having a life. There is no indication that he has any such (normal and expectable) feelings that he might prefer not to face and that could get him stuck in a morbid and guilty place. Guiltless, he does not have the inner pressure that most people would experience to stick to the convenient distraction of a party line—"Everything was going right for us and you ruined it!"

Nigel's initial period of rage, his need to hate and blame Corby, is a normal part of mourning. If it weren't Corby, it might have been the ambulance driver, the doctors, or Debbie herself. But to confront a loss fully, one must move beyond rage, which, in Nigel's case, entails returning to his love of his wife and allowing himself to feel it—and her—again. This is agonizing; he will never have her back. It may take a long time (assuming Nigel has more inner conflict than the story portrayed) before the anger, the guilty despair, the at times hallucinatory clinging have receded enough to allow life to continue in a healthy way, unhampered by depression or defenses against it. At that point, his love for Debbie has not expired, it is retrieved.

The fear that one cannot bear one's sorrow, that one must flee from mourning, haunts everyone; it is an aspect of being human, which adds a piece of instability and irresolution to our lives, as well as, in many cases, some inexplicable bitterness or depression. Experiencing the sadness is the business of mourning, but it takes strength to do so. The "Do Not Come Near" signs become more forbidding the longer they are in place. So there is an emotional imperative to keep the wounded portion of the self shut down and make off-limits much of our aliveness. To feel the sadness, to mourn, is, therefore, not only to reclaim love, but to reclaim a piece of ourselves and our aliveness.

Forgiving Corby is part of Nigel's essential journey of moving beyond anger and toward the retrieval of love and self. Forgiveness can thus be seen as a deliverance for the forgiver as well as the forgiven. Both are freed to move on.

THREE

HOLDING
OUT FOR
HEAVEN

A MONGOLIAN TALE IS A FILM ABOUT A BOY AND A GIRL, BEIYIN-palica and Someyer, both orphans, who are brought up together as brother and sister. They are raised by a foster mother, an old woman they call "grandmother." She is not, in fact, a blood relation to either of them, although she was the foster mother of the boy's father as well. Not long after the boy's mother died, the father decided to leave the grasslands for work in the city and brought the boy to stay with the old woman, where the little girl already resided, and where the three now live together as nomadic shepherds. Although both children have suffered catastrophic losses, they seem surprisingly intact. Their apparent emotional well-being is almost unimaginable from what we know about the psychological disasters visited upon children who lose one or both parents. One gets the impression from the film that it is common in Mongolian rural communities for people, when necessary, to give their children to others for foster care, perhaps due to the dislocations wrought by modern society. Possibly because these nomadic communities are so tightly knit, the children may feel that, despite their losses, their world is not in total disarray. Getting loving care from this nonfamily member, at least in the movie, is made to seem easily managed. In any case, the three become a family, and we see many scenes of idyllic pleasures as the children, who have been told, "You will now be brother and sister," enjoy a romantic childhood intimacy.

When they are teenagers the grandmother begins to worry about being alone in her old age and she cooks up a solution: You children are not related; you can marry each other and stay with me. At first the children seem to treat this as something that is too much for them to comment on. We have no idea what fears, fantasies, and longings this idea sets off in them, or even whether they intend to oblige. In any case, when Beiyinpalica goes off for eight months to veterinary school, as arranged by his father, the matter still isn't formally settled. But inasmuch as neither child has protested and the two have been like sweethearts all their lives, it seems to be silently understood that the marriage will one day take place. Indeed, at the last moment Someyer pleads with Beiyinpalica not to leave for school, as if she fears some irrevocable change will occur.

Three years later Beiyinpalica returns with his heart set on marrying Someyer (having rejected his father's wish that he go on to college). The grandmother asks him why he was away so long, and he explains that he decided to go on to get a high school education, with an emphasis on music. He seems unconcerned about the length of time he spent away, and, while away, he was apparently unconcerned about not having written.

One night while drinking with a bunch of pals, Beiyinpalica announces his plans to marry Someyer, and speaks of her with glowing pride and love. One of the other young men, a local rogue, responds by talking coarsely about Someyer, about her juicy body, about the little calf growing inside it. After a fight, Beiyinpalica returns home to realize it is all true. His sweetheart has slept with this vulgar character and is pregnant. He is heartsick. He is in agony. He can't speak to her, except to cry "Why??!!" in angry torment. The grandmother tries to reason with him; she tells him the girl loves him, that he was away so long, that many other girls have fallen for this scoundrel, that he should be mature and get over it. Her words fall on deaf ears.

Shortly thereafter he announces his plans to leave. His cherished black steed, Gangga Hara, runs after him as he is driven away, sitting atop produce in the back of an open truck. He cries as he calls his horse's name over and over again. His heartbreaking cries suggest that Gangga Hara symbolizes a larger loss.

What is this loss that is too great to be named? It is not just the loss of Someyer. He has had greater losses, and they have been awakened like sleeping giants. His mother died when he was very young, and shortly afterwards he lost his father, too, when he moved away. The movie says nothing about all this. There is no hint of a problem about early loss. In fact, it seems to suggest just the opposite. Child psychologists will tell you, though, that the child to look out for is the child who seems too well-adjusted in the face of loss. It suggests that he has cut himself off from his pain, which has become like a bomb waiting to explode.

This is how I read Beiyinpalica. His catastrophic losses do not exist for him—until he suffers a new loss as a young man, and suddenly he is flooded with pain. He cannot say, "Oh, my God, I want my mommy!" Instead he says, "I have been betrayed by Someyer, the person I loved beyond all others. She has dealt me a wound I can never forgive."

The betrayal of young love can be especially difficult to forgive. We innocently pin all our hopes for the replenishment of our losses on an idealized lover. Through Someyer, Beiyinpalica reenters paradise; through her, his mother comes back to life. With her betrayal, his mother dies all over again, and his happy universe collapses.

THE TREADMILL OF FORGETTING

Almost ten years later Beiyinpalica, a famous troubadour now, returns to the grasslands looking for the woman he left. He finds that she has given up the nomadic existence and lives in a small village, where she has a hard life and many children. She has married a big-hearted lout who drinks too much and mistreats the one child that is not his—a girl now nine, the product of Someyer's first, fateful pregnancy. Beiyinpalica likes this girl and lets her believe, as her mother has intimated, that he is her real father. Someyer herself does not show up until later in the day when she returns from an exhausting trek gathering wood beyond the mountains. When the girl asks her mother if this is her father, she snaps, "No, he's your uncle!" Nevertheless, the girl clings to the uncle and insists he sleep next to her in the family bed that night.

When the estranged lovers finally get a chance to talk, Someyer says that she's heard Beiyinpalica is famous now. Yes, he says, but it has all been empty without you and Grandma. Indeed, the folk songs he sings are about her, the land, and his horse. Someyer tells Beiyinpalica how Grandmother died, about the death of Gangga Hara, how the man who is now her husband rescued her from destitution. In the following days, Beiyinpalica becomes a part of the family and village life, very close to his niece-daughter and a guest singer in her school, where she brims with pride as he performs.

When it is time to leave, Someyer walks with him into the countryside. He says that he will be sending money for the daughter and asks her to please tell the child that he is indeed her father. In doing this he seems to reclaim his loving self and his love of Someyer. Someyer bursts into tears and howls from her depths, "Why couldn't you have been her father!" They both cry.

Beiyinpalica has come full circle. He is no longer smashed, bereft, with nothing to give. One senses he has come far enough within himself to allow some understanding of Someyer's predicament as a teenage girl. He could do more perhaps. Loss still hangs on him. But he loves again, and that is the joy in this tragic story.

As he rides off, Someyer calls after him in a frantic voice, "If you have a child, please send it to me to take care of! You know I can't live without a child to care for!" and she retreats, crying, to the village. In this parting outburst, in which she reveals her love and her longing for something of him in her life, we also get our first intimation of the emotional costs of the loss of her parents.

It seems now that Someyer has been the unforgiven not just to Beiyinpalica but to herself as well. Suddenly it hits us: She has blamed herself all along. The movie doesn't focus on her loss, but it is no less than his, both as an orphan and a spurned lover. So she, too, has a lot to forgive. Twice she was abandoned by Beiyinpalica, but the grudge she bears is against herself. She blames herself for having been unfaithful and ruining their lives. She seems haunted by regret. Her parting plea suggests, among other things, something of the cruelty that she has subjected herself to, even though she was innocent. Beiyinpalica's return, his acts of caring, especially toward her daughter, the daughter that should have been his, the daughter that he blamed her for, was a redemption for her as well as for him.

The movie ends there, without any suggestion of what will happen in their lives, other than what is already happening. Someyer's plaint, "Why couldn't you have been her father!," is ours, too, and we wish that the two lovers could have each other again. This is not only impossible, given Someyer's new family, but the author would not have it any other way. He is not angling for his character's happiness. He has another joy in mind: the goodness and sense of grace that come from the changes that have taken place in the lovers emotionally, in the form of forgiveness and reconciliation.

A Mongolian Tale reaffirms that forgiveness about injuries this deep does not come easily or quickly. There can't always be a moment of forgiveness, when suddenly our lives are transformed. We are human. We need time to process our experiences, to mourn, to separate, to grow. Forgiveness brews within us, expedited according to our own creative capacities, impeded by our conflicts, a mysterious product of the human spirit. The reclamation of love and of the forgiving self is an arduous and profound journey.

THE GARDEN OF EDEN

The losses of childhood live within us in ways we don't know, can't know, mustn't know. They represent our peculiar vulnerabilities and are surrounded by our specialized defenses and impossible, often unconscious, strivings. In this realm of hidden heartbreak, the part of us that most needs to connect is protected from the threat of connection and all its disruptive feelings. This is the breeding ground of an everyday sort of paranoia* toward others: He just wants to use me. She never loved me at all. They see me as expendable. This is where our protests, criticisms, and

---

* I use the term "paranoia" in this book not clinically or diagnostically but colloquially, i.e. the tendency to interpret others' feelings and actions toward oneself negatively.

complaints still have the ring of a tantrummy child. It is an emotional space characterized by avoidance, clinging, resentment, and revenge.

The original Garden of Eden—which we all have to lose, if not necessarily through the kind of trauma suffered by the Mongolian children—is the bliss states of infancy. Anyone who has seen a baby gazing into a mother (or father's) eyes knows this paradise. The infant is wrapped in his parents' wonderfulness, partaking of all their goodness and perfection. Like them, he is all-powerful, for whatever he cannot make happen himself they will make happen for him. I can remember my own son toward the end of his first year, still swaddled in his parents' adoring glow, lying on his changing table, about to get his tush wiped and taking a kingly pleasure in his newfound mastery of language: "Want milkie! Want blankie!" he cried exuberantly, determined to get everything just so before he would accede to a diaper change, as loving parental servants scurried to fetch. His Majesty the Baby (Freud's phrase) had spoken.

The baby needs this royal treatment. It is how he internalizes a sense of his own goodness, entitlement, and power, what has variously been referred to by such overlapping terms as "basic trust," "healthy narcissism," and "secure attachment." We all have to relinquish the exalted position of infancy, and no one ever quite gets over it. The distant, forgotten loss lingers in an (often unconscious) longing to have Mom and Dad back, the way it once was, wrapped in their caring embrace.

Erik Erikson had a wonderful theory that biting the apple, which led to expulsion from the Garden of Eden in Genesis, was a metaphor for biting the nipple. When teeth come in, the baby starts to bite, mother says, "Enough!," the baby is weaned, paradise is lost. But the loss takes place across a much broader front, especially in modern societies. As the infant ages, parents begin to seem like servants who are falling down on the job. The world becomes a harder place as we grow up, face responsibilities, burdens, limitations. Nothing feels guaranteed in the same way. We have to wipe our own tush, pick up our own clothes, wait our turn, take criticism, *share*. Who wants that! We discover that the people we worship and are supposed to worship us back—indeed, place us before all else—have other agendas. They would rather sleep with each other than with us. All this arouses hurt and angry protests.

Our gradual expulsion from Eden does not have to get in the way of a happy life. In fact, quite obviously, it is critical to a happy life. We need to move on, to experience the real world and its possibilities, to discover our own potential and to have our own life. And this need, this push toward independence, self-reliance, self-definition—*separation*—is a vital part of our makeup. We crave it. The problem is that the losses inherent in growing up, if too traumatic or not handled sensitively, threaten to undo, or at least overshadow, the fragile inner goodness that has been slowly coalescing, causing an insecurity and obsessive clinging that impairs our striving toward selfhood.

Where we end up with all this contributes significantly not only to how we feel about ourselves and what we feel we have to give to others but what we expect from and are able to tolerate and forgive in others. The question might be, Do we develop a healthy narcissism, a sense of goodness and pride in ourselves ("Look, Ma, I'm riding a two-wheeler!"), which confers a certain generosity of spirit, which enables us to enjoy and appreciate others in all their specialness, differences, peculiarities, even badness? Or do we get burdened with feelings of inadequacy? Everyone has some of this narcissistic vulnerability. It can be conscious ("If people really knew me, they wouldn't like me"), which may be accompanied by a false agreeableness. Or it can be unconscious, in which case it may emerge in famously narcissistic traits—self-absorption, boastfulness, imperiousness, a desperate need to always be in the center, and an intolerance toward anything that doesn't please us or suit our purposes. But either way, the vulnerability is there, and we are ready to topple.

Our parents' warmth and encouragement, their fairness and helpfulness, their tolerance of and responsiveness to our protests is a key factor in determining how strong our sense of goodness is. It's their sensitivity that helps us to let go of our enthronement and move toward greater independence and mutuality. Despite some inevitable scars, we learn that we can love and feel loved even if we are not constantly adored, even if our parents (and others later) want to attend to their own needs, even in the face of hurts, disappointments, and the annoying imperfections of others. We can do this in part because we carry enough of Mom's and Dad's solid, splendid early love within and because that love gets steadily replenished in various ways. We have, therefore we can give, including understanding and empathy, and the pardoning of wrongs and limitations.

SELF-LOVE

The idea of a healthy narcissism is an elusive one in our culture. To me, it means letting yourself be who you are, including your blemishes, and taking pride in and being able to enjoy the whole package. It is not bragging, smugness, or superiority. And it is not the pernicious use of slogans ("Damn, I'm good!" and "I'm happy to be me," and all that), which tend to paper over self-doubts and subsidize the flight from mourning with mindless repetition. It is the ability to know what is good about us and feel the goodness of it.

When we are able to locate and operate from that place in us where self-love resides, criticism does not devastate. We are open to criticism even if it hurts, even if it's irrational. We have access to a good feeling about ourselves and therefore are not totally dependent on getting it from others. When looking critically at ourselves, we can see what is bad, suffer the recognition, and want to change. We can feel guilty or ashamed, necessary and important emotions, without succumbing to a state of guilt or a state of shame in which the whole self is blackened or drenched in remorse.

In this realm of positive self-regard, we do not expect ourselves to be perfect. Our limitations are not a cause for self-laceration or despair. They may be a cause for sorrow and regret, but not the sorrow of depression or the regret of someone who is obsessively plunging a dagger into his chest. We have a sense of proportion. Not all imperfections are grave. To a certain extent our imperfections are part of the pleasure of who we are, even if we may be struggling to change or to grow beyond some of them. We can know we are prima donnas, gossips, materialists, thrill-seekers, penny-pinchers, lovers of dumb novels or crass entertainments, rotten housekeepers, occasional bullies or paranoids, gluttons, slowpokes, and so on, and neither feel the need to legitimatize any of it by forcing others to swallow it nor cripple ourselves with inferior feelings and self-denunciations. As I sit on my rocker with my feet up, hoping someone else (like my son, who accuses me of treating him like a servant) will fetch the ringing phone, I can feel the pull of disparate aspects of my being. On the one side, disparagement—Why don't I have more energy? Shouldn't I be more like so-and-so, the living dynamo? Aren't I a sorry excuse for a human being? On the other side a pleasure that comes from nothing more than being me. It's not about goodness or badness in the value sense; it's about acceptance and love. And just like the disparagement that could so easily replace it, it is associated with a relationship, internalized long ago, in this case one in which I am appreciated just for being me.

It is important to realize, then, that a healthy narcissism does not *equate* with goodness. Rather, it refers to the ability to *experience* the goodness in oneself. Similarly, to be troubled by a wounded narcissism, is not to be lacking in goodness, talents, excellent human qualities. We just don't know they're there (at least not in a secure, nonbragging way). We are immersed in a different sort of interior experience, where we are horrible and unwanted. Sometimes, in our misery, we can convince ourselves we have no goodness, no power, no sense of belonging or entitlement at all—and never did.

Clinging

We are never fully adults until we leave home emotionally; although, in fairness, this is always a matter of degree and the leaving process is never complete. In childhood, a sense of security and inner goodness in our relationships with our parents and other significant figures—"secure attachment"—is where this leave-taking begins, for secure attachment is always echoed by secure separation. We love our parents but we are not anxiously dependent on them, nor they on us. We are not stuck in their orbit, desperately trying to get from them or their later stand-ins what we should have had to begin with. We have learned, in effect, that we can separate while staying connected.

Secure separation begins in happy infant exploration. It is apparent later in our ability to enjoy school, sleepovers, summer camp, solitude. And still later in our ability to have a certain degree of freedom in relationships—to enjoy being ourselves and to enjoy the other person's otherness. We are not overly possessive, controlling, or dependent—all signs of the failure to separate. We can let the other person be.

Secure separation serves us well when dealing with other people's inner dramas. We are not drawn in so easily by guilt, by desperation, by all the ways that people have of letting us know that we are vital figures in their early traumas, which are playing now like real-life movies on their internal screens.

Secure separation is apparent in our ability to tolerate anger and criticism, the lack of appreciation for our musicianship or artwork, a cancellation of plans by a friend, a business trip by a spouse or lover, without experiencing them as total rejections. It's not that these things don't hurt us or make us angry. It's not even necessarily that we don't feel rejected. But that's not all we feel. Like the rabbi whose wife went back to work, making him come home every night to a dark, empty house, we can see beyond our own infantile view. We are not stuck with access to only one story about ourselves, the same old story of hurt and deprivation. We are not, in that sense, still living at home emotionally with the parent who was unfair, mean, depriving, etc. And from an early age, these aspects of separation make it easier for us to form loving relations outside the home. The insecure person—or, perhaps better, the insecure part of us—is, by contrast, haunted by separation anxiety. He can't let go.

It is one of life's great sadnesses that parents are caught up in their own torments and limitations and their children's delicate emotional needs get neglected or trampled on, with the result that children are left with painful insecurities. In some people narcissistic disturbance achieves the status of a diagnosis ("narcissistic personality disorder"), but aspects of it are generously spread through the population as a whole. We see it in the part of us that expects ourselves to be perfect, that pounds ourselves for past mistakes, that needs a perfect mate to merge with like a baby on the breast. We demand perfect attunement, a partner who knows what we feel without our having to voice it: "Why should I have to ask? If I have to ask, that ruins it."

The tendency to idealize others is an aspect of the narcissistic dilemma. A lover, a boss, a friend, or a therapist can become the godparent of early infancy who lifts us up by his wonderfulness. But idealization is a trap for both people: for the person who idealizes, because the goodness always resides in someone else and not himself; for the idealized, because they cannot be allowed to be who they are. And when they fall from grace, they are not easily retrieved.

We are all haunted to some degree by a smallness and a mortality we wish to deny. To cope, we seek applause, power, diversions, obsessions. Janis Joplin once said that she had no one to love, that the audience was her only love. The intoxication of performing for a screaming, applauding audience may be one of the experiences in adult life that approximates adoring mother love. Most people have felt it in small degrees, at a birthday party or wedding, for example, when friends and family are cheering and offering tributes. This intense injection of warmth and acceptance can banish depression, put a glow on one's skin, erase the pain and posture of age. When real intimacy is too threatening, such public adulation may be the only form of love a person can tolerate.

Power is another such tonic for wounded self-love. To be able to control, to command, to be surrounded by eager supplicants and helpers also replicates the lost pleasures of infancy. King Lear was abetted in a lifetime of narcissistic folly by the privileges of authority. Our world is full of people who thrive on power and acclamation and feel empty and worthless without it. Is it any wonder that threats to power can, much like rejection, sexual betrayal, or public humiliation, engender an unforgiving rage of infantile proportions?

Perhaps the most universal form of solace for the frailties we need to deny are the stories we tell ourselves about our lives. We soothe ourselves, consciously and unconsciously, with fairy tales tinged with grandiosity that leave us feeling less vulnerable than we really are. If you question my judgment, if you won't come when I need you, if you forget my birthday, if you raise your voice, if you don't love my dog, you may cause to collapse all the stories I've told myself about my own goodness; about the happiness, soundness, and security of my life; and about the control that I have over it. It all now seems a pack of cards. Once again, I inhabit the dark territory of depression and terrible truth, that area of unmourned loss, where I experience myself as hateful, unwanted, and alone. And *this is what I cannot forgive.* Indeed, this is why I hate you and want to kill you! To forgive you, I'm going to have to deal with the inner mess you've stirred up. In this realm of unmourned loss, forgiveness does not feel like an option. It is hostage to growth.

THE FAILURE
OF PROTEST
AND REPAIR

THE FILM *MA VIE EN ROSE* IS ABOUT A BELGIAN BOY OF SEVEN, Ludovic, who longs to be a girl. When his family moves to a new neighborhood, they have a lawn party to meet their neighbors. During the introductions, Ludovic makes a dramatic, late appearance wearing lipstick, earrings, and his sister's princess dress. His family is shocked. "What got into you?" his father demands later. "I wanted to look pretty," he says. His parents cannot grasp what he knows to be true about himself—that his boy's body is a temporary annoyance—and so he is continually at odds with them and nonplused by their reactions, as they are by his. "Never again!" his father shouts.

Ludovic has elaborate dreams of being a bride and marrying Jerome, a friend and classmate. The malleable Jerome is more of a boy's boy but he does have a crush on the magnetically sweet Ludovic. Unfortunately, Jerome's father is Ludovic's father's boss. The two boys engage in a pretend wedding ceremony in the bedroom of Jerome's dead sister, which is supposed to be off-limits. Jerome's mother faints when she witnesses the scene. Ludovic's mother drags him home.

"I told you," she says angrily, "boys never marry boys—or very rarely."

"But I'll be a girl."

"Cut it *out,*" she says sternly. "You're a boy and you always will be!" She pauses. "Ah, you're so *stubborn!*" Then, softening: "Just like your mother." She smiles at him coyly and lovingly and the light returns to his eyes.

At dinner the father strains to explain. "Jerome is Albert's son, and Albert is Daddy's boss. You are not to dress up like a girl with Jerome." Then, losing his composure: "You are not to dress up like a girl with *anyone!*" The mother and father have a row over his loss of temper, and the father storms out. Ludovic goes looking for him. Father is outside doing pull-ups to blow off steam. Ludovic approaches with downcast eyes. He offers Dad his hand to hold, and Dad takes it. "Shall we go inside?" Dad asks tenderly. They walk back slowly, their arms around each other.

This is just the start of a turbulence that will engulf the family. Perhaps because Ludovic feels so well-loved, he is not inclined to stifle himself, to pretend to be what he's not, to be falsely compliant and therefore truly bent, not just "bent" in the way the neighbors define it. The whole community, sitting in the audience at the school play, is shocked when Ludovic, having locked little Sleeping Beauty in the dressing room, takes her place in the final scene, hoping that Jerome, who plays the knight, will plant the climactic kiss on him. He is thrown out of school, and his mother is furious because now she has to take him to a new school, out of the district, on the bus each day. His father is fired. The family has to relocate. His mother, the more tolerant one at first, gets into a sustained, nasty snit with Ludovic. He tells her he hates her and wants to live with Granny, which he does for a while. They move to a new community where Dad has found a job. There he cross-dresses again. His mother goes berserk, hitting and cursing him.

Ludovic disappears after his mother's vicious attack and she frantically searches for him, eventually having an accident and getting knocked unconscious. When she comes to, she is surrounded by her worried family, Ludovic included. Warm words are exchanged, some silence, then: "I'll take these off," Ludovic says of the girl's clothes he's still wearing.

"Do whatever feels best," his father responds, his hands planted fondly on the boy's shoulders. It is a clear statement of acceptance: I finally hear you; I will stop trying to change you; I love you fully no matter what you wear or who you are, even a strange girl-boy.

Mom, still on her back: "Whatever happens, you will always be my child. Our child. I've tended to forget that lately. But not anymore."

Because of his pronounced sweetness and femininity, it would be easy to overlook Ludovic's strength in his determination to be himself, his conviction that he has the right to pursue his own wishes despite the feverish objections of his parents, and his willingness to protest their behavior ("I hate you! I want to live with Granny!") when they hurt him. Such convictions develop in the context of being secure in his parents' love, a security which, by definition, includes a right to be oneself, a right to protest hurts, intrusions, deprivations, as well as the knowledge and faith that even when love breaks down it can and will be put back together.

For all their anger and incomprehension, even brutality, what is most memorable about the parents is the force of their love. With each of them, there is always a full-hearted effort to repair the rips they've created in the loving fabric of their relationship with their son. It doesn't always happen right away, which is agonizing for the child. But it does happen, and it is never stingy.

The poster for *Ma Vie en Rose* contained the blurb "Sometimes you just have to be yourself." But that did not convey the spirit of the movie. The theme is more accurately family love, how it can hold within it hatred and rage and still survive, indeed much better than if those things were suppressed. It is also, quite touchingly, about the related processes of protest and repair, which are fundamental to forgiveness.

The Origins of Repair

Every baby attacks its parents. Small babies are unrestrained by concern for the harm they might do. The capacity for concern and guilt and the wish to repair the damage one has done only emerge over time.

The baby maintains separate universes for the good and the bad, such that every important person in his life, himself included, is experienced in two almost entirely disconnected ways—wonderful and beloved or evil and persecutory, depending on the moment. The infant does not think, Mom is really great sometimes and sometimes she pisses me off. Mom is the most wonderful being in the universe, loved beyond all reason. But when she is angry, impatient, absent, neglectful, can't comfort the baby, she's a horrible witch: She's persecuting me, I hate her, life is hell, everything is shit including her and me. This simple moral division seems to represent our only possible mode of organization at the beginning of life, of sorting out the good from the bad. The Austrian-British analyst Melanie Klein theorized that we are born with these two templates for sorting out the world. Through one template everything is imbued with a positive glow that automatically includes feelings of love, idealization, adoration. Through the other we experience danger, persecution, hatred, and envy. The result of this sorting process is not just a black-and-white universe, but a split universe. Everything, everybody, has two incarnations. When Mom is good, she is an angel, in which case one set of feelings, memories, and expectations is activated. When Mom is bad, she is a witch, in which case another set of feelings, memories, and expectations is activated. The two moms inhabit separate universes that do not know about each other.

Even in the first days of life, Klein believed, when our perceptual apparatus is not developed enough to grasp a whole person, when the key relationship is not me and Mommy but me and breast (or me and feeding bottle), we live through the same templates. The loved and adored breast loves us, wants to nourish us; the hated breast withholds from us, wants to persecute us. All the forces of heaven endow the relationship with the good breast with an eternal loving glow, while all hell screams out against the baby and the bad breast, wrapping them in a desperate struggle to death.

As perceived by an adult mind, this may seem a simple matter of different experiences. At times the baby is in a receptive, positive mood, the milk is flowing and tastes good, and the world feels like a good place. At other times, the baby is cranky, the milk doesn't flow or tastes bad, and life is hell. This is true enough, but it is not necessarily the picture the baby initially paints for himself. The overview—at times one thing, at times another—is too advanced. The binary baby does not have an overview. It experiences two different breasts, two different selves, two different relationships and is only capable of knowing about one at a time. He is not aware that he divides the world in two, he just does it by experiencing it in two different ways; and when the bad breast or bad mom is present, the good one is denied and forgotten. Likewise, when the hateful, persecuted baby is present, the happy, all-loving one is denied and forgotten. It's partially an active splitting of the world, a determination to separate black from white, partially an inability to hold an ambivalent view. Things are either good or bad, and goodness must not be allowed to get spoiled by the bad. This tendency toward idealization and demonization is never abandoned and plays a big part in the worshipfulness and adoration, the feuds and grudges of later life.

Gradually it dawns on the very small child that the mom he loves is the same person as the mom he hates, and as he awakens to this, he experiences a series of crises. He realizes that the witch he wants to destroy—indeed, has wished every vile thing upon!—and has hurt, literally, with his biting, scratching, and kicking, is the very person he loves and needs beyond measure. This leads to a depressive state, characterized by guilt and remorse. Inevitably, he also experiences a wish to repair the damage he feels he has done ("I'm sorry, Mom, I'm sorry I hit you and said mean things."). If all goes well, repeated experiences of guilt, remorse, and efforts to repair and—if his parents are receptive—success in repair, gradually lift him out of this depressive state. They help usher him into another state of being where he is able to perceive good and bad in the same person *simultaneously.* Mom and Dad are not perfect, but they still love me and I love them.

This unified internal world takes time to coalesce, is never fully built, and does not replace the earlier binary world, which both the child and the adult can easily slip into. The binary, black-and-white mentality offers the shelter of simplicity. There are good behaviors, bad behaviors; good people, bad people; right thinking, wrong thinking; righteous nations, wicked nations. The potential to live there is not only never lost; it represents a significant part of our psychic life, for many people the most significant part. It is associated with blaming, revenge-seeking, scapegoating, xenophobia, warmongering, the draconian treatment of prisoners, as well as idol worship, cult phenomena, religions of the "one true faith," and chauvinism. The paranoid instincts and the capacity to detach from the feelings of others that characterize this state are useful at times, critical to certain occupations, like espionage, and to certain periods, like that of war.

But the capacity to take a more complex view represents the entry into a realm of greater maturity, of emotional responsibility, and of the ability to accept the difficult, sometimes troubling ambiguity that is life. It is as fundamental to psychological growth as the emergence from infantile grandiosity, with which it is closely related. Indeed, the development of what we have called healthy narcissism or secure self-love is perhaps indistinguishable from this process of emerging into a unified worldview, where human frailty and error can be tolerated.

For the child in this new ambiguous world, love and hate still exist. But they no longer exist separately all the time, the love being directed toward a perfect, idealized parent, the hatred directed at a monster who cares only about herself and devours her young. The child has achieved the ability to transcend this binary state; he can bring the love and hate together. There is now an imperfect parent who can lose her temper, who can make a lousy meal, who can talk too long on the phone and yet remain a good and loved person. In addition to love and concern, we are able to feel a range of negative feelings toward this integrated parent, including fury and hatred, but all within an envelope of love. I'm hurt precisely because I love you and because I need you to love me. I'm angry because I love you. I criticize you because I love you. I hate you because I love you. I want you to be different because I love you.

In this new dimension, love is the final word. It's a much less perfect-looking place than the Garden of Eden that preceded it. But it is stabler, more real, and we do not have to slip into the hell of total hatred, persecution, and fantasies of revenge in order to experience our anger, hatred, rage, or disappointment or to hear the same from others. A kind of emotional monotheism has developed. All things, good and bad, are possible in this unified world. But it is a fragile state that is easily lost and may require considerable effort (and sometimes help) to regain.*

The ease with which our monotheism is lost is apparent in the con-

---

*I've used the metaphor of monotheism because of its implication that God is one, God is love, God runs through and emanates from all people, whether they are believers or not, whether they behave badly or not. The reality of monotheistic religions has not always lived up to this ideal, of course. Splitting has a way of sneaking in through the back door. Nonbelievers and wrongdoers are demonized, as are portions of the self, and the devil is created to suggest that there is, indeed, a dark other, a pure evil, and those who do his work.

tagiousness of paranoia. When you are hurt by me because of something mean or selfish I've done and experience me suddenly as an enemy, I am drawn to hate you back in the same black-and-white way. Like you, I now forget the goodness of our connection. Suddenly, and with crazed conviction, I experience you as an enemy as well, and I want to kill you.

We are all prone to this paranoiac contagion, although to different degrees. The more strongly monotheistic integration has been established in us, the less susceptible we are to the paranoia of others and the better able we are to hold on to our connectedness even in the face of all-out hatred. But it is a slippery business. Holding on to our monotheism and expanding it are a lifetime's work for those who wish to undertake it.

For the child, monotheistic integration makes new things possible. He can now say, "You hurt me, Mommy" or "I hate you, Daddy" without feeling that he will lose their love. In this we see the beginning of healthy, confident protest. Its development depends on the parent's openness to the child's negative feelings, no matter how ragefully those feelings are expressed. It is the parent who keeps demonstrating and re-establishing that we live in the country of love, that in this country all feelings are allowed, even hateful feelings, that we don't have to leave this country because of the other things we feel.

Monotheism allows the greatest of all freedoms, the freedom to be. It is, I believe, the essential mindset of secure attachment. The extent to which we live in it varies hugely from one relationship to another, from one psychological state to another. But at its apex, often arrived at in a relationship of ample love and trust, we approach that much-sought place where we can truly accept ourselves. It is here that we achieve our greatest tolerance and forgiveness.

The parent's steady love—which is to say the parent's own monotheism—sows these seeds of security, self-acceptance, tolerance, forgiveness. It doesn't mean that the parent never gets angry, that he never wants to throw the child against the wall, that he never protests, that he never wrestles with his faith. But he himself has a fairly strong capacity to tolerate negative feelings, the child's and his own, and even enjoy them much of the time.

When a parent is too neglectful, scary, or rejecting, the child has a hard time achieving or holding on to a monotheistic integration. He doesn't see Dad as a combination of good and bad, as someone who, overall, he loves and feels loved by despite the flaws. The goodness and badness of Dad won't come together. But if Dad never allows himself to be angry, he risks the very same thing. Is Dad all good? Is there a bad Dad, too horrible to be let out, lurking behind the good? Do I have to be all good? Does my anger mean there is a monster in me that I must not let out?

And so it is important that the parent have his aggression and yet temper it with his love and empathy. He has some feeling for what it's like to be a child, to be afraid, to have a secret, to want to flee adult control, to want to strike back. From that place of sensitivity—for himself and for his child—he can make his aggression potent and yet modulate it enough so that it does not do damage and can even be a source of pleasure for parent and child. The same sensitivity that causes the parent to modulate his anger also enables him to see the child's aggression, less tempered for sure, as something to be valued, as a charming aspect of the child's self-assertion. He is able to recognize in it the development of the child's own point of view, of his spunkiness and ability to protest.

The parent also needs to be able to handle being experienced by the child as *bad*. If that is too threatening, if it destabilizes the parent's own sense of goodness, then the child is put in an untenable position. Not only can't he get the relief that splitting affords him (Mom's bad, I'm good), but his tendency to split, to idealize and demonize, is reinforced. Badness, he learns, cannot, after all, be tolerated. It kills goodness and kills love. Mom's hostility proves it.

When the parent is firmly situated in the zone of connection, being bad is not so threatening. He is in touch with his own goodness and not dependent on the child's view. He doesn't need his child to be loving and easy to affirm him. He is not ruled by his narcissistic fragility, his fear of arousing his unmourned losses, or his dread of separation. He is able to stay lovingly connected regardless of where the child goes. He doesn't demonize himself or the child even if he has to reprimand or punish him. He remains confident that love is the umbrella, the overarching truth of this relationship, regardless of what else is felt or expressed.

The parent's monotheism allows him to set limits, to say no, to be firm in the face of tantrummy demands, and to feel good about himself in the process. He does not feel guilty because he is still in touch with his love—indeed, he is operating out of that love; and he doesn't have to overindulge the child to convince himself of it. He also knows that the child, in all his ire, is still ardently in love with him, even if the child himself has lost touch with that. So the parent doesn't live in fear of an unbearable loss, which might make him alternately clinging and rageful. When the parent operates out of this place a good enough percentage of the time, the child discovers, much to his relief, that his negative emotions—his anger, his complaints about being bored or not liking what he's been given, his sulking, his jealousy, his hatred—are neither damaging nor a terrible reflection on his character or soul. All these things can live within a loving relationship. Without that confidence, loving relationships feel confining. Love demands that you always be on good behavior, love demands that you always have to be pleasing, and so on. The confidence that he can be all the things he is without fear of shame or rejection, on the other hand, allows him to grant that freedom to others. It is the cornerstone of a forgiving spirit.

The parent's monotheism also means knowing the difference between thought and deed. He doesn't have to feel guilty and batter himself for wanting to wring his child's neck, nor does he have to batter the child for having the same impulse. He understands the child's inclination to regress, to demonize, to overreact; he gives the child space to come back and repair, and he welcomes the child's efforts to do so. In all of this, he creates a safe place for the child's own monotheism to develop.

Just as the parent has been able to tolerate and to welcome the child's anger and hatred, the child learns that he can tolerate these emotions in himself and others. When anger or hatred is directed at him, he may be rattled, he may even feel persecuted, and that may be true for the rest of his life, but there is some resilience, some ability to bounce back. He can live with people who have an attitude toward him that is critical or unfriendly; who believe things about him that he knows are untrue; who hold a grudge, who don't forgive, etc. He doesn't depend on them for his sense of goodness. He doesn't get wound around them in hopeless perpetual protest. Nor is he so dependent on his own view of himself—I am good, I haven't done anything wrong, I have nothing in common with the unjust caricature this person holds of me—that he cannot entertain another point of view and believe he might learn something from it. He can say, The girl I like thinks I'm a playboy and won't date me, or My colleague thinks I'm out to get his job, and still have a positive feeling that this is a person I care about, am connected to in some way, can get things from, and that our future may be better than the present. He can say, My cousin doesn't like me, and I can see why, without feeling that the unlikable things his cousin has seen in him invalidate him. In the zone of resentment, ruled by the gods of shame, guilt, and blame, goodness comes from being able to prove others wrong. In the realm of security and connection, goodness is just there, it's the monotheistic envelope in which all sorts of bad or regrettable things can live without making us worthless or turning others into committed tormentors or deprivers in our eyes.

The parent's ability to impart such a view is not always conscious or verbalized, although it certainly can be. It may never have been learned in words. It is often a spontaneous part of his or her emotional makeup. So that when the mother runs after the kid with her hand raised, chasing him downstairs and out the front door, threatening to knock his block off or tan his hide, the child knows that he is in big trouble but that he is still loved. Or even if he forgets that for the moment, he soon regains it. He does not feel a depressing fog of misery, badness, and isolation settling into him, the terror of exile and excommunication. He still has his mother and his loving connection with her, and somehow things will get worked out.

All parents foul up. They cross the line in their rage such that their love is no longer protecting the child. Such moments are like a crisis in faith. The envelope of love seems to disintegrate, and feelings of rage, paranoia, hatred, and revenge spill out in undiluted form. We've all experienced it. "My mother could freeze me out with a look." "When my dad felt disappointed in me, he made me feel like two cents." We saw that in *Ma Vie en Rose* where both mother and father were horribly rejecting toward Ludovic at one time or another and seemed to literally forget their love. But both of them were able to cross back and repair the damage.

The confidence to repair and to believe that our efforts will be accepted suggests a knowledge that, even at our worst, we still have a right to love and to feel okay about ourselves and to know that if we make amends, our love will be accepted and returned.

Repair is inherent in the new monotheism of the developing child's emotional life. It can be seen as the beginnings of both forgiveness and apology. Throughout our lives we eject people from the loving circle, and then, in forgiving, apologizing, owning up, or just reconnecting with our own connectedness, our hearts go out to them. But repair does not always occur, and, in childhood, its failure leaves scars.

These scars are universal, a part of the human condition, even though their extent and their overall effect vary vastly. Every life is a crazy quilt of splitting and paranoia, of terrible feelings of guilt and badness that seem as if they cannot be dispelled, of hopelessness over the prospect of repair, of idealization and escapist fantasies of perfection, but also of the monotheism that enables us to stay in the zone of connection and be a force for keeping our relationships together. Whether the crazy quilt adds up to an essentially healthy disposition, where we have enough access to our own creativity, where we have enough awareness of our own goodness to be able to give, where we are not too threatened to entertain another point of view, including an angry or critical one, depends in large measure on what we meet up with in parents, siblings, and other crucial people in our early lives and on the work we do later, as adults, to improve whatever childhood has bequeathed us.

I WANTED TO BLOW UP
THE WHOLE WORLD

Small children often feel the need to get even before they can forgive. Their primitive sense of justice demands satisfaction: I felt hurt and rejected by you and now I'm going to do the same back. But they can also be quick to return to love. At three my son had a strong will and a temper to match. He easily flared into outrage: "I don't like you! I'm not going to play with you! I'm not going to be your friend anymore!" Whereupon he would march out of the room to find his mom. But five minutes later we were pals again.

The little research that has been done in this realm suggests that between the ages six and eight children still see a tit-for-tat solution as the essential response to unkindness. From nine to fourteen they are more likely to look beyond retaliation and take a more nuanced view.

F. Clark Power of the University of Notre Dame tells a ten-year-old girl about the apocryphal druggist, first mentioned in Chapter 1, who hid the drug that might have saved a man's wife because the man was too poor to pay for it. The man's wife dies. Should he forgive the druggist? The girl answers that doing so would be "hard" and "might take a long time," but it would be "nice," "as long as the druggist apologized." Power then asks if it would be okay for the man to retaliate in kind if at some point in the future their situations were reversed. No, the girl says, because "two wrongs don't make a right." A ten-year-old boy agrees. He says that he would want to be forgiven if he made a mistake. And, besides, the druggist should be forgiven, because he "is going to feel sorry for what he did, and life goes on."

We see in these youthful and still somewhat naïve responses a huge advance in cognitive and moral development—the struggle to see both sides, to balance justice with charity, to put oneself in the shoes of the guilty person and empathize with his (presumed) suffering, to forgo revenge in favor of the resumption of a cooperative connection. That these children are able to reason this way probably owes a lot to being taught moral values at home, at school, in church. Moral education, formal or informal, helps the child to think more complexly about intentions and circumstances, to take a view of relationships and of others that goes beyond the immediate, to understand that everyone errs, and to see things from other perspectives. There is no guarantee that this will yield authentic forgiveness: It could promote a coerced, ingratiating forgiveness, wherein the child learns to simply fold and forgive when faced with bullying or guilt-tripping. But, if conveyed with gentle encouragement and respect for the child's conflicting feelings, a moral education invites the child to struggle creatively with hurts and what to do about them. It promotes that side of his psychology that wants to move beyond the primitivity of good-vs.-evil, of paranoia, and of revenge; it gives him something more complex to reach for.

For many bright, sensitive children, understanding the concepts involved in forgiveness can easily outstrip their ability to forgive. The fact that ten-year-olds are able to think that a miserly druggist who behaved heartlessly should be forgiven does not, of course, mean that these same children would be forgiving themselves—if, for instance, they entrusted a friend with feeding their pet while they were away on vacation and he forgot to do so, so that the pet died. Indeed, far less grievous offenses can generate bitter hatreds and feuds at this age. What if the friend "stole" her best friend? Or humiliated her in gym class? So the question is not just how do children learn to think about complex issues like justice and forgiveness but, also, why do two children with a similar intellectual grasp of moral issues behave differently?

Children are deeply pained by injustice. I have been impressed by the way many parents I know have attended to their children's protests in this regard. They acknowledge the child's feelings. They own up about their own mistakes. When they lose their temper with the child, they try to deal with that first, independently of whatever crime the child himself may have committed.

When my son was three, a memorable event occurred one morning when I was taking him out to the playground. When we got downstairs, he decided he didn't want to go to the playground after all. He wanted to go in the opposite direction, up the hill, and on my shoulders. This was something I did not want to do at all. We made a deal. I would carry him as far as the canopy of the next building, and after that, we would turn around and walk back to the playground together. When we got to the canopy, I said, "Okay, Rafie" and began to put him down; but he pulled my hair and scratched my forehead with such ferocity that I yelled out in pain and furiously hurled to the ground the large red plastic fire chief's car I was carrying for him. I still remember the wheels of the car bursting off and flying into the street and the face of a passing adult who coldly scrutinized me as if I were a child abuser. I told my son angrily to get back to our building at once. He ran back crying as I picked up the pieces. Once inside and upstairs, I cooled off and told him I was sorry for having become so enraged. Rafie said, "That's right, Daddy, because I'm just little." It seemed that he wanted me to know both that he needed the room to misbehave and that my rage was too much for him. After that, we talked about our fight many times, told and retold the story, until it gradually lost its negative charge and became a piece of family lore:

> The time Daddy smashed Rafie's car
> (after Rafie scratched Daddy's face and pulled his hair).

One night during this stormy period, when I was putting my son to bed, my wife encouraged me to use this time to work out any altercations from earlier in the day, and this soon became a routine. Not surprisingly, it would sometimes turn out that he had held onto some incident more than I had guessed. He would tell me I hurt his feelings when I displayed some anger, and he would be relieved by my apology or display of caring, as if it helped him to release a dammed-up hurt. He would also want to tell me that he felt bad about the mean things he said to me; and he would earnestly agree if I said, "You don't want to hurt Daddy."

Such exchanges with a child help him to understand the emotional turmoil he is struggling with. It is a way of learning that you can hurt and be hurt by and hate the person you love without that love being destroyed. It helps build cognitive, emotional, and behavioral pathways to healthy protest—I have power, I can be heard and understood, I can make a difference. It reaffirms the possibilities of repair.

Another father describes dealing with an even greater level of rage toward his small son:

> Around the time of his fifth birthday, about eight months after my wife and I separated, I took Jerry to the Jersey Shore for a week with my extended family. He enjoyed himself with everyone but me. I could not do anything right. He accused me constantly. He rejected me. He twisted my words, making them into the opposite of what I'd said and then took offense. He wouldn't listen. Rage welled up in me that I didn't know what to do with. I tried a formula—to let him have his anger no matter how crazy and irrational it seemed, but to firmly disapprove of random acts of disrespect. It worked at times. A couple of times, I blew up at him when he was dissing the hell out of me.

Jerry actually seemed relieved by that. I needed a lot of help to get through the week.

One of my relatives who was there that week told me that after his separation from his first wife, his daughters were similarly furious at him and that it took some time for them to get over it. It had been months since the separation, and Jerry had not exhibited much anger until now, but François pointed out that this was a loaded situation. On our previous trips to the Shore, we had come as a family, and now for the first time his mother was not there, while all around us were intact families, one of them with a new baby who was getting tons of attention.

A few days later, after we returned to Philadelphia, I said to him, "Jerry, I think I know why you were so upset with me when we were at the Shore." He was interested. I said, "It was the first time we had gone away without Mom. You must have been very upset and angry with me, especially being around all those families that had mommies and daddies together." He said, "Yeah, it made me so angry I wanted to blow up the whole world! And then if some other little bad thing happened, it made it that much worse." His response amazed me. I thought it totally right on. After that, the air seemed to have cleared.

No one did any apologizing in this conversation; there was no overt forgiveness. But there certainly was repair. Father and son got to something that had been a wedge between them. Jerry knew he had been acting cruelly toward his father, could not help himself, and was grateful his father did not turn against him or leave him stuck in all the badness he felt about himself. Jerry had slipped into demonizing his father, which must have been costing him a lot emotionally; for if Dad is a demon, he no longer has a good dad. It was not a place Jerry wanted to be, but he needed help getting out of it. His father's words liberated him from the primitive defense of projecting his rage onto his father and then reacting peevishly against it. They rescued him from an inchoate feeling of being a bad and difficult boy. They were a valuable lesson in the benefits of speaking one's feelings and working things out, and, more subtly, of the importance of being able to define the complexity of one's feelings and not settle for something simplistic. In Jerry's newfound clarity, there was also a newfound legitimacy. Of course, he wanted to blow up the world! It is the unspoken, the supposedly forgotten, that becomes the seeding ground for guilt, shame, bitter hurt, silence, and, eventually, more explosions.

The child needs his protest. His protest begins in crying, tantrums, and physical attacks. As he gets older, he learns to use his words. His verbal expression of anger, like his biting and kicking before, can be ferocious. And he needs that ferocity, too, at times, especially considering the size and power of his parents and what he may be up against in them. Through gradual limit-setting, modeling by the parent, and positive experiences of repair, he learns to modulate his rage. Ideally, he becomes a connoisseur of anger. He recognizes the variations of feeling within himself, from being so angry he wants to destroy to an anger that is looking for and expects the redress of his grievances. He may learn how to modulate his anger to protect the other person, how to lighten it at times with humor. He may learn how to speak his anger without enacting it and how to protest without anger—in each case because he has faith that he will be heard and that something good will come of that. He learns, also, how to hold on to his protest when he is not understood without becoming murderous or depressed. He discovers that there is something good in simply having his say, even if he is not heard. He can feel sad: It's disappointing when someone you love can't or won't understand, can't or won't give you what you need. It hurts. But better to hurt than to be shut off and bitter. This is an ideal picture, of course, but it gives some sense of the directions in which a positive experience with protest can take the child.

The constructive use of anger and the knowledge that connections do not have to be damaged by it represent an advance in a child's development. Anger becomes a means of staying connected instead of lapsing into depression and resentment or both. We learn about the goodness or badness of anger not only by how our parents receive our anger but also by how they use their own, especially with us, but also with others. A woman recalls that when her mother had a fight with a friend, she never spoke to that person again. "It took me a long time to learn that if some-one got angry at me it didn't mean he didn't like me or love me any-more."

Children need their parent's anger. It is an essential part of the par-ent and the parent's relationship to the child, and the child wants to know the parent in all his aspects, even if he gets scary at times. A par-ent's healthy access to anger, his ability to warmly, even hotly, express his own protests, is an important model for the child and lets him know that he can have his anger, too, that it doesn't have to obliterate or ruin, that it can be helpful to a relationship if used constructively, that it does not have to be shamefully hidden, that even if it hurts it won't destroy, and even when destructive there can be repair. "Go ahead, use it, try it out, have fun with it, it's not bad!" is at least part of the message. Even when it is bad and we seal ourselves off from each other, we can still come back.

Protest, which is what anger is all about, is a natural and necessary part of nonnarcissistic connections. People aren't perfectly attuned to us, they don't do the right thing by us all the time, they can be mean and vindictive or simply wrapped up in themselves, and protest is part of the way we negotiate and correct relationships.

THE PRETENSE OF REPAIR

In *Ma Vie en Rose,* Ludovic's parents always manage a loving repair. I don't think that is the norm for most children, at least not in our culture where so much militates against it.* In some homes a kind of Stalinist repair dominates. The child does something that irks the parent. He may be fussing or tantrummy or just extremely annoying, as children can be; often it's the child's anger that the parent cannot tolerate. But whatever the cause, the parent loses his temper, goes into a rage, perhaps becomes physically violent. Now the parent feels guilty. He wants to erase what's just happened. He wants to be forgiven. But he cannot accept responsi-

---

* Like the tendency of parents to be on heavy working schedules, the increased pace of life and pressure of time, and the absence of extended-family networks to take the strain off the parent-child bond.

bility or blame. It will make him feel too ashamed, too terrible about himself. So he doesn't fully soften; he doesn't relocate his love. He doesn't say to himself, Oh, my God, I've been a monster to this little person I love, and now I want to do everything I can—own up, apologize, soothe—to nurse this sobbing child back to repair. This avenue feels closed to him. Besides, the parent experiences the child not as a child but as a persecutor. So he is locked in his accusatory anger. And it is from this place of wanting to fix the damage he's done but having to keep the blame on the child that he approaches the task of repair: It is time for the child to confess his sins.

If you confess, if you recognize the bad thing you've done, we can be friends again. It's like a Moscow show trial. The child is bullied into acknowledging his badness, the parent is relieved, and now he is warm again toward the child. Life resumes. But the child has just learned a rotten lesson. Forgiveness, apology, and other forms of repair emerge not from the power of our love but through weakness. Also, that the powerful can spill their rage all over without remorse, that only the powerless apologize, that forgiveness comes at the price of submission. Meanwhile, the child does not feel loved or even really forgiven; he feels used and manipulated, and his rage has nowhere to go. There is no legitimate avenue of protest. And so before long he refuses to listen, or drops a plate when cleaning the table, or leaves his dirty clothes in the living room, or makes a rude, mocking face, or worse, and the cycle starts again.

Similar in a way to Stalinist repair is clutching repair. Again the parent goes berserk. But now the principal thing the parent feels in the midst of her meltdown is guilt coupled with the fear that she will lose the child's love. I recall a mother and daughter like this. After smacking the kid, the mother would pull the daughter to her, pet her, and kiss her: "My sweetie, my darling!" But there was little or no attunement to the child. She was not operating from a place of genuine concern. She had no interest in what the girl had experienced, in hearing her speak her hurt, in finding out what it is really like to live with a mother who behaves as she does, and the very last thing she wanted was to let her daughter have her anger. Indeed, she was dead-set against it, and her lavish affection was partly an effort to smother it.

This mother did not want to experience what she had done, let alone embark on a process of personal change. She wanted to cut all that off and go straight to the loving embrace that she herself needed. She was a person who could not tolerate sadness, could not allow herself to mourn—either in the immediate sense of seeing her own shortcomings, seeing the damage she was doing to someone she loved, and feeling bad about it, or in the fuller sense of processing the wounds from which her own monstrousness emerged. She harbored an unconscious belief, as many of us do under similarly threatening circumstances, that the price of self-awareness and growth was too high; and that if she ever moved inward to reexperience the sobbing child within herself, there would be nobody there to hold her.

The daughter in this pair felt stifled and used. She also felt confused and bad about herself for rejecting her mother's apparent contrition. Meanwhile, she had learned something about her own power. She could see that her mother was desperate for her love and approval, and she saw that she could withhold it for the sake of revenge. This became a strong current in her psychology, reacting with coldness when her mother (and others) mistreated her, which was certain to elicit the mother's clutching despair. She learned that satisfaction comes not from forgiveness and the rekindling of love but from getting even. She became turned on by the excitement and intensity of inciting anger or abuse, going cold, and then arousing guilt and abandonment panic in the other person. This was where the heat was for her; this was where she and Mom got really close.

What happens in many cases of false repair is that instead of expecting and welcoming reconciliation, the child learns to move in another direction—toward a masochistic submission or the power implicit in holding a grudge, or both. In extreme cases, where parents are not only insensitive but abusive emotionally, the child may come to hate the thought of apology or forgiveness and associate them with abject surrender.

In some families reconciliation is accomplished by letting things drop. The child bullies a playmate or tells a lie, which enrages the parent because his control and moral authority are being challenged. The parent blows up. Some kind of repair is needed. But the parent knows nothing about how to repair, has no sense of the child's need for it or even of his own need. He may not even know he has done anything wrong, may feel perfectly entitled to his own tantrums. I had a mother say to me, regarding her loss of temper, "It never would occur to me to apologize for that!" To her, her outbursts were like a good bowel movement—they relieved her, and she went on. Another parent told me, "After I blow up, I just keep trying to push down all my anger until finally I'm just not angry anymore." At that point the child is let out of the doghouse, and normality returns. But the child's hurt is untouched, as are the dark conclusions (I am bad, I have no rights) that form around it. He never gets to speak about what made him behave the way he did, he never gets any help in understanding himself and his experience. And he never gets the apology that is rightfully his under the circumstances. Why should he apologize to his playmate, then? Except under coercion?

Parents can be ruthless in their use of guilt. A kindergartner who has just learned to write his name scratches it absentmindedly into a small pewter tray on the coffee table. When his mother enters the living room and sees it, she acts devastated, as if her life has been ruined. The child feels horribly guilty and horribly bad. But the parent just leaves him there to be defined by her anger, her self-centeredness, her judgments. The mother is ruthlessly enacting an inner drama about her own victimhood. When she feels like a victim, nothing else matters, including her child's devastation. The child apologizes. It is an apology that emerges in part out of authentic concern. He has hurt his mother. But it is also an apology of the damned, of a bad, mother-destroying child, hoping against hope to be released from hell.

Children are constantly being defined by their parents' emotional states. Living with a rageful, unforgiving parent continually emphasizes the child's badness, makes him feel as if he is too bad to be embraced. He feels inadequate, ugly, unworthy, not good enough to be loved. There is a deep sense of shame, which may be largely unconscious. But unconscious does not mean inoperative. The child becomes susceptible to the belief that he deserves to be locked out, excommunicated, put into solitary confinement; that he must be stripped of his membership in the family and humanity. That is the proper fate of one who is so wicked, unworthy, or unlovable. In the future, when reprimanded or rejected by others or regretful about something he's done, he will return to this terrible box and sink into depression. Or he will try desperately to stay out by holding on to an irreproachable or grandiose image of himself or engaging in some kind of power struggle, like a blaming-match, the purpose of which is to put the other person in the box.

All people have some of this shame embedded in their psychologies. It is part of the scar tissue that forms out of childhood trauma, and even in good families children get traumatized, at least to some extent. Our defenses exist, in part, so that neither we nor anyone else can know the truth of our shameful badness. The continuum between emotional health and dysfunction in this regard can perhaps best be defined by certain questions: How much shame are we struggling with, how rigid are our defenses against it, how entrenched is our depression, how available are the avenues of repair (such as opening up about our shame to someone we trust and regaining a sense of goodness)?

Living with a parent who keeps the onus on the child, who doesn't own up, who doesn't help the child out of the terrible places into which the parent's anger may thrust him, more or less guarantees that the shame will be deep-seated, that the child will feel little hope for a way out, and that he will relive the various dramas of his badness with others. In this sense, rageful, unforgiving parents are not only traumatic but exceedingly hard to separate from psychologically.

EMOTIONAL STALINISM, clutching, and avoidance are but three examples of the ways in which parental psychology—including the unprocessed traumas from the parent's past—can compromise the child's developing monotheism. If a parent cannot bear the agony of seeing himself at his worst, if he needs to make the child the problem, there are innumerable ways to do it, and some of them can be quite disguised.

In the worst cases repair is not even an issue. The parent's will must not be toyed with. The small child commits a minor infraction and is shut up in his room for the day. The ten-year-old misbehaves in school once too often and is grounded for an entire summer. Or the child is locked up and told she cannot come out until she says the thing that will show that her will has been broken. There is no mercy, no going back on these terrible sentences.

In some families the child does not do anything, and he is not even overtly punished. The parent is just locked in his own bitterness or self-concern and rarely budges from that place, so that the child has the eternal experience of knocking on the parent's door to no avail. Nothing she does is good enough to get Mom or Dad to see her.

If you're protesting, you're still loving—all the more so the more furious the protest is. But parents who have difficulty with repair can have a hard time grasping this. That's why many of us weren't allowed or encouraged to protest and so moved into a defensive and deadened place. One of the most devastating things we experienced with our parents was the rejection of our protests—they were dismissed as wrong, irrational, illogical, rude, insulting, disloyal, ungrateful, and so on. And we were told so to the point of parental fury.

The result of these traumas is not only a stunting of protest, but a perversion of protest. The perversion can take many forms. Narcissistic protest may take the form of a demoralized, irreversible disappointment: You should have known what I needed, you should have known that would hurt me. You are not the ideal friend or lover I thought you were. It's over. The implication here is that one should not need to protest, that the very need for protest proves the relationship was bad. Paranoid protest has a similar quality, but now the emphasis is: You did it on purpose! Or, Aha, you've finally shown your true colors. The other person is convicted in advance and there is no opportunity to work things out. Depressive protest is more outwardly defeated: There's no hope of going up against this person who hurt me, there's no hope of redress, but if I destroy myself, he may feel guilty. All three have a murderous and unforgiving quality.

As healthy protest atrophies, knowing what hurts and why is often lost to us. "I don't know, I just don't like her" replaces "She's always putting me down." "I don't like her body" replaces "I hate how withholding she is with me." "I don't respect him, he's too weak, his family controls him" replaces "I'm hurt that he never puts me first." "It's just time for me to go, Baby," replaces "I could kill you for not being exactly what I need you to be." This confusion about what we really feel and why is part of a general loss of a sense of legitimacy. We may complain or hate with all our might, but somewhere inside we fear that it is we ourselves who must be wrong.

The fate of anger for that part of the self that grows up in relation to the unforgiving parent is not a good one. Anger becomes unavailable in the context of love. Love has a kind of subservience, an enforced goodness to it, which allows no room for hate or anger. Love itself can feel like a prison under such conditions, while hatred and anger, ravenous and uncontrolled, become the coin of another realm, part of a secondary self that feels persecuted and murderous. Most people try to avoid that secondary self which they feel is bad, shameful, not really them. When they can't contain themselves anymore, their anger bursts out from the covers with a machine gun. It operates outside the monotheistic envelope, unmodulated by caring. A similar avoidance and dread are also experienced in relation to the anger and hatred of others. It is intolerable. It must be warded off. There's no room for it.

In the Dutch movie *The Vanishing*, a sadistic man, getting even at the world for God-only-knows-what early agonies, kills two young people—first a pretty woman he snatches from a roadside stop, then, three years later, the husband who has been searching for her (Mom and Dad?). But he not only kills them. He entombs them in coffins, buries them alive under his garden table, and sits with satisfaction, eating his lunch over their living graves. To be locked in a trauma box, buried alive, their protests unheard, abandoned by the people they love and who should love them—this is the kind of torment that children suffer at the hands of parents whose behavior is destructive, irrational, rejecting. Their anguish is great, as is their hopeless rage. Without authentic apology or repair, it stays with them, and it haunts their later relationships.

THE BIRTH
OF THE
INNER DRAMA

ATTACHMENT THEORY EXPLORES THE IMPORTANCE OF LOVE IN human psychology and relationships, especially as it pertains to the developing child. In a famous attachment research procedure called the Strange Situation, one-year-olds are taken into a playroom with their mother and are separated from her for several minutes on two occasions. Most of the babies become very upset during these breaks, but they have different reactions on her return. Babies who are believed to be securely attached typically reach for their mother, get picked up, mold to her body, and accept her efforts to soothe them. The scene is like a microcosm of a successful protest followed by what might be considered a rudimentary sort of mourning via Mother's care. The babies feel heard and loved. They let go of their misery and resume the loving relationship with their mother, themselves, and the world.

A second group of children also want to get picked up by their mothers, but instead of molding to her they arch away and fuss angrily, sometimes kicking or hitting. Their mothers cannot soothe them. The protests of these babies have a built-in futility, as if their anger has gotten the better of them and will not let anything through. A significant portion of these babies develop into children who are clingy, fretful, and panicked by small separations. They act as if they can never be certain of Mother's love, as if it might be taken away at a moment's notice. They have not been able to internalize her love and carry it around with them as part of their psychological makeup—at least, not enough—and so they must hang on to Mother herself. They never seem to get past the normal separation anxiety of infancy.

A third group of one-year-olds in the Strange Situation first struck researchers as precociously independent. Some react indifferently upon their mother's departure and all are indifferent upon her return, even if they were crying miserably when she was gone. But their independence is only apparent, and other measures show that in fact they are highly distressed. They seem to have learned that it is futile to go to Mom when they're distressed, and dangerous to protest her lack of care. Their only way to soothe themselves is to make her less important. But neither their distress nor their anger is resolved. Here, too, there is no opportunity to mourn and move on. These babies stay locked in their rage, and follow-up research suggests that, assuming no significant change in their home lives, many of them will develop into aggressive and defiant children, often isolated and unpopular, with a stunted ability to seek comfort or love.

The assessments done in the Strange Situation at age one do not necessarily reflect what the child's relationship with his parent will be like in later years or what issues will trouble him as an adult. But they do show us the kinds of insecure patterns that can and do develop, patterns that we instantly recognize as being relevant to adult psychology. It is in those insecure places that the resistance to forgiveness takes hold.

Both types of insecure children have become enmeshed with the parent, most obviously with the bad part of the parent, and this enmeshment can be remarkably enduring. They are tormented unconsciously by having wanted Mom and her love so awfully and not having been able to have her, at least not the way they needed her. One type of insecure child says, "And now she's all I can think about." Another says, "She's no big deal." Often the two responses are interwoven in various ways within the same person.

To the degree that such insecure attachment orientations get woven into character—and that happens to everyone to some degree—we get caught up in repeating the wounding relationship, repetition being the inevitable alternative to mourning. We do this by roping others into the drama of "Wounded Me and My Bad Parent," although it may go by other names, such as "Bad Me and My Bad Parent," "Bad Me and My Perfect Parent (Who Never Has Time for Me but Through No Fault of His Own)," or even "The Most Wonderful Mom in the World and the Daughter Who Took Care of Her," in which idealization walls off the trauma from consciousness and from feeling. Each of our stories comes to represent a different organizing principle for the self. When we are in the self-state associated with that specific story, no other aspect of us seems to exist. Indeed, important in all of this, as important as the orbit of the rejecting parent, is the eclipse of the loved and loving parent—often the same person—who is still there, waiting to be retrieved, and the eclipse of the loving self.

A person's inner dramas may be complex and contradictory. The stories often include more than one person—the sibling who was favored, the parent who stood by while the other was mean, the grandmother who came to the rescue, and so on. But most relevant to the subject of forgiveness is how our dramas define the wounding we anticipate from others, especially others who get into certain roles with us, like lover, close friend, boss. Of course, it is not limited to such people. If you do not feel entitled, then anyone may be the depriver who was once your dad. If you're guilty, then anyone may be the jailer that was once your mom. If you're self-hating, then anyone may be seen as reproachful. If you're a martyr, then anyone may be taking advantage of you. If you must save those who are in distress, then anyone can become your burden. If you're the less loved sibling, then anyone may be seen as playing favorites. If you have internalized an indicting voice, then anyone's criticism can make you the defendant in a hostile court.

The inner drama also incorporates the particular ways we hold out for the heaven of infantile bliss, where our own creativity and agency become a nonissue, where we rage over the flaws and failures of others and long for them to become the perfect beings they are supposed to be and make our lives right. The inner drama is the place where we get stuck in relationships, held hostage or imprisoned by unresolved aspects of our relationships with our parents. It is also, inevitably, the ground in which we indulge our need for a black-and-white universe. Embroiled in these unconscious blueprints, we find it much harder to see the true texture of another's personality or motives. When someone is rejecting or hurtful, the insecure self that developed in childhood has no sense that "we can work this out." In the heat of conflict, all he knows is that he has been turned against, that it's hopeless, and he either becomes desperate or feels, "Get out of my life!"

The things people do that hurt us hurt all the more because of this psychological self we inhabit. Dad was judgmental and put me down, and, now, when you do it, I reinhabit my traumatized self and feel destroyed by you. You become a big person, and I become a small wounded person. I cannot sidestep your shenanigans, know that it's you, refuse to take it personally, refuse to take the bait. Nor can I protest effectively. My protests are not spoken with warmth and hope, but with murderousness, open or disguised, with pleading desperation, or some combination of the two. You cannot say these things to me, you must not; I can't tolerate the put-down, the rejection, the disrespect, the manipulation. The shame, the guilt, the sense of imprisonment, the humiliated fury are too intense. I feel like a three-year-old pushed out into the cold with the door locked behind me. You must take it back! You must open the door! I'm going to die out here!

Or my character has developed somewhat differently, so that I feel deprived, fucked over, and angry, and I'm going to fly at you like a demon. Or I feel dismissed and controlled and I turn my misery into contempt. But whatever form it takes characterologically, I cannot let you have your wrong and hurtful point of view, your annoying habits, the ways you disappoint me. The mean or critical things you do or say flood my identity. I cannot stand separate from them.

The inner drama is the mental representation of emotional scar tissue. If not seen and not worked on, it becomes a way in which we lead separate lives, missing each other, missing who we really are and what could be between us.

REPETITION

The inner drama is not brought to life solely by direct assaults, or what we take to be such. We are able to imprison ourselves with much subtler provocation. Allen, a young man in therapy, is tormented by murderous feelings toward his girlfriend in England who refuses to join him in the States. He came here for a unique educational opportunity, it would be ruinous for him to leave, and he is infuriated by her intransigence: She does not want to be four thousand miles away from her mother. He tells me that he is dying for sex and can't bear to see all the girls in their summer dresses. He is also finding that life in New York is much more to his liking than life in Leicester, which was too slow for him and to which he doesn't want to return. Everything feels hopeless.

When I ask him what would improve his disposition, what would make him feel less miserable about his life and more loving toward his girlfriend, who will be arriving soon for a week's vacation, it is obvious that he would like more freedom, "at least to be able to get laid." Then he'd feel a lot less resentful about how little they see each other. Would he also like to be able to take the freedom to explore other women more seriously, given the stalemate he is in with her? Yes, but the guilt if he ever left her would be too much to bear. "Did your mother give you the impression she would die without you?" He laughs heartily. She gives him that impression to this day.

So Allen is creating his own imprisonment. True, his girlfriend would be unlikely to tell him, Go, have sex, Go, explore other women. But the very need for her permission is an aspect of his inner drama, in which Mother will abandon him if he strays. The freer he can allow himself to be, the less he will experience his girlfriend as the person who is ruining his chance for happiness. Released from his grudging resentments, he will be freer to enjoy her when they are together, to love her wherever things between them may go.

The failure to separate from the traumatic parent is not solely a matter of having old wounds reopened. It is also a matter of choice, of choosing to live in those wounds. A therapist will see this in patients at times, when they rush right past him and the relationship they have with him in order to plunge back into the stream of their resentments. Others cling to a different sort of inner drama.

Joyce often feels hurt by her mother and readily cries, but she is not angry at her. She adores and dotes on her. Her caretaking, which includes preoccupying thoughts about her mom's well-being, is her response to a mother who was both monumentally narcissistic and unavailable and yet openly pathetic and needy, so that her little girl came to believe that if she took good enough care of Mommy, Mommy would eventually be healed and be able to love her. Joyce is not a woman who will fail to cry at her mother's funeral. On the contrary, she is already crying in anticipation of her mother's death, even though her mother is young and healthy.

This morning Joyce is hard to reach; we agree that there is something almost autistic in her untouchableness. She did something yesterday that has left her feeling ashamed and self-hating. She called a neighbor to ask her to check on her sick dog. The neighbor is an older woman who has had a protective attitude toward Joyce at times but is not a warm person and, as Joyce says, "has a short attention span for connection." After several calls to the woman about the dog's condition, Joyce felt the woman's coolness and immediately knew she had overstepped the bounds of propriety. She had pushed for too much and all because of her hateful insecurity. The dog was not going to die and she could have waited to check his condition when she came home from work.

I say, "Well, you were worried. You get anxious." But this doesn't seem to do much for her. She looks preoccupied with her shameful inadequacies. I ask her whether she had a right to be an anxious person, to be insecure, to do "bad" things. She doesn't allow herself any of this, but sees how it might be allowable. "What if you could see that you felt rejected by this woman and recognized that the intensity of it came from your childhood experience, but that you didn't go to the next level of bashing yourself for your insecurity? Where would you be then?"

I wondered if she might say, "Well, if I didn't feel so bad about being so insecure, then the shame wouldn't be so overwhelming and I would feel free to go to you or my husband"—two people she remains peculiarly detached from—"to be taken care of: I did something dumb, I got hurt, I'm feeling bad about myself, I need to be held."

But that was not what she said. She said that if she weren't bashing herself for being so insecure, she would have to go back to that woman to be told that she still loved her. And this despite what she's told me about the woman's essential coldness. This captures for me some of the human tragedy of holding on, of failing to separate psychologically from those aspects of Mom or Dad I've labeled "the bad parent." The reject-ing woman represents the rejecting mother, and only she can make it better. Such ongoing enmeshment keeps us stewing in our resentments. It robs us of our capacity to take in love, which in turn robs us of our ca-pacity to mourn and be healed.

IT IS UNDERSTANDABLE that we would want to recreate the good in our experience with our parents—to become loving parents like them, to be-come heroic police officers or teachers like them, to tell jokes and play ball like them—but why do we so obsessively hold on to the bad? Why do Joyce and the rejecting neighbor take on more importance than Joyce and the loving husband? Why does Joyce so strongly identify with and live out aspects of her mom—like withholding herself from the people who love her—qualities that she hates in her mom?

This can be understood in many ways, but, like our wish to repli-cate the good, our re-creation of the bad draws much of its power from our tremendous love and devotion. We don't want to walk away from our parents, what they're about, and what we were about with them. We want to be like them, even in their badness, and we want to stay with them, even if they're bad to us.

Obsessively repeating the past is, however, a river with many tribu-taries, and a second significant tributary is separation anxiety. We find it hard to let go of our parents and move on without feeling securely loved by them. This is one of the fundamentals of human psychology and of early attachment experience: The internalization of parental love is what gives us the security to move outward and to expand our love affair with the world. Absent that, we are left unconsciously clinging, struggling to get it right, to be accepted by the rejecting parent or parents, to make the bad parent good and to thereby make ourselves good. If we could but have their goodness and love inside of us, we could let go; we could be free to be.

The truth is we do need to get that goodness inside of us. It is, in-deed, the antidote to obsessively reliving trauma. The love that was not established solidly and securely enough in childhood can be strengthened later through new loving relationships that reconfirm and bolster our security—which is, at core, about feeling loved and loving. But that task can feel unworkable, like trying to swallow one's tail, partly because of the impossible dramas we enact, which tend to elicit everything but love and make us feel everything but loving, and partly because, to the extent that we remain embroiled in the past, the only love that is acceptable is from the rejecting other, the bad parent, in one guise or another. We are, as the Scottish analyst Ronald Fairbairn noted, drawn to the only sort of passion we know. We want to be there, where the excitement is, however sickening it may be. This is what love, this is what passion is all about to us, and so, as if magnetized, we plunge back with gusto into the stream of early experience as it has become encoded in our inner dramas.

In all this we see, too, a natural resistance to change. There is a perverse human preference to stay where we are, stuck in this deadened or contentious place, where we are always feeling wronged and unresolved or safely unalive. Love hurts; it gets us too close to our pain; it shocks us with the knowledge of how lonely and unloved we've been, which floods us with sadness and demands mourning. We are reluctant to go through that. To take in love in any form—appreciation, gratitude, caretaking—is to leave oneself defenseless, and that can be a very hard thing to do. Besides, love is not where we belong. We might get shot down. That would be unbearable. Better to stay with the tragic security of the wounded and the dead.

And so we play and replay our inner drama and insist that others play it with us. Even if they make significant efforts to alter their own bad habits, we may remain unimpressed. "Too little, too late" is the motto of the wounded self, still secretly holding out for the Valhalla of perfect love and attunement, who, for the eternal meanwhile, has made its home in resentment.

THREE GENERATIONS OF ENMESHMENT

Norman came into treatment because his three grown sons were combative, distant, or openly rejecting of him. He was consumed by the injustice of it and ripped apart by the loss, especially since they were his great loves; no one else meant as much to him. He believed that two of his sons had been poisoned by their therapists and was worried that I, too, might be a parent-blamer, as he assumed they were. He let me know that whatever my ideology, such thinking would be wrong in his case since his sons' experience with him had been uniformly good. He never punished them. He was always available. His wife had died when the boys were very young and he took on the roles of mother, father, provider. Most people were impressed, even awed, by the job he did. In short, he let me know in the first session how important his official story was to him and that I'd better not tamper with it. It gave me my first sense of what his sons might have been up against.

I took an immediate liking to Norman, who had a genuine warmth and lively sense of humor. I liked that I could play with him and be aggressive with him, that I could say what I had to say and, in most cases, he would not blow me away for it. He told me he could tell right away that I liked him and that that made hearing me easier. But there was clearly another side to Norman, and the minute I challenged The Book of Norman too directly I felt myself to be in the presence of a defensive person who could not bear to see his shortcomings and who, contrary to his firmly held self-image, could be a not-so-subtle dictator who could threaten you with a tone. In much of life, he presented himself as a charming, endearing man and lively conversationalist; but he was shadowed by a judgmental, blaming dismissive werewolf that sprang to life to attack any perceived flaw in him or others and leapt at the throat of any critic. In this, he was very much like his own father and determined not to see it. That he harbored a wolf was something he could only grasp at moments. The fact that it had played a role in his relationship with his sons was anathema.

Norman had been verbally battered as a child, and, as if to erase all that and give it no chance to befoul his own job as a parent, he had diligently raised his boys on the sunny side of the street. He was the Good Dad, and they were the Perfect Boys. But when one of his sons displeased him, he could not tolerate the threat this posed to the fantasy of goodness and superiority that he depended on to ward off his demons. If Norman scolded and the boy acted wounded and turned from him, if he refused to own up, to smile, to reembrace his father, Norman's inner drama sprang to life. The boy now crossed over in Norman's (partially unconscious) mind from Perfect Son to Rejecting and Abandoning Child. At that moment his battering father was doubly reborn—in the person of the child and in Norman himself. His temper would flash and he would become scary.

Flaring up this way was unbearable for Norman and made him feel as if his life were falling apart. His method of repair was to quickly suppress his rage and do what he could to smooth things over. But the boys got the message that he was not to be toyed with. When they finally mustered the will in adolescence and early adulthood to be angry and critical of their father, they, like Norman, had developed no healthy channel for the expression of anger. They only had two modes: Everything's Perfect, or Time to Kill. Their untamed rage collided with his, and a falling out occurred from which neither side knew a way out.

The two older boys, Robbie and Steven, like Norman himself, were confident, even grandiose, on the outside, but secret self-haters. He had praised them ceaselessly when they were young—their talents, their intelligence, their goodness—the implication being that they were superior to other children. This praise was a trap and a burden for them. They didn't feel seen and appreciated for who they were. They could not tolerate or struggle with their flaws. They became addicted strivers, trying to live up to Norman's fantasy of perfection and wanting as little contact with their core selves as they could manage. Both were cruel toward Norman and could not stop harping on his faults. The enormous, adoring affection that they felt toward their dad as boys was still in them, but they could no longer feel it. The fun they had with him, his patient explanations, his being there for them when they needed him were like the memories of another person. This inability to feel a love that is so profoundly a part of us is a terrible form of unforgivingness. You've hurt me, you've disappointed me, I can't do anything to make you change, the frustration is too much, I feel overwhelmed, unsupported by anyone who understands my plight, so I shut down and shut you out. I make you unimportant so that you can't hurt me anymore. Meanwhile, in various respects, I become you in the process.

Norman's third son, Paul, did not fit the pattern. He could not keep up with the first two and was a constant disappointment to himself and his father. "I tried so hard not to let him see it," Norman told me, but the boy nevertheless felt like a misfit, even though, officially, he was included in the circle of perfection. He became surly and oppositional, and created problems. Norman tore his hair out trying to make things right with Paul, but he could not give him the two things he most needed. One was being appreciated and loved for who he was. The other was seeing his father for who he was. To be found wanting, to be the target of angry disapproval is bad enough. But at least at some point you may be able to break free and say to yourself, This man is impossible on the subject of schoolwork and achievement, I can't make it with him, I'm going to stop trying to live up to his crazy values. But Paul didn't have the satisfaction of knowing, with any real confidence, what his father was about. (And, in fairness to Norman, there was no second parent to provide some perspective.) The pretense that Paul was not the black sheep of the family, that he was included in the golden circle, confused him, made him not trust the evidence of his senses, made him feel as if the hatefulness he was feeling originated in him.

Norman wanted his sons to forgive him, which, in his mind, meant going back to their Valhalla of mutual adoration. It took a long time for him even to begin to see that this worshiped past was not worth going back to; that he was responsible for much that had gone wrong between him and his sons; that, as nasty and as unpleasant as they were, they had a lot to be angry about. He had not been able to let himself or them be who they were. He had not been able to tolerate their anger. He had used them as substitutes for a mate. In short, he could not allow them to separate from him. To this day, he could not relinquish his dependency on them; he was more focused on getting his boys to be what he needed them to be than on finding a woman, the prospect of which filled him with pessimism. I did not doubt Norman's love for his sons, but because of his own unprocessed trauma, he had never been able to love them at a distance, a crucial requirement of parenting as small children get bigger. Rather, terrified of abandonment, he clung harder at every sign of their maturation.

Like any parent, Norman needed to invite and hear his sons' protests, even though their protests threatened many of his cherished views of himself. He needed to strap himself to the mast, like Ulysses, and force himself to listen without striking back. True, they were treating him poorly, and he should not have to submit to their disrespect. Learning how and where to draw the line was going to be a complicated process for him. His submission to them grew out of his own slavishness, his fear that he would lose them further if he protested, as if, as ever, they would become the frightening, abandoning father of his youth. He had a hard time grasping this, how terrified he was of being turned into that rejected little boy again, just as he had a hard time grasping that he had anything to be sorry for.

Norman also had a hard time understanding that his two older boys were afraid of him. Like many parents, Norman could be quite unforgiving when hurt by his kids. And he would act it out by turning into his own rule-making, indicting father. His steely eyes would say, Bad, disrespectful son! when they weren't properly gracious to him at a family gathering.

For all their self-importance, Robbie and Steven were still like children with him, still frightened and unable to deal, except like passive-aggressive teenagers. They would rather duck out of a room than say good-bye to him and risk getting trapped in an unpleasant encounter. Norman needed to blame less and allow himself to feel the sadness of this enmeshment they were all trapped in. That alone would be an act of forgiveness: I don't like it, I wish they would grow up, but I understand what my sons are up against in me and in themselves and why they behave the way they do. It's not so different from what I went through with my father.

Norman progressed, but because of his fragility, the threat of self-awfulness that hung over him like a Sword of Damocles, he understandably resisted seeing many of these truths about himself as a parent. To see them would be to lose the precious sense of purity that held his self-esteem together. For people whose identities have been forged in the extreme circumstances of abuse, the grip of a black-and-white view can be hard to shake. Splitting, enmeshment, rage, avoidance, all mediated through a pervasive and unseen inner drama, become the way of life.

That there was something deeply lovable about Norman, a lovableness associated much more with his hated vulnerability than with his treasured grandiosity (Dad of the Century!), was nearly incomprehensible to him. His resistance in this area impeded his need to mourn; and without that mourning, he could not be in a position to forgive himself—at least enough to co-exist with and work on the things he wanted to change. Any flaw would be too threatening.

Mourning and self-awareness naturally arouse wishes to repair. But, at its best, the wish to repair includes the element of self-care and self-acceptance, because there is no real love without self-love; that's where our giving comes from. Thus: I hurt you, and it hurts me that I hurt you; I want you to know that I know it and that I feel bad about it. But I am not telling you this out of my need for you to make me whole. That need may exist, but it is not my governing motivation. I have enough self-love to care about you and want to touch you with my caring in order to repair some of the hurt I caused.

From such an empowered place, Norman could move toward repair without dissolving into self-hatred. It would support his efforts to retrieve in a more secure, nongrandiose way, what is really good about him as a man and as a parent. Eventually, he could perhaps speak from the heart to his disparaging, contemptuous, rageful sons and say, without indictment: "Can you allow me my flaws?"

PART II

THE
LANDSCAPE
OF
RESENTMENT

The More
We Blame the
Further We Get
from Ourselves

A GROUP THERAPY SESSION. IN THE OPENING MOMENTS, PEOPLE were talking about the visit, the previous week, of a former member who had quit the group six months earlier because she was moving to another city. Back in town for the holidays, she had waited outside the building and met the group members as they emerged. Several people, speaking in a casual, chit-chatty way, said it was great to see her and to catch up. But one man, Mark, felt left out of the good feelings.

Mark hesitated to speak. He seemed tormented. Coaxed, he spoke bitterly about feeling mean and hateful, like a moralistic prick. Why? Because he had not been at all pleased by the visit; he had experienced it as an intrusion. He had, in fact, walked right by the visitor, with whom he had had a meaningful connection when they were in group together. He had actually quite liked her, even though he accused her of being "ruthlessly superficial" and "chirpy" at times when he felt something much deeper was going on. He felt that again with her visit, as if she was crashing an intimate setting that she was no longer a part of. As he spoke, Mark revealed a state of fury, and one could feel the moralistic dimension he disliked in himself. He spoke as if the visitor had committed a crime, was contemptible, and should be shot. But Mark exhibited that same fury toward himself, a fury laced with feelings of shame and humiliation. In the face of everyone else's apparent delight with the visit, he saw himself as a cur.

The therapist eventually responded to the self-hatred. "Why don't you have the right to your boundaries? And to define them in a way that feels comfortable to you? And to get angry if you feel they're being violated? Group is a special setting for you, which you treasure. You get very vulnerable and very exposed here. And you've been intruded upon a lot." Mark brightened up on hearing this. He had been molested by his grandfather when a child and had a mother who did not believe in privacy, who disapproved of closed bedroom or bathroom doors. He came by his sensitivities honestly. He had a right not to want an outsider to burst through the door smiling and shaking everybody's hand, like a mother who wouldn't let him poop in peace. And he had a right to be angry at the rest of the group for tolerating, even embracing, such behavior, like an oblivious father so besotted by his wife that he never told her to back off from their son. But Mark had always felt unheard and unvalidated in this realm. His complaints had been turned against him—What are you so uptight about?—and so they had become a source of bitterness, a bitterness directed simultaneously toward the world and himself.

With the therapist supporting him in his feelings about the visit, Mark felt he could allow those feelings to himself. The right or the wrong of them, their rationality or the irrationality, whether they were neurotic, didn't matter so much anymore. This was how he felt. His shameful sense of being a moralistic prick seemed to evaporate.

His attitude toward the other group members changed, too. Minutes before he'd been in a horrible place with them—small and stingy alongside their largeness and warmth. He had also felt persecuted by them, as if they were flaunting their superior qualities and reveling in his badness, while cruelly ignoring his hurt. But now he experienced a shift, as if into another self-state. From having to nail the others, which came from his ancient inner drama (persecuted, ugly me and my bad parents), he moved toward a sense of caring for himself and wanting that caring from the others. This had its origins in another aspect of his early life, the relationship between himself and the caring side of his parents. The others, liberated from the magnetic pull of Mark's inner drama and liberated from the threat of Mark's indictments, which emanated from that drama, found themselves pulled toward a more caring place as well. Mark was no longer a weird guy who got all worked up over nothing. Appreciating his truth and the fact that they had not been sensitive to it cost them nothing of themselves and opened them up to him.

Mark's displeasure with the visitor remained, but it was not the same. It now came from a stronger, more entitled place. His new attitude, if it could be put into words, might be summarized like this: "I don't like her coming here. It makes me feel violated and angry. But maybe, even if I don't like it, she still has a right to visit. If I can have the right to be me, then I feel more inclined to let her be her."

Mark's struggle has many elements to it, but one aspect clearly relates to the powerful force that blame has in his life. Can he have strong feelings about the visit and the visitor without having to denounce, control, and shackle her? The more entitled to his feelings Mark felt, the more the world opened up to him. Yes, he was moralistic; yes, he was feeling hateful; and yes, that's a lousy way to treat yourself and others. But beneath it was a legitimacy, and the moralism and hatefulness emerged at least partly from a denial of that legitimacy. Once Mark found his legitimacy, once he found a basis for self-caring, he emerged from his shame into three dimensions; he was no longer simply a self-righteous policeman. His inner world became a more complex and interesting place to him, and the outer world did, too. He began to have a more nuanced view of the visit: "I hate it, and I have a right to hate it, but is it a crime? I'm not so sure." He got back in touch with what always bothered him about this former group member ("She treats everything like a ladies' tea!"), but, at the same time, also began to remember the woman's humanity as well. Somewhere in that person whom Mark found so annoying, was a woman Mark liked and enjoyed, even admired in various ways, especially for her capacity to enjoy herself, whom Mark once wished he could know more deeply, who has her own struggles, and who, in any case, has the right to be who she is—which may include a disinclination to go into things as deeply as Mark might wish, as well as the desire to visit her old friends in the group. All of which is to say that Mark emerged into a more fluid, alive, dynamic world, a world where embracing himself obviated the need to police others. Blame, by contrast, collapses the world. It makes it rigid and binary, with moral winners and moral losers, and the imperative to control.

The need to blame (ourselves or others) runs so deeply at times that it can feel like a basic necessity. Part of the need arises as a defense against shame. As shame encroaches, fending it off requires that someone else be proved the villain. And it is not enough that we protest what they're doing, that we have our say. We have to nail them to their crimes, make them confess, make them feel bad and promise to be better. Only then can we finally have the satisfaction of being free of the denunciation we direct at ourselves, which is now safely directed at them.

Self-denunciation arises out of early experience, as does the pernicious and obsessive need to be right. One can almost feel the child's struggle: With a parent, for instance, who won't hear his protests, so that if the child can't prove he's right and can't lock his rightness into place with a stubborn, blaming fury, he will be oppressed and have no point of view at all, no leg to stand on. Also, with a parent who finds fault, who pins the tail back on him, a parent who cannot tolerate being wrong and establishes his own rightness by denying the child's and making him out to be malformed in some way. In his blaming struggles with others, he becomes both the parent and the child.

In such a worldview, there can be no owning up, no honest communication, no real connection, no expansions into the appreciation-and-forgiveness-building realms of self-knowledge and other-knowledge, just the cold landscape of the courtroom.

Knowing oneself is integral to growing up. But, to the extent that we live in a blaming system, we do not want to know the truth about who we are and, therefore, resist growing up. We don't want to know our own murderousness, selfishness, greed, envy, because all of these very human feeling states have been made a source of so much guilt and shame that they lead at once to total condemnation and self-rejection. We can't know them, and we can't know how we came to them. As a result, we miss out on the experience of self-empathy and self-care, which might be the basis for doing something new, for beginning to emerge from these things we don't like in ourselves but which hold us prisoner.

Some of what we do is bad and should be changed—the way we bully, deny, manipulate, shirk, indict. Mark was right to question his moralism and even be revolted by it, and so was the group. But if we make every misdeed or character orientation into a capital crime, into evidence that our very being is worthless, we will not be able to let ourselves know the full complexity of who we are. If there can be no mercy, no leniency, no understanding, no forgiveness, no simple tolerance for the magnificent complexity of being human—if we face every flaw or disliked quality as evidence that our blackened souls require rejection and banishment—we will not be captured by our own awareness and motivated to change. The blaming system, therefore, puts a brake on a fundamental area of growth. Our energy goes elsewhere—into repression and dissociation and the rather useless, wasteful obsession of hammering at ourselves or into making someone else the problem. To the extent that we inhabit a blaming system, we are naturally drawn to furious bouts of who-did-what-to-whom. Between siblings, in married couples, this can become an unending imbroglio, and when the latter come into couples therapy, they each have the same expectation: that the therapist will serve as a judge and find in his favor.

The tendency to blame is reinforced in a culture that is full of finger-pointing. Whether it is the political correctness of the left, which may criminalize one man's wish to marry a much younger woman or live free of emotional commitments entirely or another's wish for wealth and power, or the moral righteousness of the right, which may criminalize a woman's decision to have an abortion or work during motherhood, we are awash in an intolerance that poisons our intercourse. Who should pay when a man and a woman go out on a date? When is the right time for them to have sex and which sort of contraception, if any, should be used? What is the appropriate time for them to make the relationship an exclusive one? Such questions can become intense, ideologically laden debates, full of judgments and denunciations (spoken or not) that are supported by a political movement or point of view. They ride roughshod over the unique sensitivities, wants, and disappointments on each side and evaporate any sense that our moment is uniquely and personally about us.

In November 1999, the *New York Times Magazine* ran a piece by Jacob Weisberg about the ongoing battles between left and right over the McCarthy era, which suggests how passionately we hold to beliefs that help define for us who or what is good and who or what is bad. Even with the Cold War over, it turns out, many of the old combatants cling fervently to its battle cries and denunciations. Blame and the refusal to acknowledge any wrongness have remained far more compelling for them than the wish to take stock, to reconcile, or to recognize frail and strong humanity on each side. To do so, perhaps, would represent a letting go, a greater acceptance of ambiguity, a degree of mourning. It would entail facing what one was and wasn't, saying good-bye to a beloved cause that helped organized one's life but that may no longer be meaningful, or acknowledging to oneself that the crusade to which one was devoted has proven to be defective or even barbarous in some ways. As we've seen over and over again, such acts of mourning, such movements away from the certainties of splitting toward the uncertainties of monotheism, are difficult to tolerate and rarely undertaken voluntarily.

Blame defends against mourning. A case comes to mind, concrete, at least on the surface, in which a beloved family cat fell out of an apartment window and died. The mother was devastated by the death, as was her nine-year-old son. But she could not keep herself from blaming the boy. Why had he left the window open? She had told him never to leave that window open because of the rain. And he knew the cat had a tendency to want to escape. She didn't want to express her rage at him because he was already miserable. But the more she tried to restrain herself from actively scolding him, the more her thoughts about his stupidity and carelessness obsessed her. She was absolutely dying to tear into him. She was also thinking, somewhat less consciously: I never warned him explicitly that the cat might fall out the window. I never actually said it. Why didn't I? It's really my fault. So she was torn between clubbing herself and clubbing him. But why did anyone have to be clubbed for this tragedy? Partly because this is the way she learned to deal with loss.

Blame is very absorbent. It soaks up sadness. It dries the tears. It provides an opportunity and a target for fury which is felt as preferable to experiencing pain or loss—whether the loss is a cat, a spouse, an aspect of physical health, a loved object, a piece of work, a good night's sleep, an election, a colony, or a war. Blaming and vindictiveness are ways of not feeling one's sorrow or shame and, by corollary, of not caring for oneself. Blame is the anti-mourn and, hence, the anti-self.

Blame can become for us an habitual means of relating to the world—a defense, an avoidance, a way to renounce responsibility. One can't acknowledge any fault or wrongdoing because the stakes are too high, so one frantically looks about for someone else to pin the fault on. The sense that one is going to get blamed at every turn is an aspect of the inner torment that keeps the system going. The blame, of course, is coming from within us and from the parental voices we've internalized. One patient described this condition as walking around with an amphitheatre in his mind full of 50,000 dads all roaring their disapproval. But the amphitheatre is externalized. The world becomes Dad. The spouse becomes Dad. The child becomes Dad. The boss becomes Dad. The therapist becomes Dad. The frail Dad of today, the eighty-year-old Dad, becomes Dad, the omnipotent Dad of old. And each one is a constant threat to blame, to sneer, to abandon.

Blaming fogs our perception of others as profoundly as it does ourselves. People don't act out of confusion, or mixed motives, or weakness, or ineptitude. They have no just cause, nothing that they are responding to in us. It's impossible that they genuinely care about us but also are selfish and narcissistic and even mindlessly treacherous at times. They are just bad. Through and through. Someone has to be good. Someone has to be bad.

The blaming, usually learned at home, is, ironically, applied later to the parent or parents themselves. If it weren't for their meanness, their selfishness, their abuse, my life would be okay. Meanwhile, the grown child continues to live in the orbit of the traumatic parent, unable to remember the good parent that was also there, however badly obscured, and, more important, tragically hampered in his ability to activate the self that lives in relation to that good parent, the secure self who is loved, whose love is valued and powerful, who has the confidence to make good things happen. Without the powerful and insistent stimulation of another significant relationship, he may be unstirred by thoughts of leaping through the scary fog of this confining system, having the faith to reach out to the goodness in others, taking initiative despite his paranoia, getting good things for himself despite the felt certainty that his destiny precludes it. He stays where he is, he dwells on the past, he makes excuses, he blames.

I was seeing a young man in treatment whose life was bent out of shape by a determination to get his due from a father who had been too authoritarian, too short-tempered, too distant, too tied up in an important job throughout my patient's childhood. I had met the father, who was tight, undemonstrative, and still authoritarian in his thinking, with a send-him-to-boot-camp view of dealing with psychological distress, but a warm man, nonetheless, who clearly loved his children. But he had been unable to be sensitively connected to his very sensitive second son, and the result had been disastrous for the boy, who was fixated on Dad and remained so into his adulthood. At thirty-eight he seemed every bit of sixteen. In ways that were both obvious and disguised, he was letting his life slip through his fingers as a direct result of his obsession with his father, whom he wanted to murder and whom he loved and wished to be embraced by more than anyone on earth. I had an image of him, suspended over a vat of acid, his father watching in horror nearby as he gradually lowers himself into the broth. As his flesh disappears to the ankle, he cries accusingly, "See! See! See how you've ruined my life!" and he lowers himself a little farther. Meanwhile, his mother, with whom he is overly identified, another person who has lived excessively and ruthlessly through her victimhood, with whom he has an unhealthy mutual dependence, looks on with a nod of approval. I once said to him, "When you're lying in the gutter with a bottle in your hand, dying at forty-eight, you want to be able to say: 'Dad was such a bastard!' Not: 'Boy, did I fuck up my life!' "

One of the things that pained me all the more about this patient was that he was a bright, warm, lovable guy who was turning himself into a mental case because of how lost he was in his traumatic attachment to his father. I frequently felt that if he could have had more—a career, a girlfriend, any real sources of satisfaction in life—his dad and his need to either vanquish him or have him in just the right way would have felt less imperative. But he was too preoccupied and debilitated by his hostile dependency on his father to seriously seek such things; and besides, it made no sense, for to get better would mean giving up the leverage of his despair.

In some people, the tendency to turn one's blaming voices against others is weak, there is a stronger pull toward depression, and the blaming system is turned more against the self. Rather than desperately fighting off the horrible truth about oneself, one embraces it. But this is no improvement, for the truth that is embraced is partial, unforgiving, destructive ("hateful, moralistic prick!") and takes no account of the deeper truth of who we are. This is the truth of intolerance, reductionism, scapegoating.

Like the blaming of others, self-blame is often a means around accountability. There is no useful taking of responsibility, no enlightenment, no repair. To blame oneself like this is to disappear from the playing field, to limp away wounded and unavailable, crippled and useless. "Yes, yes, I am terrible" can be an infuriating way of not being there, like someone turning out his empty pockets and saying, "I have nothing to give." It is not a constructive response to criticism. There is no effort to take in the complaint and make use of it, so that the other person feels heard and cared about. It's much more narcissistic than that. It's like taking the complaint and turning it into a dagger to plunge into one's own chest. "Look how awful I am" coexists quite nicely with "You don't exist at all." It is also a not-so-subtle act of aggression: "See what you've done to me! You've made me commit suicide!" Here, too, the blaming system yields a collapse of initiative and connection, as well as the flinging off of any chance to get closer to knowing who one really is.

REGRET

Is there room to be imperfect? To not have achieved? To have erred? To have hurt the people we loved? To regret is normal. We all make mistakes we wish we hadn't made and wish we could rectify. Regret can stir us to do better, to right wrongs, to go after what we've missed. But like shame and guilt, regret can also be an obsessive form of self-blaming and self-nulling. I never studied. I wasted my youth. I neglected my health. I got caught up in a cult or a cause and wasted years of my life in the process. I threw away love. I slept with him too soon. I had an abortion I should not have had. I missed the stock market boom. I made terrible mistakes.

Whack! Whack! Whack! Whack! Why can't we look back in sadness, feel the pain, and move on? It is, again, the problem of failed mourning, now in a slightly different form.

Earl, a friend, nearing fifty, describes a source of regret that has haunted him since his college days. Earl went to Columbia University and in his junior year became best friends with Arthur, a talented and charismatic young man from a wealthy family who would one day become a Broadway producer. The two were inseparable and part of a crowd that included other wealthy, intelligent young people, several of whom would also go on to impressive and glamourous careers. Earl and Arthur planned to write a play together. But because of his infatuation with Arthur and his doubts about himself—"I was afraid it would become Arthur's script and I would become second fiddle all the time"—Earl procrastinated and sabotaged their plans. Arthur was infuriated, quickly hooked up with a new coauthor, and never spoke to Earl again.

Even now, almost thirty years later, Earl remembers Arthur as smiling, sweet, diplomatic, creative, loaded with generosity and energy. He exudes a kind of sad worship when he talks about him. He sees himself as having been at his peak when he was running with Arthur and their mutual friends, especially Iris, who also abandoned him after the split with Arthur. Although Earl has many talents himself, has a good marriage, and is in no way a failure by most yardsticks, in the inner world of him and Arthur, he is a wannabe who had his chance and blew it. "Arthur and Iris are now friends in New York, and they go to hip downtown parties together and are part of the same social world. I have this feeling that when I broke with Arthur, I lost entrée to these people for whom he was my protective coloring. When the story got out of how I had shown this weakness and shameful behavior with him, and he rejected me utterly for it, all that was over. And I'm left with this feeling now that my life could have been different."

Earl's story raises questions. Why can't he look back and respect his choice (I didn't want to play second fiddle, I didn't want to be overwhelmed), even if he lacked the self-assurance to own it at the time and convey his decision to Arthur more directly? Why can't he look at the fiasco with Arthur, learn something from it and move on? Why can't he see the cruelty in Arthur's unforgiving response? Why does he join Arthur in that cruelty by seeing himself as unforgivably weak and shameful? Why has Earl made his own behavior a crime and Arthur's so understandable? Why has he made hanging out with stars and living the life of hip cocktail parties such a fetish that, at his worst moments, he lays waste to all the goodness he has created for himself? Why does he believe so firmly that he could have been a star player himself, but only through the auspices of a greater one, a true star, who would discover him and offer "protective coloring"?

It is not enough to say that Earl suffers from a pernicious and poisonous regret. He also must suffer from an internal relationship with some other worshiped, disapproving figure, some other person who looked benign but was capable of locking him out cruelly when wronged, some other person who could be stubbornly unforgiving and who imparted the feeling that status was more important than whatever was natural and good in him. This is, of course, a recipe for shame, with which I believe obsessive regret is often closely linked.

Russell, another friend, also suffers from regret. He thinks highly of creative work, like fiction writing, and believes it is his natural calling, but he has never taken a real shot at it. Russell is not sure whether to attribute this to lack of talent or lack of courage (that disapproving internal figure again). But he stabs himself over the failure, becomes depressed and demoralized. These feelings hold him back from writing. It all should have been done long ago. He should be much further along now. Who wants to begin at forty? Too late, too late.

Obsessive regret, therefore, has a paradoxical quality, in that it is often a way of continuing the very thing that is regretted. You blame yourself because of what you didn't do back then. But why back then didn't you do it? Because you were in some unentitled, anti-self, depressive hole. Regret keeps you in that hole. It bears the mark of enmeshment. It is a way of not separating.

Like other forms of blame, through regret we deny ourselves the space to be. There is no right to explore, to struggle, to make mistakes, to not know. There is no forgiving voice that says, You were being you, and that was all you could be at that time. There is only bitterness and grudge. Obsessive regret is how we submit and get defeated. Often, it is little more than revenge against the self.

COLLUSION

A woman came to see me six years after her marriage had collapsed. It ended abruptly when she discovered that her husband was sleeping with another woman. Such separations are almost always traumatic. For Pat it was particularly wrenching, first, because she had been in such a state of denial about the problems in her marriage that it hit her as if from outer space and, second, because her husband was leaving her for her own assistant, whom she had counted as a friend and confidante. Pat was thirty-six at the time and had hoped still to have a family. Now she expected that she would be childless and her faithless friend would have the babies that should have been hers.

After a period of rage she turned against herself. The question Why do I deserve this?, at first an uncomprehending lamentation, now turned into an accusation. An implication of badness and shame washed over her. She gnawed over all of her failings, real and imagined. This was not a constructive reassessment. It was pure indictment, and the only defense she had against it was to hold to her story of innocence and persecution. Her depression was paralyzing, causing her to neglect and eventually lose the business she had spent years building. Then from the depths of her misery a new resolve formed and a new cause: a punitive divorce action. She would make her husband pay for her losses. She would exact a vengeance that would somehow make her whole.

Six years later, she and her husband had still not come to an agreement on the division of assets. In our work it became apparent that Pat had helped plant the seeds of separation herself. Emotionally speaking, she had been no more available to her husband than she was to the men who were showing interest in her now. Her behavior with me was indicative of her don't-get-close-to-me policy. She could not ask for what she needed; she could only punish for not getting it.

Almost two years after we began working together, Pat walked in the door indignant and ready to chew me out. She had gone over the last bill I had given her and discovered that I had charged her for a session that she missed because she had been stuck in traffic. She loudly told me off, likening me to the worst sort of money-grubber, and I found myself tightening up and wanting to defend myself with a cold recitation of my policy on missed sessions. I asked her if she knew what she was doing with me.

"I'm being angry."

"You're not just being angry, you're trashing me."

"Well, I'm angry, Bob. Come on, that's what people do when they're angry."

"You could tell me that you're angry, you could tell me that you're upset and hurt, you could say you need to talk to me about the bill without wiping me out."

It was one of the remarkable things about Pat that, as defensive and aggressive as she could be, she could snap out of it if spoken to fairly and directly. She welled up. "I could never say that, Bob," she said.

"Why not?"

"How could you say that in my house? My mother would have said, 'Grow up!' " She used her mother's screechy, dismissive voice.

"And you would have felt . . . ?"

"Like I always felt, like nothing, like I didn't mean anything to her."

I asked her how she would expect me to react.

"Kind of the same way," she said.

"Which means I feel what about you?"

"That I don't matter, that I'm just a walking billfold."

The pervasive sense of being a nobody, whose feelings, whose very being meant nothing, was augmented by the conviction that she was physically unattractive. Her mother, an envious and insecure beauty, had jealously guarded her queenlike position in the family. There was to be no rival princess, no little girl trying on her jewelry and her lipstick or stealing Daddy's affection. Sadly, Pat's father acquiesced to her mom's demands and steered clear of showing Pat the attention that would upset his wife.

Pat felt like the ugly duckling, and she remained so tightly connected to the traumatic, rejecting aspect of her mother that into her forties she was still riveted to evidence of her ugliness. The fact that ample numbers of men had always shown interest in her did nothing to disconfirm her belief. She reacted to men with a sense of ugliness and the surety of rejection. She avoided making eye contact and sent them signals that their approaches were unwelcome. She had a deeply subtle way of conveying, I am ugly and you don't want me. If they got past such barriers, she usually found a way to discard them. She would catch a whiff of ambivalence. She would take offense at small things. She would hear criticism when it wasn't there and interpret actual criticism as an attack. And then she would counterattack in ways that made my jaw drop when she related them. Inevitably, she would either engineer the rejection she feared or see the man as a lost cause and write him off. Consciously, she thought, Men just want to use me; they want to marry starlets. Unconsciously, she seemed to have decided, I would rather not have a man than to have my hideousness confirmed by his rejection.

With Pat there was always a subtext about worthlessness, about not being able to identify with her beautiful mother, and becoming particularly involved with the rejecting aspect of a man because this brought her back to Mom. Like the young man whom I imagined lowering himself into the acid, only through the symbolic vehicle of the men in her life, Pat was waiting for Mom—and Mom only!—to remove the hex, to tell her that she was, after all, a lovely, embraceable girl. It was not something she felt she had any power to effect on her own or would allow anyone else to effect except momentarily.

Pat warded off her feelings of being an ugly nobody with a kind of ballsy insouciance. She was almost always on the attack, often in small and funny ways. One Sunday, when I was working in my office, I got a call from Pat. She was intending to leave a message. When she heard my live voice, she burst through the phone with an exclamation of surprise and dismay: "Bob, what are you doing in the *office!*" "Writing," I said. "Why are you picking up the *phone!*" she screamed. She seemed downright indignant: What was I doing working on Sunday when I should be having fun! What was I doing picking up the phone! Although it was ostensibly caring, it felt like an assault. It was an experience I had come to know well with Pat, and I had spoken to her about it. She turns all her unwanted feelings into assaultive high spirits.

Contrary to the image she projected of being a free spirit, Pat was timid about her feelings. She was not just a little nonplused or embarrassed to be intruding, she felt horrified over what she had done. So while part of her was concerned about me and about intruding on me, she was also made suddenly anxious about having gotten in my way. Unconsciously, she anticipated a rejection, a cold slap coming through the phone, as befits an annoying pain in the neck. This aroused not only hurt but resentment. Her trumpeting scold of concern both managed her anxiety and enabled a disguised attack: "Why are you picking up the phone, damn you, and putting me in this horrible position!" (and if she had blurted that out, straight from the unconscious, it would have felt a lot friendlier).

One of our goals in therapy became to get her to stay close to that crushed place inside of her, that walled-off child, unwilling to be touched, afraid to let anyone care, who is convinced that no one could. As in any therapy, the goal was met in fits and starts. But as the picture became clearer to us, her attitude toward her husband softened. It wasn't that she lost sight of his betrayal and how cowardly and hurtful his behavior had been, but she had some perspective now. She remembered how supportive he could be and how she used to brush him off. She also took note for the first time of his limitations, which included difficulty being assertive or direct with her, and this, too, made her feel less blaming, more forgiving.

She could still get into a fury over what he'd done. She told me, "In some way I don't know if I'll ever forgive. There's a piece of me that can still catch fire thinking of them and what they did." I knew what she meant by "catch fire"—that she could wish them the worst sort of death. But such moments were less frequent and the fire less consuming. Now, she sometimes pined for her husband and felt sorrowful over the chance she'd missed to have a good marriage with him. I asked her what she thought would dampen the flames once and for all. "Finding happiness," she said. I took this as a sign of progress. Instead of obsessively holding on to these spoiled relationships and gnawing away at her own wound as if it were a precious bone, instead of reveling in her victim status, which conferred upon her the holy right to get even, Pat was seeing herself as having other possibilities.

This work of letting go is perhaps the final task of mourning. Letting go, in Pat's case, would not be limited to letting go of her husband. (Indeed, it might not, under some circumstances, have to mean that at all. If she wanted to reopen things with him and if it were possible, that would be fine.) But rather letting go of a way of being and, more deeply, of inner, victimized relationships with her mother and father where this way of being is fostered. Her way of being was something she constructed as a child; it was how she coped. It got her through, albeit at the expense of her feelings. But she was not a child now; she had more resources. She could do something else. She could feel the pain and survive. She could have this part of herself back.

What this meant, of course, was reexperiencing her brokenheartedness as a child. The past lived in Pat in a way she had never understood. Facing it facilitated her ability to imagine moving on, imagine seeing herself differently and having a different sort of life, where love could be satisfying and dependable and conflicts could be addressed and resolved. This had been unimaginable before. Glimpsing the possibility of it enabled her to let go of her legal battles and negotiate a settlement with her ex-husband. If she didn't entirely forgive him, she did begin to release them both from the tyranny of her grudge.

A CASE AGAINST THE GODS

Why is life so unfair? Why do others have so much more? More beauty, more money, more love, more talent, more luck, more pleasure? Why do some people experience this unfairness more acutely than others, to the point of feeling persecuted? Two close friends get pregnant at the same time; they look forward to an expansion of the friendship into a new realm as they become mothers together. But after two and a half months one miscarries. She now refuses all contact with her friend and experiences her as an enemy. Why do her loss and her envy take her to such a place?

The feeling of being a Have-not is a terrible thing that has deep psychological roots. When envy and a feeling of having been cheated and left out, marked by the gods for bad things, become pronounced in one's psychology, it typically has its beginnings in a formative relationship, where one felt cheated and left out by a parent or identified with a parent who felt cheated and left out, or, quite commonly, both, so that this condition comes to feel like one's destiny. It can lead to a bitter feeling about the world, a perpetual sense of having gotten a raw deal, a cramping possessiveness toward anyone who is loved, and an envy toward others who are unconsciously experienced as having it all but refusing to share. In *The Idiot,* Dostoevsky drew a portrait of someone like this in Ipolit, who was dying of consumption but seemed to have felt robbed of life even before he became ill. In *Till We Have Faces,* a re-creation of the Cupid and Psyche myth, C. S. Lewis also addresses this theme. Here, Orual, the ancient queen of Glome, tells her story, which she sets down as an indictment against the gods.

Orual, who never knew her mother, was raised by a scolding nurse and subjected to the tempers of a shallow, unloving father. From her earliest years she heard things that made her guess that people thought her ugly. When a Greek slave was purchased by her father, he told the captive that he would one day have a son for this learned man to educate. Until then, he could practice on the king's two daughters. "Especially the elder," he said of Orual. "See if you can make her wise; it's about all she'll ever be good for."

The children briefly had a stepmother who died in childbirth, bequeathing the king a third daughter. "Girls, girls, girls!" the king bellowed. "And now one girl more. Is there a plague of girls in heaven that the gods send me this flood of them?" In his rage he caught Orual by the hair, shook her to and fro, and flung her aside in a heap. This was the misery of her childhood.

The new baby was called Psyche, and she became the love of Orual's life. Her beauty was beyond measure, and her temperament was sweet. Orual narrowed her focus to Psyche and their Greek teacher, nicknamed "the Fox," whom she also loved, and with them she spent many contented years. But ill times fell on Glome: A drought, and then a pestilence, with enemies pressing in on the kingdom, and the sick and starving people swelling around the castle, threatening, and demanding relief.

The pestilence struck the Fox, and Psyche nursed him back to health. The people heard the story and believed that she had healing powers. They demanded that she come out. The king sent her to attend to them, and the people fell on their knees, awed by her beauty. Some died, some recovered. Word of the recoveries spread, and Psyche was worshiped as a goddess. But, as things worsened in the kingdom, the tide of opinion turned against her. They called her "the Accursed," and the priest demanded that she be sacrificed to a local god, the Shadowbrute, who, rumor had it, would make her his bride and devour her.

Orual and Psyche have a last meeting before the sacrifice. Psyche, who has gone through inner transformations, now seems serenely adjusted to her fate. She has discovered something in her core, a spiritual longing that no one had guessed before. Orual is miserable to the bone over her impending loss of Psyche and furious at Psyche for not reacting the same way. "Oh, cruel, cruel!" Orual wails. "Is it nothing to you that you leave me here alone? Psyche, did you ever love me at all?"

Psyche no longer seems like a child. As she discusses her fate, especially such things as the longing she has always felt for the holy mountain where she is to be sacrificed, Orual cannot bear her detachment. "I felt (and this horribly)," Orual narrates, "that I was losing her already, that the sacrifice tomorrow would only finish something that had already begun. She was (how long had she been, and I not to know?) out of my reach, in some place of her own. . . . I felt, amid all my love, a bitterness. Though the things she was saying gave her (that was plain enough) courage and comfort, I grudged her that courage and comfort."

Psyche talks hopefully of what she calls "the sweetest thing in all my life," her longing to reach the mountain, the place "where the beauty comes from." Orual protests bitterly, brokenheartedly, "And that was the sweetest?" Psyche asks her to "look up once at least before the end and wish me joy. I am going to my lover." Orual responds, "I only see that you have never loved me. It may well be you are going to the gods. You are becoming cruel like them."

The loss of Psyche leaves Orual crushed and hopeless, hating the gods and all their earthly representatives, with their horrible rituals and unctuous chicanery. After recovering from a long illness, she convinces the king's lieutenant to take her to the mountain to gather Psyche's remains. As they make their way up the holy road into the mountain, a strange thought comes to Orual: "Why should your heart not dance?" She reflects that "The freshness and wetness all about me . . . made me feel that I had misjudged the world; it seemed kind, and laughing, as if its heart also danced. Even my ugliness I could not quite believe in. Who can *feel* ugly when the heart meets delight? It is as if, somewhere inside, within the hideous face and bony limbs, one is soft, fresh, lissome and desirable."

But Orual's heart, momentarily tempted, sinks back to its sadness. "My heart to dance? Mine whose love was taken from me, I, the ugly princess who must never look for other love, the drudge of the King . . . ?" To believe in such a thing would be to set herself up to be dashed down again.

When they finish their climb and arrive at the place where Psyche was sacrificed, Orual, to her astonishment, finds Psyche herself, healthy and radiant, standing in a valley just beyond the sacred river. In her joy, Orual has only one thought: to get Psyche back to Glome. But Psyche is happy where she is. She insists she is the god's wife and cannot return. She lives in his palace and invites Orual in. Orual, however, cannot see it and is horrified when Psyche insists it is right before her eyes. "Stop it, stop it, I tell you! There's no such thing. You're pretending. You're trying to make yourself believe it."

Orual later admits that she actually was not so certain. "How did I know whether she really saw invisible things?" Besides, Psyche was healthy, coherent, impressive in her directness and clarity, with no sign of hardship about her. But the whole thing—to have found Psyche and to not be able to have her—felt terribly cruel. "And now," Orual narrates, "she was saying *he* every moment, no other name but *he,* the way young wives talk. Something began to grow colder and harder in me."

The sisters part, Psyche urging Orual to visit her again. Orual finds her companion, and they prepare to encamp for the night. Thirsty, Orual takes a drink from the "sacred" river. When she lifts her head, "I saw that which brought my heart into my throat. There stood the palace." Orual is frightened and determined to go back to the palace and ask forgiveness of Psyche and her god. But as she rises, the whole structure disappears into the mists, and she decides it was a mirage.

When she returns to the mountain months later, it is with a new resolve—to convince her sister that she is either the prisoner of the Shad-owbrute, a loathsome, otherworldly, creature, or the chattel of a criminal and depraved mountain man. She demands that Psyche disobey her husband-god by doing that which he has expressly forbidden: to dare to gaze upon him. Orual insists that Psyche take a lamp secretly to bed and steal a look at the god while he sleeps; only then will she know the truth. She pulls out her dagger and warns Psyche that she will kill both Psyche and herself if Psyche refuses her challenge. Psyche, furious over this manipulation, informs Orual that she has no physical power over Psyche in this realm and cannot possibly harm her. But she will risk her happiness rather than let Orual harm herself.

"I had won my victory," Orual writes, "and my heart was in torment. I had a terrible longing to unsay all my words and beg her forgiveness." But she holds firm. Night falls. Disaster follows. Terrible lightning, storms, and ragings, and the pitiful sounds of the weeping Psyche tell the outcome. The horrible husband-thing, Orual realizes, might destroy them both now. But at least Psyche would know. "She would, at worst, die undeceived, disenchanted, reconciled to me. Even now we might escape." Through a flash of lightning the god appears before Orual, looking upon her with "passionless and measureless rejection." He makes it clear that he sees that "all my doubtings, fears, guessings, debatings" were all "trumped up foolery, dust blown in my own eyes by myself." Psyche is sentenced to wander in "hunger and thirst and tread hard roads."

Orual now knows without doubt that the gods exist and that they hate her. They dealt her a bad hand, they took away her only love, they refused to give her a clear sign of their existence when she most needed it, they tricked her into dreadful errors, and they mocked her with the implication that she should have known better.

Orual returns home, eventually becomes queen of Glome, and dons a veil that she never removes. Never again does she have to deal with the shame she feels over her ugliness; the covering also gives her power and helps her conquer her fear. Not even those closest to her are allowed to see her face. She runs the country in exemplary fashion, bringing to it a level of justice, prosperity, peace, and security unknown before. Glome becomes a model kingdom.

But Orual lives in spiritual exile. Hers is an empty-feeling, obsessive life, in which work takes her further and further from herself. "I locked Orual up and laid her asleep as best I could," she writes, "somewhere deep down inside me; she lay curled there. It was like being with child, but reversed; the thing I carried in me grew slowly smaller and less alive."

Decades pass. Old and shriveled, Orual begins to see things about herself she never guessed could be true. Wrenching occurrences make her recognize that she misused and misunderstood even those she loved best as a result of her blinding self-centeredness. All that mattered, after all, was that she had been dealt a bad hand, that she was miserably deprived, that the gods did not smile on her. Why should she have a care for all those others, be seriously concerned with their needs, when they lived in the sunshine of the gods' smile and she lived under a cloud? She had never thought to tell the Fox that she loved him or how much it would have meant to him to hear that before he died. She had never allowed her military chief, whose company and counsel she so valued, to have any time with his family. Instead she had made herself miserable with the thought that she was just a duty to him and that his heart was with the "wife and brats" he went home to. Of her younger sister, the pretty, yellow-haired Redival, Orual also experiences a revelation. She had always seen Redival as shallow and treacherous; after all, it was Redival who had started the people against Psyche, by whispering that she was setting herself up as a god. But Redival was lonely. She had had Orual to herself as a little girl. But Orual fell in love with the Fox, then Psyche, and Redival was left out. "I never gave a thought to Redival's loneliness; after all she had her locks."

Near the end of the tale, Orual has her day in the gods' court and is able to present her case against them, the very book that we have been reading. But what comes out of her mouth, uncontrollably, is not all the words she had carefully, logically, written and always believed she believed, but a litany of envy, jealousy, and possessiveness spoken in a poisonous flood.

"You said a brute would devour her," she cries about her beloved Psyche halfway through her tirade. "Well, why didn't it? I'd have wept for her and buried what was left and built her a tomb. . . . But to steal her love from me! . . . It would be far better for us [humans] if you [gods] were foul and ravening. We'd rather you drank [the] blood [of those we love] than stole their hearts. We'd rather that they were ours and dead than yours and made immortal. But to steal her love from me, to make her see things I couldn't see. . . . The girl was mine. What right had you to steal her away into your dreadful heights? You'll say I was jealous. Jealous of Psyche? Not while she was mine. . . . But to hear a chit of a girl who had (or ought to have had) no thought in her head that I'd not put there, setting up for seer and prophetess and next thing to a goddess . . . how could anyone endure it? . . . Psyche was mine and no one else had any right to her. Oh, you'll say you took her away into bliss and joy such as I could never have given her, and I ought to have been glad of it for her sake. Why? What should I care for some horrible, new happiness which I hadn't given her and which separated her from me? Do you think I wanted her to be happy, that way? It would have been better if I'd seen the Brute tear her to pieces before my eyes."

And so she raves until the judge says, "Enough." The room is silent. Orual looks down and sees that her book has become a tiny insignificant thing in her hands and that she has been reading it aloud over and over. The voice she read it in was strange to her ears, but she understands with certainty that this is, at last, her real voice—envious, possessive, murderous, anguished. It is the beginning of a stirring awakening, heart-rending realizations, an extraordinary reunion with Psyche, and a touching self-forgiveness. It is an awakening for the reader, too, for as much as we may have been rooting for her, and as sad and unfair as her plight seems, we recognize that Orual chose to be bitter and to live inside her trauma and her grudge.

A wiser Orual eventually decides to amend her book. "I saw well," she now writes, "why the gods do not speak to us openly, nor let us answer. Till the word can be dug out of us, why should they hear the babble that we think we mean? How can they meet us face to face until we have faces?"

I HAVE BARELY TOLD the skeleton of C. S. Lewis's story, and I hope that anyone who takes up the book will find its dramatic and spiritual value unspoiled by this preview. But I think this portion does capture a truth that reflects on our struggles to forgive. Our complaints against others, deeply believed and repeated like an incantation, come from a self we do not fully know, are bitterly determined not to know. It sometimes takes a great work on our part to dig it out.

REVENGE OF
THE WOUNDED

IN 1983, DURING THE NUCLEAR FREEZE CAMPAIGN, AN UNUSUAL event took place at a Manhattan high school. Before an audience of peace-movement activists, the Performing Artists for Nuclear Disarmament put on a show consisting mainly of singers and skits with movement messages. But the second skit itself hit the audience like a nuclear bomb. It was a piece of a play called *Dead End Kids,* which had had a successful run at New York's Public Theatre. It featured a vulgar, fast-talking master of ceremonies who assailed the audience with his manic game-show-host-type personality.

A sense of threat rippled through the large room in reaction to his slick, aggressive presence. To a young woman in the front row: "Tell me, sweetheart, what's the difference between a pastrami sandwich and a blow job? Aha! You don't know! Well, I'll see you for lunch tomorrow! Hey, hey! All right! We're having fun tonight!" He now proceeded to violate every prejudice, political assumption, and cherished conviction of the people in the room.

The skit, which presented a noir picture of American culture, was the sort of thing this crowd would normally have loved. But by an amazing bit of bad luck, the performance was not taken as a theatrical depiction of an ugliness they were fully prepared to hate, but rather as the ugliness itself, something that was being done to them, right there, in real time. It was as if the emcee was slaughtering sheep before vegetarians or urinating on the cross before a gathering of the devout. The stunned audience began to hiss, then grew louder and angrier. An old woman cried, "Get 'im off! We don't want this pornography!" Others walked out. The emcee heroically carried on until he could no longer endure it, then abandoned the performance.

The houselights went up on a scene of huge and mounting confusion. The PAND president, Florence Falk, looking somber and distraught, came forward and said she would like to invite the author and director of the piece, JoAnne Akalaitis, a rising theatre person in the city at the time, who was present, to explain what the misfired skit was supposed to have been about. But an emotional transformation had taken place for many in the room. They had moved into another state of being, one in which they were rageful, unforgiving victims and determined to remain as such. *Dead End Kids* was over; The Revenge of the Wounded had begun. Akalaitis walked forward amidst an harangue of howls and protests, as if her very presence was an affront. People rushed into the aisles to denounce her. They demanded that she be removed. Grace Paley, the short-story writer and pacifist leader, tried to calm the emotions and encourage a dialogue. She, too, was shouted down. Teary and defiant, Akalaitis exited amidst a rain of indictments.

The eviction had been swift and stunning, and people who might have wanted things to turn out otherwise hardly had time to assess what had happened. The room that night was like a person torn in two directions. A wish to be fair, to be generous, to take responsibility, struggled weakly against a potent rage, a rigid, wounded innocence. The indignant segment of the audience, safe in its ideological positions, powered by ancient injuries, and gorging itself on moralistic indictments—Sexist! Pornographic! Disrespectful!—overran the befuddled opposition. Misshapen parents, bullying and violent cops, narcissistic ex-husbands, the Internal Revenue Service, Richard Nixon, Joe McCarthy, the Women's House of Detention, John Wayne, Mayor Ed Koch, Hugh Hefner—all stood before them now in the person of JoAnne Akalaitis. It was a sobering lesson for anyone seriously interested in peace and reconciliation among nations and peoples. For here were a group of activists for peace and reconciliation, many of whom had slipped into a murderous state in which one of their own had become a demon in their eyes, in which they could not tolerate hearing her offer an explanation or make an effort to repair an offense; while others, who may have desired a different outcome, could do nothing to stop them. It is similar to what can happen *internally*, to the kind of conflict that can at times define an individual psyche.

ON BEING A VICTIM

The psychological experience of being victimized is different from real victimization, in that we take a piece of reality and use it to symbolize the whole. All I know is that you hurt me: I have been cruelly and intentionally wronged, your attitude toward me is one of heartless disregard, I am powerless and played no part. This sense of victimization is widespread, endlessly varying, and perversely delicious.

Years ago I co-ran a workshop on power and intimacy. June, one of the participants, was a woman I knew through a neighborhood organization and counted as something of a friend. In the second of the six two-hour meetings the leaders answered a question about missed sessions, indicating that there was a single fee for the whole course and that there would be no refund, regardless of the reason. This displeased June and several of the other participants. The two leaders, both of us young and inexperienced, tried to hold our ground and, feeling threatened, were probably rigid about it. June became enraged and yelled at us with a startlingly disturbed look in her eyes. After some back and forth, she said, "You guys have our money and you're going to do exactly what you please!" Her tone screamed "victim." I said, "June, have you paid yet?" I knew she hadn't; she timidly admitted as much. I said, "You're totally in control. You can quit, you can fight with us some more, you can do what you like. But you're so determined to experience yourself as being victimized that you feel and act as if we're holding your money when we're not."

From the point of view of her inner drama and the victim self she inhabited there, June experienced herself as dealing with people who were irrational and all-powerful. She felt as if she was already submitting to us, could already feel her knees sinking into the carpet. A complaint or protest of any kind coming from such a place is bound to sound victimized, wounded, accusatory, blaming, indignant—better characterized as an attack than a protest—and this did not invite a sympathetic response. It invited a defensive response. The leaders felt under the gun, our own anxieties about being bad and tossed aside were activated, and we might easily have reacted accordingly. We didn't have to react that way. We didn't have to take the bait. But that was certainly the direction in which June's protest beckoned us.

As the workshop proceeded we discovered that June was not alone in experiencing an irrational sense of victimization. All of us did at times, and several of the participants were veteran victims with a litany of grievances and an arsenal of retaliatory weapons, weapons that some spoke of ruefully at first but obviously loved. Thérèse, a woman nearing fifty from Lynbrook, Long Island, was able to recall every person who had ever injured or offended her. Her selective memory and her propensity to plunge with relish into negative interpretations of people's responses to her made me think, Here is someone who never passed up a chance to taste the poison.

Thérèse spoke rather poignantly of one grudge of six years' standing against an old friend named Mona with whom she had gone to college and who had obviously been one of the most loved people in her life. The friendship had foundered when Mona's daughter was Bat Mitzvahed. Thérèse had helped prodigiously with the preparations, but when the photographer came, Mona ran around getting photographed with everyone but Thérèse, and she neglected to mention Thérèse's helpful efforts during the many toasts that followed.

Shortly afterwards, as planned, Mona and her family moved to Atlanta, her husband having been transferred there. Thérèse received cards from Mona and her daughter thanking her for her gift and her help, but Thérèse viewed these as insults. She said Mona's note was the kind of thank you you send to an acquaintance. A few weeks later when Mona telephoned, Thérèse was cool. From Thérèse's point of view, Mona had crossed over; she had become an enemy, someone who was determined to deprive and humiliate Thérèse and act all the while as if nothing had happened. Her reaching out, therefore, struck Thérèse as a hollow imitation of friendship, an ugly charade. With a hurt, prosecutorial face, like a bitter hawk, Thérèse suddenly addressed the group members as if they were Mona's defenders: "Come on!" she said, looking fiercely from face to face. "No apology, no explanation, *nothing*. I mean, really. This was not a friend." By the time Mona called to say she would be in town for the holidays, Thérèse's rage was as hard as a diamond, and she avoided seeing her. Gradually, Mona stopped calling. But all these years later, Thérèse still seethed.

Thérèse's story aroused the group. Some recognized the victim's style and became very agitated, entreating Thérèse to, if not exactly forgive Mona, at least open herself to the possibility of reconciliation. They wanted her to recognize that one wounding experience is not a basis for discarding a valued friend. Some eventually perceived that this was not only about Thérèse. Thérèse's story provoked them because it portrayed an aspect of their own inner lives. Although Thérèse had taken on some characterological qualities of bitterness—her face itself was a mask of unforgivingness much of the time—the struggle she described was universal, and none of us could legitimately count ourselves free of it. In the meantime, of course, much work was done to try to argue Thérèse out of her position.

Group members asked Thérèse why she hadn't told Mona about her hurt feelings. ("She *knew* what she was doing," Thérèse said.) They offered explanations for why Mona may have acted the way she did at the Bat Mitzvah. (One theory held that Mona had been caught up in her own excitement and accidently overlooked Thérèse, only to feel guilty later and not know how to handle it.) Some had suspicions about the way Thérèse had behaved based on things she'd done in the group. (Did she remove herself in some way, so that Mona would have had to search to include her? Had she said, "No, no, don't bother about me" at some crucial point in order to live out her woundedness and test Mona's devotion?) They had explanations for why Mona didn't apologize. (She may not have realized how much she had hurt Thérèse, she may have hoped unconsciously that everything was okay even though she knew it wasn't.) They had reasons for Thérèse to be hopeful. (Mona may have responded well if Thérèse had confronted her—and indeed might still do so if Thérèse would take the risk.) They even thought they detected in

Thérèse a sadness over the rift with this friend and some hurt that Mona had moved so far away. I thought I saw Thérèse flinch when Mona's moving away was mentioned, but she denied it. Indeed, she would have none of any of this. She refused to believe any interpretation but her own, in which she and her former friend were engaged in a victimization drama, in which Mona had used her, indeed had always used her, and then cast her aside. Nor could she accept that freezing Mona out had been a potent form of revenge. ("What else was I supposed to do?") Few were surprised, as the workshop progressed, to discover that Mona was not the first or the last person to betray Thérèse, to be viewed as an enemy, or to be banished.

Toward the end of the workshop, Thérèse was doing a role play with one of the men in the group. They were enacting a dating couple, negotiating how they would get to the theatre that night. The man was angling for Thérèse to meet him there, and Thérèse was playing hard for him to pick her up. Eventually, she seemed to acquiesce in a faintly shruggy sort of way, and her partner was naïvely about to go along with it. At that point, I interrupted and asked her, "But what's going to happen, Thérèse, if he doesn't come get you?" She raised an eyebrow and said with a little smile, "Well, that will be it for *him.*" The group erupted in laughter at the pleasure Thérèse was taking in creating a new victimization for herself and a new opportunity for revenge. Thérèse displayed a sheepish enjoyment of this sudden revelation and seemed to gain some insight from it.

Victimhood is an immense source of power, even if it can do its user no real good. It is poisonous in both directions. It is pronounced in people with personality disorders but it is no stranger to anyone. And it is antithetical to forgiveness. The catastrophic energy that can get wrapped up in victimization is apparent in the crimes of passion that fill our newspapers and airwaves.

The Seduction of Crime

In March of 1996 Mike Tyson fought the champion Evander Holyfield in a much-anticipated rematch for the heavyweight title. Holyfield had mastered the feared Tyson in their first match, and by the third round of this fight he appeared to be doing so again. Then, as much of the world knows, a remarkable thing happened. With the two men leaning into each other, Tyson bit off a chunk of Holyfield's earlobe, causing the other man to leap and howl. The referee gave Tyson a warning and let the match continue. But moments later Holyfield leapt like a jackrabbit out of another clinch, holding his ear and hopping in pain. Tyson had bitten again. The referee stopped the fight and declared Holyfield the winner.

In the aftermath, Tyson painted himself the victim, speaking resentfully of the repeated head butts he had endured from Holyfield in this fight and the previous one that the refs had done nothing to stop. He said he had no choice but to retaliate. "This is my career," he said. "I've got children to raise."

In his heyday Tyson had dominated the heavyweight field through terror, causing some opponents to lose before they entered the ring. Tyson's physical abilities were abetted by the immense rage he carried with him at all times. It was the rage of a bully who dominates weaker men and sadistically humiliates them. He spoke of wanting to break his opponents, wanting to see them "cry like a woman." An orphan from the streets of Brownsville, one of New York's toughest ghettos, he had been savaged as a kid. In his world, you were either a brutal intimidator or a humiliated, whimpering emasculate. In Holyfield, Tyson ran into a man whom he could not bully, who offered him a real contest. But to Tyson, a real contest was a defeat, and a defeat was a loss of manhood.

The victim in Tyson was always apparent. He felt perpetually unloved and persecuted. He identified with Sonny Liston, the last heavyweight champ to emerge from a world of crime, a most unbeloved champion who collapsed before the vibrant Cassius Clay. Tyson watched and rewatched old Liston fights, as if anticipating his own doom. His victim self and his bully self were, of course, one and the same, but in his ongoing contest with Holyfield, the victim aspect emerged as dominant. He will probably go to his grave determined to believe that he did not intentionally foul his way out of the fight, but rather was done in by the refs and others who wished his downfall.

A similar sense of victimhood and humiliation drives some men to kill the women who are unfaithful to them or who leave them for other men. Men who have felt battered, manipulated, controlled, or rejected by their mothers and are therefore quick to boil when hurt by a woman have a visceral understanding of the psychotic-like rage that might cause an ex-lover to go to such extremes. The feeling of being a victim, the shame that often comes with it, and the self-righteous fury that explodes out of it and seeks to erase it brings to mind what the sociologist Jack Katz has referred to as "the seductions of crime." As I write this, there is a story in the news about a man from New Jersey who shot and killed a schoolteacher who he erroneously believed was having an affair with his wife. He based it all on a single encounter between his wife and the dead man and a Christmas card sent to his wife by the dead man's wife. It is tempting to dismiss this as paranoia, which of course it is. But that would miss the more universal point of how powerfully a desolate and persecuted aspect of one's inner life can gain ascendance, overwhelming and transforming the evidence of one's senses.

Suicide, too, is often a crime of revenge. Over the years I have heard about a number of suicides or attempted suicides by parents of small children. In one case a single mother recently rejected by her lover slit her wrists and was found in the bathroom by her child. In another, a mother who had just lost a custody battle for her child jumped off the roof of the building where she lived, landing where her husband and child might easily have stumbled upon her body.

Suicides like this suggest not only unendurable pain but also the humiliated fury of a small child who feels she is being crushed by a cruel adult. Unconsciously at least, they usually include the wish to retaliate—against the lover or the husband, obviously, but also against a parent or parents who retain a tyrannical, indicting presence inside the suffering person.

A person who kills herself may be stuck in a state where she feels so insignificant that she forgets she has importance to anyone. She may slip into such an isolated, devalued, disconnected place that she loses touch with the very fact that she is a parent or that her absence will matter to her child. But it is possible, too, that the suicidal parent knows at some level of consciousness what her death will cost her child. That she goes ahead anyway suggests the extremes to which victimization can take us.

The child himself may be experienced as a victimizer: He doesn't love me. He won't even care if I'm gone. He's happy despite my misery. He loves his father more than me. And so forth. In such a frenzied, infantile state, a parent may not only abandon the child she loves but risk his finding her corpse on the sidewalk.

RATHER BE A HAMMER THAN A NAIL

A young man, Jeff, comes in to see me. We've been working together for two years. He's smart, insightful, and, in his connected mode, when he allows himself to get close to his vulnerability, quite lovable. But he can be hard to reach, and he has a haughty contemptuous air. He can't focus today. He is preoccupied, eaten away really, by struggles with a girlfriend and a business partner, both of whom he is now actively hating. But he hasn't expressed this yet, he is keeping his hatefulness to himself, and the session seems to be going nowhere. I say, "I feel like you're a stray cat and I'm trying to offer you some milk, but you don't seem interested." "No," he says. "What I would really like is to have my enemies here so that I can destroy them."

Jeff is a successful man. He drives his employees hard and he is quick with contempt for anyone who does not live up to his standards, a failing he virtually equates with sabotage. He has found power in hatred. Nothing is more exhilarating to Jeff than high-octane hate. People fear him. They succumb to him. They fall bloodied and beaten before him. All this gives pleasure to the manufacture of enemies. He has raised "I'd rather be a hammer than a nail" to a credo. But his love of revenge is not just about the pleasures of aggression or of getting even. Revenge is a way out of mourning. It is a way of not feeling pain, not looking at your life, not dealing with an incipient depression that might otherwise engulf you.

Jeff is consumed, unconsciously, by early injuries. He was the love of his parents' lives until age three when his younger brother was born. His mother, overwhelmed by two children, dropped all his baby privileges at that time. She demanded that he stop needing her and become a little man. He became clingy, accident-prone, oppositional. His father was repulsed by this behavior and withdrew from him. Jeff wrapped himself in a bitterness that still shapes him. At times, he evokes hateful behavior in others, which he then obsesses over and which gives him fresh opportunities for revenge. He's like a child who saw his whole village, including his parents and everyone he ever loved, wiped out by a heartless enemy and has devoted his life to them; it's the only thing that gives pleasure. Sadly, the enemies of his childhood were his beloved parents themselves. In holding on to victimhood he is also holding on to his love of the cruel, sadistic, abandoning aspect of his parents; in seeking revenge he acts out his identification with this side of them. Tragically lost in this process is his memory of their goodness or his capacity to identify with it.

Whenever I pointed out his murderousness, he would get furious at me and demand that I recognize that he was the hurt party. And there was an emotional truth to this, for he did feel like a crushed baby. But his behavior was that of the parent who crushed him. This is what children do. In feeling so weak and so devastated, they strive to be strong like the loved, abusive parent, and they often use the parent's weapons to achieve it.

When I say he is consumed by early injuries, I do not mean in the sense of going around angry all the time, although that's part of it. Rather he's enmeshed with his parents, magnetized by them, can't get them out of his mind, even if he does not consciously think about them. He re-creates his relationships with them with virtually every other important person in his life. He's always on the lookout to turn someone into Mom or Dad. Thus, Jeff reads into his girlfriend those qualities in his mother he most hates and feels persecuted by. He then feels manipulated, undermined, humiliated, abandoned, betrayed, etc. He seethes obsessively over her wrongdoings, complains about them in treatment, plots his counterattack, and executes it with prosecutorial zeal.

It's not that Jeff's girlfriend is totally innocent. He's not making things up out of thin air. But he's choosing to become most engaged with the parts of her that replicate what is negative in his mother. This is what it means to make a mountain out of a molehill, or to see the mote in someone else's eye and ignore the beam in one's own. It's as if his girlfriend's eyes are like his mother's, and he is transfixed by those eyes. So transfixed that he cannot see the rest of her face. He focuses on the eyes and fills in the face accordingly. And suddenly, *voilà!*, a perfect replica of the monster herself! This is the essence of what is known in psychology as transference.

When Jeff feels wounded, he gets into the trauma zone that he carries within, and at that point it is no longer possible to have a dissatisfaction, to be angry, to want to straighten somebody out. It becomes a case of "You're destroying me and I want to destroy you." It's as if he's going back home and dragging the offender with him, with no sense that the current situation is not remotely the same as the original where he was powerless and his parents in control.

At moments when Jeff feels wounded, he is so disgusted by the image of himself as traumatized, weak, out of control, he can't even look at it. It gets him back to feelings of being worthless and unwanted by those he loves most in the world. This sense of humiliation makes it feel impossible for him to express a reasonable protest—"That hurts me"—or to try to work things out. He wants to stick to the strong place, in which he plays the fury. When he feels wronged by me, he seems, Clark Kent–like, to go through a transformation into another self, a self at war, but a self profoundly at peace with being at war, a self without anxiety. A gleam flashes from his eyes that says, Make my day! At such moments he seems to be operating from a place of: "You hurt me, but I don't feel the hurt because I am so excited about getting even."

Jeff told me about a fantasy he had of meeting up with his first boss, Aaron, who treated him shabbily. When Aaron was critical, Jeff ran after him trying to make it right, which seemed to give Aaron a sadistic kick. Now that Jeff is powerful and successful, he would like to meet Aaron again. He would like to show him what he has become, he would like to dare him to be condescending once more, he would like to rub his nose in the fact that he was a bad manager and a poor leader who did *everything* wrong. Jeff was surprised that I thought there was anything amiss in this fantasy. Isn't it natural to want to correct an injury?

If you've been bullied by someone, and you stand up to him, you feel good about yourself. If you don't, you may feel untrue to yourself and want another chance. This is not exactly about revenge or annihilation. It's about setting something right. You want to establish your rights and your boundaries, you want to show yourself that you can stand up to a threatening person, but you don't necessarily want to become like him or kill him.

But Jeff is after something different. He hasn't seen Aaron in twelve years, but he hasn't let go. He wants revenge, and his appetite for it is unabated. He hates the fact of his having been obsequious with Aaron, "like a scurrying mouse," much as he hates that he sucked up to and clung to the mother who was awful to him. His inability to forgive himself is implicit in his need for revenge. But unlike standing up to a bully, such revenge cures nothing. How can shame be erased by vengeance when the root is childhood trauma?

Self-forgiveness and release from shame lie in another direction altogether, but it is difficult for Jeff to go there. The dread of humiliation makes it hard for Jeff to open up to me about a painful experience or, much worse, to cry in front of me about what he has suffered. Indeed, in a way, Jeff does not want to be touched by me at all. As much as he longs to be loved, he cannot bear to open himself up to it. To be that vulnerable, to risk being smashed and ejected all over again frightens him too much. Warmth and appreciation, although he craves them, never reach him. For to take them in requires a kind of defenselessness, the ability to trust enough to be open. Jeff will not allow that openness. Besides, he has come to enjoy his rage and even his sadism. He loves to get into his bitter self, to go down the road at ninety miles per hour on the wrong side, to play the victim, to blame, to kill. Why give that up?

But there is another reason Jeff cleaves to his childhood home and the paranoia and antagonisms that characterized it. He takes this journey through hell partly because he is in love. He's in love with the parents who hurt him. To him, the hurts are associated with the love, and so he wants to stay close to those hurts. The hurts are the intensity that recall his connection to Mom. The hurts are the opportunity to keep fighting to get the bad mom to be good. And—in his unconscious fantasy at least—when the bad mom passes every test and turns good, truly good, the milk that stopped flowing eons ago will flow once more and the world will be made of love. Such is the infantile fantasy of return.

This is what people tend to do with the unmourned, unresolved, traumatic experience with their parents. The externals may be different. Whereas Jeff breathed entitlement but could readily feel like a piece of shit, for others the sense of being shit, of being envious and deserving of nothing, predominates. Their revenge may be explosive, unplanned, and even regretted. But they, too, feel compelled to dive back into the primordial muck, to be with Mom, to manipulate Mom, to get from Mom, the only person who really matters. The obsessiveness with which a wounded child clings to a parent, either literally or metaphorically, is reminiscent of Toni Morrison's novel *Beloved*, in which a murdered infant returns years later as a young woman to haunt the mother who killed her. She is like a single-celled animal capable of only one compound thought: I must have mother, I must be taken in her arms and nourished by her unendingly, I must demand explanations from her ad infinitum, and I must have revenge on her.

Jeff and I had a connection that was nourishing to him at times, but it repeatedly slipped away as he obsessed over his unavailable or imperfect lover. If the fount of all goodness is the parent or her stand-in, then it is hard for someone in Jeff's position to take in nourishment anywhere else. It either doesn't hit the spot, isn't noticed, or is too threatening. With other people, too, if a positive connection forms, Jeff may find it hard to hold onto it because the psychological slant he lives on more or less demands that he slide toward persecution and retaliation. Early in our work I pointed this out, but a thousand rationalizations came back to meet me. Now, he sees, and he struggles, and he is getting somewhere with it.

Jeff told me about an incident in which he was furious at his girlfriend for manipulating him. He called her on it, and she owned up in a sweet way that made his heart swell with affection. But he did not express the affection. He is uncomfortable with the vulnerability of love, and so he found himself continuing to drive home his point when it was no longer necessary. It was a measure of his growth that he noticed something amiss in this behavior, could take in my interpretation, and want to change. That he could say, "What I really want is to have my enemies here so I can annihilate them," that he could allow this into conscious-

ness and speak it to me, also represented an advance for him. At least
now the problem was accessible and could be worked with.

A Passion for Enemies

The need for enemies is an integral part of the magnetic pull toward victimization and revenge. Richard Nixon apparently loved having enemies
so much he compiled lists of them, as a miser might compile lists of his
holdings. He abjured taking responsibility for what befell him, seeing in
all that went wrong for him the insidious work of Big-money Jews or the
Eastern Establishment or the Kennedy Cartel. In his famous speech after losing the gubernatorial race in California in 1962, Nixon put his
barely controllable paranoia on display for the nation, blaming the press
for having a vendetta against him. Then, his lips curling in a tortured
smile, he suggested that the newsmen would be sorry to lose him, because, after all, "You won't have Richard Nixon to kick around anymore." Nixon's sense of persecution was so acute that, on this occasion,
it extended to his own campaign workers, whom, he insinuated, had betrayed him by failing to get out the vote. He seemed destined to enact
in public life the disturbing tendencies of character that others, like
Thérèse and Jeff, exhibit, perhaps less floridly, in private, and still others
feel but keep in check—tendencies that we can all identify with in some
horrible way.

The state of mind exemplified here is the black-and-white universe
of the baby, where hate and fury exist in pure states, unmediated by any
awareness of mitigating circumstances, good intentions, human limitations, or what happened the day before yesterday, and where love is
equally immaculate. As we've seen, it is emotionally satisfying for the
child to divide his mother in two, so that when she is abusive, she is a
hideous monster he wants to kill and when she is kind, a saint who deserves canonization. (Nixon referred to his mother as "a saint.") In adult
life a similar need may cause a man to see his wife as a horrible bitch and
have a fantasy lover (an actress or a married friend) who is perfect. Then,
like the child, he can hate full throttle and pine full throttle and not be

troubled by ambivalence. Or he may see his wife as a monster when she's angry or demanding, a goddess to merge with during sex. Meanwhile, he can project all of his own hatred and sadism onto the ugly, persecuting witch and remain pure himself. This is what infants do, what developing children do less and less, what remains a factor in adult psychology, especially under stress, and what is a larger factor in disturbed psychology, especially strong perhaps in what is known in psychiatry as borderline and schizoid personality disorders.

A passion for enemies and revenge is an aspect of this mind-set, and it can be addictive. Having an enemy gives you full access to negative emotions of immense power. You don't have to hold yourself back to evaluate or consider the other person's point of view. You never have to second-guess yourself or feel guilty. This is a world without self-doubt, without compromise, and certainly without forgiveness.

If the romance novel emphasizes the positive side of the black-and-white universe, the popular entertainment that plunges most enthusiastically into the negative is the action movie. One of my favorites, because it does a pure distillation on the theme of revenge, is Mark Goldblatt's grade-B thriller, *The Punisher,* based on the Marvel Comics anti-hero of the same name. The plot, as usual, is a comic-book model of simplicity: The wife and daughter of a police detective are wiped out by a car bomb planted by the mob. The cop, insane with grief, quits the force and retreats into his private hell. He dedicates himself to revenge, which consists of slaughtering Mafiosi all over the city, year in and year out, to the point where he is single-handedly wiping out the underworld. Needless to say, unlike his former partner, still on active duty, who is distraught about the homicidal path his old pal has taken, the audience does not disapprove of this righteous mayhem. Far from it!

The avenging officer, played by mammoth Dolph Lundgren, is mighty, virtually invincible, almost like death itself, indeed much as we would wish ourselves to be in such circumstances, and the wise guys seem like hopeless nitwits as he outfoxes and demolishes them, leaving behind his signature weapon, a tooled dagger, in their chests, their foreheads, their necks. When not out killing, he lives in a secret crypt in the city sewer system, his own underworld. With his naked body glistening, he prostrates himself before an altar that includes a photo of his slain family and rededicates himself to the gods of justice and revenge. Like many of his action movie compadres, he is a seethe of uncompromising hatred, hatred in the name of love. And this is the twisted truth in these dramas. Hatred and revenge, even the wish to blow up the world, emerge out of wounded love. I say "twisted" because the action movie, like the infantile mind, divides the world in a fictional and satisfyingly simple way: We worship what is lovable to the point of perfection; we want to destroy what is hateful to the point of perfection. That we love and hate the same person, that we want to kill that which we also adore, is forbidden to enter this picture. It would be a blasphemy. This carefully enforced simplicity is very appealing; these movies sell big.

The Punisher speaks to that part of us that is bitterly committed to our wounds and won't make up; the part of us that wants to turn away from the hand outstretched for forgiveness, reconciliation, or help; the part of us that knows that with love or openness comes a new and unbearable sort of pain; while bitterness, in all its cramped loneliness, provides an endless, if sickening, fulfillment. Some people make a home for themselves in this place. It is invulnerable, loaded with energy, and provides a consistent and reliable *raison d'être*. We see this in people who spend their lives in litigation, like those who get fired from a job and develop a long-term legal obsession with the company who released them.

A subplot in this movie concerns a bunch of kidnapped children whom the Punisher rescues from the clutches of hi-tech Asian gangsters in Ninja suits led by a woman of unimaginable fiendishness. Lundgren shows little interest in the children themselves; his heart isn't stirred by them. He saves all his passion for the bad guys, and, of course, all of our passion is directed toward them as well. In our aroused state, we would boo the picture off the screen should it stray from its lethal duties.

I have seen a similar tendency in patients who have had an abusive parent. Sometimes they will have violent fantasies when they see a mother abusing a child in public. They imagine swooping down on that mother like an angel of vengeance, raining terror on her for yanking the child by the arm or shrieking it into submission. But in these fantasies there is no swooping in to care for the child. The child is ignored—no consoling, no tenderness, no love. The passion is directed entirely toward the parent. Needless to say, there is something very wrong here. Because just as the abusing parent in the supermarket is a stand-in for the abusive aspects of one's own parent of decades past, so, too, the cowering, devastated child is a stand-in for oneself. The punisher (speaking generically now) has no interest in the self. The punisher is only interested in the other.

Like blame, only more terribly, vengeance leads us away from the self. We brush aside the puny, pathetic, ugly little self that is us—no goodness, no power, no capacity to make things right—in favor of a fierce (if sometimes only fantasized) pursuit of the longed-for, life-giving, wonderful-terrible parent who crushed us. If blame is anti-mourning and thus anti-separation and anti-growth, an obsession for revenge is all that locked in at a deeper, more passionate, more committed level. It can be hell to let go of.

The Punisher's secret sewer chamber and his prayer-like rededication to vengeance are particularly masterful contributions that this movie brings to the genre. For it symbolically captures the hidden, unconscious, dark manner in which we worship at the altar of our primitive commitments. When Jeff tells me that what he really wants is not a connection with me but an opportunity to annihilate his enemies, he is revealing a loyalty, a dedication, and a love as ardent as the Punisher's.

In the movie, we can openly root for the Punisher because his battle is so unambiguous. The flashbacks to his family, like all flashbacks in such films, reveal a beautiful wife and child who—we know this instantly!—were engaged with him in mutually adoring relationships. (Thank God, we don't pause to compare this to our own relationships; our envy would poison the fun.) We know this bliss. And we are suckers for the battle cry that asks us to avenge its loss. Because it is our loss, too. We have all been ejected from the Garden. It was the heaven we inhabited before our maturing psyches put an end to a neatly divided universe, and before Mother and other caretakers began to move us off our infant's throne. We may have forgotten the Garden, we may even dispute that it ever existed, but here we are, in a heightened state of arousal, panting and carrying its flag.

The Punisher's innocent wife and child and his innocent love are cruelly exterminated by a fiery bomb planted by evil, loveless men. This, too, is perfect! In real life, the people who hurt us are rarely so obligingly evil; they are often, at worst, klutzes like us. So we are constantly adjusting, forgiving, making allowances or, at least, torn. But action films bring us back to paradise, where hatred breathes the pure air of paranoia. And the bad guys, there they go—blessed, unmitigated evil!—just begging for extermination.

Metaphorically, who are these killers? Just like the innocent mother and child blown to bits in the bombing, they, too, are stand-ins in a way for parents. The action heroes and bad guys take us back to our first relationships, to our first loves and hates. They offer the opportunity to escape what maturity expects us to remember—that people, including ourselves, are a complex of good and bad, that we collude in or have some sort of responsibility for much of what befalls us, that justice and revenge, while important in their contexts, have only limited application to much of our affectional lives and can never replace or undo the necessity for mourning.

PARANOIA

What we would call paranoia in an adult is a normal feature of infantile emotional life. Where suffering exists, a sense of persecution cannot be far behind. "You don't love me, Daddy!" "You did that on purpose!" "You want to hurt me." "You always speak mean to me!" Such declarations from young children to parents may seem unfair, but they accurately represent an aspect of the child's feeling and experience at that moment. Never mind that it can blow off like a mist moments later. The child feels persecuted. At four or five, of course, the child may know at some level—depending on the child and the circumstance—that there is more to the story than these dreadful proclamations. But he is still capable of sinking into a dark place.

Although some people inhabit this paranoid primitivity on a regular basis, most of us have experienced enough love to tolerate a world of imperfection and disappointments. But the emergence from the primitive is never fully settled and we find ourselves periodically reengulfed by feelings of persecution. This was evident among the peace movement veterans who wanted to bomb JoAnne Akalaitis back to the Stone Age, in Thérèse's hardened heart, in Jeff's and Nixon's obsessions with enemies. In each case we see not a clinical condition per se, but a return to the primitive, the reemergence of paranoia, the whisper of psychosis in everyday life. We might be tempted to consider this realm abnormal, but, more accurately, it reflects the natural insanity of early splitting to which the human psyche is forever susceptible.

Psychologist Michael E. McCullough of Louisiana Tech University, in an article he co-authored on forgiveness in the *Journal of Psychology and Christianity,* offers a moving description of this quality and how it gets linked with moralistic indictments:

> I am, generally, a mediocre forgiver [McCullough writes]. For all of the ink I spill about forgiveness, one might think I were better at it. Despite five years of training as a psychologist, I make all the mistakes that we tell our clients not to make. I frequently assume the worst of people, attribute intentionality and malice aforethought to innocent oversights and carelessness, allowing petty differences to become large rifts in relationships. When I was recently injured by the actions of a friend, my bitterness about those actions quickly spread through my perceptions of the person, crowding out my friend's humanness and good points, until I was unable to see the offender as a complex but human combination of good and bad. Friends told me that my "righteous indignation" was irritating.

For many people the experience of paranoia takes place at an unconscious level or in various dissociated states. The kind of dissociation I'm talking about can be illustrated by an incident from childhood. When I was four years old, a little friend in my building was having a birthday party, and I must have been crushed to find out I wasn't invited. While the party was in progress, I was alone with nothing to do. With no one attending to me or my predicament, I wandered down the flight of stairs to her floor and went up to her apartment. Without any conscious thoughts, I knelt down and began peeling the wallpaper outside the door. Laura's grandmother came out and saw me doing that, got very angry at me and lectured me. Just because you don't get invited to the party, this is the way you behave? You destroy the wallpaper?

I couldn't respond. It was as if she had woken me from a dream. On the one hand, I knew I was caught, but on the other hand, I was incredulous: What was this about? The psychoanalyst Philip Bromberg refers to this kind of experience as having entered another self-state. It is a common feature of emotional life that we tend to be quite unaware of. In such an alternate state, our experience of others can go through sudden and radical transformations. If I move into a persecutory zone and unconsciously envy or resent you, I can walk by your car while hoodlums are breaking off your antenna and be secretly pleased, even though you're my best friend.

A colleague describes another example from his experience. It concerns changes he sometimes goes through when a friend fails to call.

> A mature response to wanting to speak to a friend is to pick up the phone. But I have been poor at times in keeping in touch with friends. I don't make the call, but hope to get a call. I may not even be aware of this longing, because it puts me in a vulnerable place. So I don't call but I wish for a call. And when it doesn't come, a resentment grows inside me. I start to feel like a sullen, unhappy boy. I find myself envying, hating, and feeling persecuted by the friend who hasn't called and attributing to that friend the growing hatred that I am feeling toward him, until I come to and shake myself free of it or, in the worst cases, my heart grows hard and the friendship may actually suffer. I let all this happen despite the knowledge that the paranoid fantasy is false, that I am equally at fault for not calling, and that I never give this much thought to how my friends feel when I don't call them.

In fragile personalities, paranoia's inroads can be ruinous. It is easy to imagine how it grows into a defining preoccupation, as with Thérèse or Nixon. Invariably, there is a strong element of projection—seeing in the other the uncaring or murderous impulses that we disavow in ourselves. In many social movements, paranoid-style thinking takes on a peculiar imperative. They are the action movies of our political process. The language of the anti-abortion campaign sometimes has this quality, whereby those with an opposing view, women who seek abortions, doctors who perform abortions, are demonized to the extent that clinically paranoid people who get attracted to the movement may commit murders in its name. Abortion is an especially magnetic topic in this respect because it invites identification with the most helpless of human creatures, unborn children who (in the most extreme view) are being crushed by the uncaring monsters who are supposed to love them. This is an almost textbook replication of how the suffering infant, the victim of earache, or a diaper pin, or cranky overtiredness, his blood boiling with hurt, rage, and persecution, constructs his view of the world.

Primitive politics and action movies make excellent bedfellows. *Rambo* is a masterpiece in this respect. It is the story of a sensitive, noble, childlike man who also happens to be a formidable killing machine (much like my son at four and a half). He feels that he was horribly misused by his country in Vietnam, and, after giving everything he had for her there, was snubbed and reviled when he returned. Now that same country is asking him to go back into the jungles with nothing but a camera and a loincloth to bring back evidence that our prisoners of war are being held there. He agrees, but once again he is betrayed by the country he loves, which is using him for political purposes and doesn't care at all about him or his starving comrades wasting away in bamboo cages. Rambo is captured and tortured by diabolic Vietnamese and Russian military personnel; he falls in love with the angelic Vietnamese girl who serves as his guide, saves his life, and loves him purely, only to see this innocent love taken from him by a Communist bullet; and when he manages, through awesome heroics, to free the POWs—huddled innocents, cast off by their own motherland like so many discarded children—and lead them to the pre-arranged pickup site, he is met with another betrayal. The American helicopter that has come for him is ordered to abort its mission when the authorities realize that Rambo has succeeded too well in his. They thus leave him and the forlorn POWs in the hands of the encircling foe, as Rambo reaches up, crucifixion style, looking like a helpless, bewildered fetus. If a suffering infant could compose a screenplay, this would be it. It drips with paranoia, with purity and evil, with parents who care only about themselves and leave their children to be done in by monsters, if they don't eat them themselves.

At the movie's end, after he wipes away all his foes and returns with the POWs he has saved to face his betrayers, Rambo delivers the grief-stricken speech that has inflamed and delighted many a paranoid heart. In his choked-up, husky voice, he declares that all he wants of his country is the same thing those broken-down, forsaken POWs want: "For it to love *us* as much as we love *it!*" (Now give me my blankie and my bow and arrow, I'm leaving here for*ever!*)

Political paranoia coalesces around different causes, right or left, but it boils down to the same thing: the sense of being persecuted, of being a victim, of being betrayed, of hating and wanting revenge—and of getting gratification from being in that place. It's a perverse sort of gratification, associated with feelings of being threatened and getting screwed, but symbolically and emotionally it keeps us close to the hurtful parent and it liberates a self-righteous anger and a hatred that might otherwise have to be suppressed.

What George Santayana said of fanaticism—that it "consists in redoubling your efforts when you have forgotten your aim"—applies equally to paranoia. For the more vicious and improbable one's accusations, the more one must be committed to them. Annihilation fury is like an express train that is not easily derailed. Either you're bad or the other guy's bad, and if you can't keep the badness in him, it's going to be in you. Once out of the station, the train needs to find that badness. And if it develops that you've been in a rage over nothing, then the nightmare comes true: You were the problem all along. And since we're talking about states of mind in which there is no tolerance for wrongness, badness, imperfection, no tolerance for ambiguity, there's no such thing as spreading the responsibility around or meeting errors with understanding. You have to face that train. Under such circumstances, owning up feels like suicide, which leaves only one logical response: escalation. You must jack up your level of paranoia, not dare to consider the evidence of the opposition—and they can be sly! with their parsed explanations and partial apologies!—for you don't want to see the headlight of the express bearing down on you.

PULLS TOWARD GROWTH

Many years after our first encounter, I met Thérèse again. She had been in therapy for some time and was looking for a couples therapist for her and her husband. By coincidence, her psychologist recommended me. She seemed less rigid and hawkish. She told me that the workshop experience had been meaningful to her and that it had made her think about the stance she had taken with Mona. Her work in therapy had helped her to see that she was doing similar things with her husband and grown daughter.

Thérèse and Bill were an interesting couple. They had a genuine affection and commitment to each other, but a tendency toward resentment and tirades on one side, and submission, passive aggressiveness, and temper tantrums on the other. Bill complained that there was no room for error with Thérèse. "Last weekend we were going to her family, and I was supposed to pick up pastries from her favorite place on the way home from work. I forgot. So this was a major crisis. I said, 'We'll pick them up on our way tomorrow. So it will take us fifteen minutes out of our way.' But she looks at me as if I'm a killer, like I just intentionally pushed her onto the railroad tracks in front of a train." Thérèse would hear nothing of this, but during our second or third meeting, she saw something that caused her to soften toward Bill and toward herself. This brought to mind the story of her and Mona. She spoke again about that critical relationship, this time revealing not just the love she felt for Mona but the childlike idealization that Mona, in the end, could not live up to. She also displayed a softer, more reflective side of herself that was surprising and endearing:

"It's as if there are parts of my mind that I don't reveal and I don't want to reveal—and I feel like I don't have to reveal. Or let me put it this way: There are certain things I know that I can't be expected to know— so then, I don't have to say them. Does this make sense? I knew that Mona had a good heart, I mean a *totally* good heart, I knew it the whole time we were doing that stuff in the workshop, but I was not going to say it. Mona is very sweet, but she was absorbed with her daughter during the party and just didn't think about anyone else. I had seen this before, and it irked me whenever it happened. It made me feel furious really, furiously jealous. I wanted her to be focused on *me*. It was like, *I* wanted to be the daughter at that Bat Mitzvah. I can say this now, I couldn't say it then, or even when we did the workshop, but Mona is a very nurturing person, and I always wanted her to myself, and it just filled me with bile if she gave herself to someone else—even her own daughter!"

I asked Thérèse if she could imagine that Mona did not have a perfectly good heart, that perhaps she had in fact used her.

"Don't let me go there!" Thérèse said. "That's where I lived for years."

"But what if she had? What if she used you for your terrific energy and organizational ability and really didn't think much about you as a person. How awful is it?"

"Because then it just burns me up, and I go into a total grudge state, and I can't get out of it."

"So it burns you up, you make a fuss, you have it out, something happens or doesn't happen. But why can't you go on being connected? Why does this have to be the defining thing?"

This was not an easy concept for Thérèse to grasp. That we all use each other at times. That we all say or do hurtful things to each other. That Bill is a son of a bitch sometimes and only thinks about himself. But that it doesn't have to lead to isolation and grudge. It doesn't have to define the relationship.

Thérèse understood the logic, but at the feeling level it was as if I was telling a child that there was no justice on this planet and she should accept torture and humiliation. In future sessions we would explore some of her early experiences with her mother and the agonizing internal places she went to when she felt hurt or betrayed by someone she loved. But on this day Thérèse revealed more about her identification with her mother and how she used her mother's tools against anyone who defied her.

"Grudges are good!" she said with a laugh. "If I hold a grudge, I think it will somehow get the other person to capitulate." She shrugged sheepishly toward Bill. "I think that is what happened with Mona. Mona was kind of naïve, and I knew I could bully her and make her feel guilty. So that's what I tried to do. It always worked before! I played the guilt card for everything it was worth, and I knew, even as I was doing it, that I was caught in a horrible trap of my own making. It was as if I was going to hammer her into confession, into total apology, at which point the victory would be mine, but I would feel empty and sick. But that's what I was after. And if she hadn't moved away, she probably would have apologized profusely, and I would have accepted her back, and we would have gone on being friends. And I'll tell you, that was part of my anger, too, that she didn't keep playing the game."

Bill, who had suffered plenty with this side of Thérèse, moved closer to her on the couch and took her hand.

PART III

THE
LANDSCAPE
OF
CONNECTION

EIGHT

THE
REDEPLOYMENT
OF LOVE

SHORTLY AFTER JUDITH AND VINCENT WERE MARRIED, THEY FOUND themselves in a conflict over a single event that they could not let go of for years. Neither one understood the implications of the conflict, although it was clear to Vincent that it implied Judith was not fully available to him emotionally.

I had an opening for my first-ever exhibition of my photographs on a Thursday [Judith recalls], and we had a dinner on Saturday for out-of-town friends and family. My sister and her husband came from D.C. and they brought their video camera. Vincent and I lived in a loft where all of his artwork was up on the walls, and he didn't want his artwork filmed. He was exhausted from having worked so hard to help me with the opening and make all our travel arrangements—we were about to go on vacation—and then to get the dinner together. He asked her a couple of times not to film. And she said, "Oh, don't worry, I'm not," but she was. He said, "Please don't film my art," and she said, "Well, I'm *not* filming your art." He asked her three times to put the camera down, and then the last time he just blew up at her and said, "Put the frigging thing away!" And my sister went into another zone. She left the dinner, walked around

the block a few times, she was extremely upset. She and her husband left, and we didn't get to say good-bye. And when we got
back from our trip a week later, we had a long, single-spaced letter from her demanding an apology. I didn't take Vincent's side,
I didn't say, My sister, what a jerk. I felt like he did owe her an
apology for blowing up at her. And he really resented that I took
this position. And I think it hurt him tremendously.

Judith had, in effect, rejected Vincent's freedom of expression, an aspect of his masculinity, in favor of her castrating sister with whom she
identified. All this was intensified by a family cultural bias against ex-
pressiveness. Whereas Vincent came from a working-class Italian family
where displays of anger and other emotions were common, Judith came
from a polished Protestant family in which people did not lose their tempers. To them, his behavior was inconsiderate and crass. So Vincent had
not only violated her sister but he had brought shame on Judith by revealing himself as a primitive to her whole family. And Judith let him
know this in her cool, measured way, which seemed to say, "You're an
ape, not a person."

Where I come from that kind of behavior is unforgivable.
How could he expect me to take his side? People just don't fly
off the handle like that. Or maybe they do, but I don't. And I
blamed him. I felt, Well, maybe you've got some kind of gripe,
but you've ruined my relationship with my sister. The fact that
my sister had played a big part in the whole thing, maybe really
the bigger part, I could not see. I felt very loyal to her, I felt kind
of identified with her, and I was also—I realized this later—
frightened of her and afraid of losing her. So I wouldn't give in,
and this really tormented him.

The conflict took years to resolve. During that period, Judith herself
experienced friction with her sister, who found numerous reasons to
disapprove of her and resent her efforts toward independence. Vincent
helped her to see how competitive her sister was with her, how determined she was to keep Judith in her place. If her sister visited, Judith

dropped everything to cook for her, shop with her, cater to her. But Judith never seemed to notice that the caretaking and accommodating never went the other way.

Vincent helped me to see how much I idealized my sister, what a puppy I was with her, and how much she hurt me. I would get horribly depressed after her visits and think I wasn't good enough in some way. I never thought, She's mean to me. Before Vincent, I never asserted myself with her. For most of my life, she told me what to do and how to live and who to be. She's a bossy older sister, and, in looking back, I gradually came to see the original conflict from that perspective. She came to New York from Washington thinking, "My little sister's having her first show, and this is all about *me!*" And I think Vincent was right that it was hard for her that I was the center of attention, very hard. And it was even harder for her to accept that someone else was becoming number one in my life. And it wasn't just my sister that Vincent helped me with. I started to realize that I didn't have such a great relationship with other members of my family as maybe I thought I had had, that they weren't as nice as maybe I thought they were, and they had reasons to want to keep me to themselves, keep me young and unattached, and the peacemaker who could be depended on not to make waves and to help keep them all together. Vincent's input had a lot to do with my seeing this. It's been a journey for me. And in the process I think I have come to rely on Vincent and trust him and have him be the most important person in my life, but it was not something that just happened overnight, it's something that happened gradually.

It was not easy for Judith to erase the image of Vincent as the boorish Italian, *El Duce!*, who had entered the scene like a bull in a china shop, embarrassing her, oppressing her, disrupting the goodness of her perfect family. This image was repeatedly, if subtly, reinforced by her siblings and by Vincent himself, who had a bad temper and could go overboard. But her caricature of him, which represented her own hostility and grudgingness, was softened by gratitude. She *needed* a courageous and unbridled vitality like his in her life. He had helped her to see that she had been living as her sister's sidekick, and that her loyalty to her family had restrained her own development. Since living with Vincent, her work had become bolder and more original, and she had begun renegotiating her place in the family. She was less confined as a person, and she knew he had played a big part in that. Judith was grateful for Vincent's love, for his ability to hold on to his love even when he was angry, for his straightforwardness, for his persistent, unbitter protest in the face of her withholding. Her gratitude—grudging at first and, even now, not everything it could be—helped her to understand him better, understand the pain of his position, and to forgive him for whatever wrongs, real or imagined, that had caused her to withhold. Implicit in this was a wish to repair: It hurts me that I hurt you, and I am sorry because I love you.

A HAVE IN THE REALM OF LOVE

I said at the beginning of the book that forgiveness is an aspect of the workings of love. I could equally have said that forgiveness is an aspect of staying connected, of reconnecting, of repairing broken pieces of a relationship. By connection, I am referring to a state in which our fundamental caring position toward the other person remains active in us, no matter how angry we may be with him. It means, in a sense, relating to others from an inner place of secure attachment: I am good, I belong, I have power, I am a Have in the realm of love. I don't need to revert to an infantile binary state and excommunicate your badness from my life. In this inner configuration, sadness and hurt, anger and hatred, can all exist. One does not feel persecuted and bitterly alone. Enough caring remains to act as a brake against self-loathing, as well as against nursing or misusing one's anger.

Studies have tended to suggest that people are defined by a certain pattern of secure or insecure attachment, and this seems true to a point. We have our built-in expectations and ingrained ways of relating. And yet it is equally true that no one's psychology is entirely defined by security and trust, just as no one is wholly defined by insecurity and resentment. We have our prominent patterns, yet we are capable of much else. We are different with different people. We are altered by circumstances. We enter and exit different states of being under different emotional conditions. In some states we can only experience resentment; in others secure connection and the capacity to tolerate and forgive emerge more readily.

When we operate out of a secure zone, we can feel an inner goodness and connectedness that escape us at other times. In this entitled, empowered state, we do not seek goodness elsewhere to make us good; we have it and we are free to take it to whomever we wish. We do not need the Perfect Other to make us whole. We are not dependent in the same way, so we are not desperate in our wanting nor so unforgiving of flaws.

We may feel securely connected with only a spouse, or a child, or a therapist. We may feel it with certain friends and less so with others. We may feel it only if we are able to keep certain walls in place; with a lover, for instance, only as long as we live separately or are free to explore elsewhere. If certain subjects are raised or past events remembered, if anger, demands, or criticism comes into the picture too strongly, paranoid or persecutory feelings may return ("This is not a person who cares about me and values me; this is someone who wants to hurt and discard me").

Except perhaps in cases of extreme disturbance—psychopathic personalities, for instance—there is usually a hidden element of security even in the most insecure profile. But it is a security one doesn't connect with and indeed *resists* connecting with. That's the crux of the matter for most of us in our resentful states. It hurts to love. We hold on to the rejecting parent and the perverse security of resentment. But there is more to us than that.

In a state of connection, forgiveness is not the arduous struggle it often seems. We have an essential kindness and generosity to draw on— not just toward the other but toward ourself and our hurts. This makes it easier to hear and be reopened by expressions of contrition, remorse, or empathy: "I was wrong," "I understand how you feel," "I'm sorry I hurt you." Such statements, even if unspoken, even if only implicit in a caring attitude, are enough to enable us to let go of our hurt and anger and move on. Once we have crossed over to a persecuted place, however, forgiveness becomes a more complicated affair, and even an obvious display of concern may leave us unmoved.

We have our ways of coming back, some of them more reliable than others. A roaring fight, sex, time spent apart, hearing a third opinion, recognition of the other person's suffering—any of these things may enable us to have our protest without the murderousness implicit in indictment and withdrawal. Some people rely on a few drinks (or some other enhancing substance) to revive the glow of connection. It may be the only way they know to break the spell of persecution and be filled with the feeling of inner goodness that allows charity and forgiveness to thrive. For Judith the catalyst was the gradual growth of appreciation and gratitude, moved forward by Vincent's warmth and persistent protests.

Sometimes love comes on like a sudden liberating breeze. I saw this happen to my father not long before his death, his bitterness triggered by typical irritations, at odds with himself and the world. My son read him a poem, which he had written for him, filled with love and concern. My father was jolted out of his irritableness and acrimony and used a word I had not thought was in his vocabulary: "I love you, too, little one," he said with feeling, and his mood changed.

Living in the zone of connection can make us feel like a very different person from who we are in less trusting states. We have the same personality, the same sense of humor, the same tastes, the same interests and habits, the same passions, energy, fears, peeves, and desires that have always made us who we are. But some fundamental emotional tone is so different we feel like a different person, more endearing to ourselves and more tolerant of others. Even the bad things, the things we feel remorse or regret over, do not compromise our essential goodness. From this position it is easier to forgive, partly because we have more and, therefore, have more to give. It is easier to apologize, to own up, to admit our badness—to have our badness—because we do not feel at risk of being demonized by others, which is often a projection of the demonizing we do to ourselves.

The connected state also comes with a set of memories and perceptions somewhat different from that of resentment. It's not that Cinderella, redeemed by the prince's love, looks back at her stepfamily and thinks, What a loving bunch! But the thought of them no longer fills her with the same sense of smallness, persecution, and hatred.* They were awful, but she no longer takes her identity from her experience with their awfulness. She is loved and she is loving.

She may, if she has healed enough, even find that she has some sympathy and affection, now and then, for one or another member of her original family, based on newly remembered aspects of their vulnerability or goodness or based on some recognition of their own misery. She might also see some fault of her own in her conflict with her sisters that softens her position toward them.

Because she no longer needs to cling so tenaciously to her victimhood and the high moral ground that goes with it, Cinderella may also recognize that she wasn't entirely unloved as a child. Although to this day her (step)mother may remain an impossible person, insensitive, relentlessly selfish, murderous when feeling wronged, Cinderella is able to recognize that, in her own weird way, her mother loved her. More important, she is able to recapture her own love for her mother, as well as the heartache she feels to this day over wanting her mom and not being able to have her. To allow herself this pain and this love is an aspect of reowning her own goodness as a loving person. It represents a move away from resentment and toward healthy sadness and mourning: "I love her, but I can't have her, not the way I want her; she is just too awful, and this is a great sorrow for me."

As usual, an act of mourning like this, which entails returning to a painful place in a caring mode, also becomes an act of separation and growing up. Cinderella is at last laying down an unconscious, obsessive clinging to the bad mother. The clinging may have taken the form of "I hate her," or "She disgusts me," or "I really couldn't care less if I never see her again," but it is clinging all the same. In laying it down, she is reowning a vital, if heartbroken, aspect of her self. It is her ability to do that—and only this ability really—that keeps her from being an emotional replica of her mother.

---

*I assume all this is in her, even though there is no room for it in the story, which is, as ever in fairy tales, soothing and binary.

The father figure in Cinderella stories is either kindly but absent or ineffectual and oblivious. But if we think of this as the memory of a wounded child, we can also image that some elements may have been forgotten. This limited, inadequate, perhaps somewhat cowardly dad who was never around may have loved her the best. (Could this have been why the others came to hate her?) And his love may have helped save her from being like them. As her connection to her own connectedness grows, she may retrieve memories of his comforting her at times when the others had been brutal, of his helping her in her internal struggles—Am I bad? Is Mom bad?—by letting her know he thought her mother could be bitter and punishing. To recognize Dad's goodness is another way in which she recovers a piece of her loving self and moves toward a place of secure attachment. She feels a flowering in her chest that not only gives her back a father, but makes her feel like a different person, more entitled, more powerful, more a Have in the realm of love.

Other recollections may flower: the gardener who was kind to her, a man who as a little girl she secretly wished to marry; the affectionate shopkeeper she saw daily, who she dreamed could be her mother, and whom she wanted to grow up to be like. Why had she forgotten them until now—or remembered them with so little feeling, so little sense of nourishment?

This subtly—but profoundly—altered memory set is like an alternate psychological history, based on the love she had to cut herself off from in order to survive in that horrible climate of abuse. In this alternate history, she is not a stepchild at all. She had to make it that way.

OWNING ONE'S INNER DRAMA

People grow in their capacity to forgive by expanding their zone of connection. A piece of that territory where intolerance and splitting once reigned is conquered and imbued with caring. It is added to our monotheistic world, where people can hurt us, disappoint us, have hated habits and flaws, have what we feel are absurd and wacky opinions about us, use us at times strictly for their own purposes, neglect us, even hate us for qualities they find hateful, and yet still be appreciated and loved, still recognized as people who care about us and whom we care about, not enemies we wish to crush. Their peculiarities, their odd ideas, their nutty habits are experienced less as annoyances and more as fascinating and enjoyed aspects of who they are and of the endless, inexplicable variety of human psychology and experience. Monotheism, in replacing a black-and-white perspective, can, at its best, embrace the full rainbow of human experience.

The tentative moves toward expansion, the retreats and the gains, can be seen in the course of a single psychotherapy session. Thérèse gnashed her teeth repeatedly over Bill's inadequacies, his withholding, his endless capacity to disappoint her. At times, when we were in session alone because Bill could not make it, I protested that, listening to her complain, I felt under assault myself, even though Bill was the ostensible target. When she was in that roiled state, she treated me like an object, a dumping ground for her misery. Confronted with this emphatically enough, Thérèse would begin to emerge from her murky rage and become present with me in a different way.

There is a scene from Charlie Chaplin's movie *The Gold Rush* in which he and his partner, a good-hearted but very big and dangerous man, are stuck in a cabin in a snowstorm and haven't eaten in days. His partner, prone to bellow, "I must have food!", has become delusional and periodically hallucinates that Charlie is a large chicken. He chases this feathered meal with a gun, as Charlie pleads with him to recognize who he is. Suddenly the partner comes to, wipes his eyes, realizes his error, embraces Charlie, and the threat is over, at least for a while.

The scene can be read as a wonderful metaphor for the hold that transference and identification have over us. For Thérèse, Bill easily becomes the all-powerful, withholding mother and she becomes the powerless, persecuted child; and in the grip of this transference there is no punishment too severe for him. In her sessions with me, the transference was somewhat reversed. Thérèse would fall into identification with her self-centered, bitter, complaining mother who rained down her misery on everyone around her, including her hapless child.

But now, hearing my protest, Thérèse softened. ("Oh, my God, I thought you were a chicken!") She laid down her weapons and the whole intense and resentful worldview that went with them, and we reconnected. Internally, a similar transformation was affecting her relationship with Bill. As we discussed the changes she had just gone through, including how she was reenacting her childhood relationship with her mother, she became reflective. She spoke about Bill with a sweet regard that I knew was in her but that she normally had a hard time accessing: "All I ever do," she said, "is bitch at him for not being there for me—*me, me, me.* I'm not there for him, and I feel bad about that, because he's an insecure sort of guy who really needs me."

Here, emerging out of a number of important internal changes—including separation (in the sense of moving away from her tight enmeshment with an unloving, murderous mother) and mourning (in the sense of experiencing the pain of that relationship in the context of a more caring attitude toward herself)—was an aching and heartfelt wish to repair. She was taking responsibility for her behavior, she was empathizing with Bill, she wanted to reach out to him, to comfort him, to salve some of the wounds she herself had opened. From this position, I imagined she could protest Bill's behavior toward her without having to annihilate him.

Again, this was not a permanent transformation. It was ground that Thérèse would have to reconquer many times. But a change was beginning to take hold. She was starting to understand that her feelings of persecution were an aspect of her own psychology. It was her inner drama, a struggle that she needed to engage in with herself and not externalize by making a demon of ineptitude and withholding out of Bill.

Thérèse's dawning ability to recognize her inner drama as her own—and to, therefore, take responsibility for it—was an important step toward a more forgiving attitude. It could be summarized like this: "My resentments seem so real to me that I cannot resist them. My mistrust and fear of being touched does not mean that people do not wish to touch me. My feelings of inner badness and unentitlement are my struggle. They are not symptom's of Bill's withholding, even though he can be withholding and I have to find a way to deal with that."

Thérèse's growing awareness of these issues meant that they were less likely to become the hidden focal point of many of her communications with Bill. She could now begin to speak her paranoia to Bill rather than live it out. When she did this, it allowed him more freedom. He felt less guilty and less under the gun, and his heart was more likely to go out to her. It also made it safer for Bill to reconsider his own official story, with its victim themes and justifications. He could begin to acknowledge and reveal more of his own inner drama, which slowly brought their relationship to a new level of caring and intimacy.

Expanding the zone of connection reverberates all across our emotional terrain. It represents an enlarged capacity to relate healthily and lovingly to another person, as well as to oneself. It implies that some work of mourning has been done, so that one achieves a greater separation from the inner parents with whom one has been unconsciously entwined. Again, I want to emphasize that by separation I do not mean detachment, distance, or coldness. Separation means a growing freedom from an obsessive involvement with a rejecting aspect of the parent, a place where we live unhappily, predictably tormented by the same themes, in relationship to ourselves and others. (It is also, simultaneously, a growing freedom from an infantile dependency on the idealized parent, a parallel, if sometimes less obvious, part of every unconscious enmeshment.)

One day Thérèse had to go to the hospital for a special exam to rule out ovarian cancer. She was frightened, panicked really, and took the unusual step of asking Bill to accompany her. Bill declined, saying that his absence from work that day would be a disaster. Thérèse said nothing but her anger grew steadily, until, backed by a friend who thought Bill's behavior unconscionable, she went into a fury of self-righteous indignation. Bill warded her off with a combination of logic, condescension, and guilty withdrawal. For three days they didn't speak at all; a kind of hell descended around them. The next day Thérèse did a big favor for Bill, graciously offering to pick up his car at the garage, which cost her over an hour, while he was working late at the office. By doing so she was not forgiving his behavior. She still felt angry and unresolved, she still wanted him to see what he'd done, to see that it had hurt her. She couldn't wait to get to the next couples session so I could tell Bill how bad he was. She was incredulous that he could have done something so heartless and she wanted to understand where it came from. But part of her desire to understand included some openness to his side of the story, which was new for her. Meanwhile, if she had learned nothing else in her therapeutic work, she knew that her ballistic, indicting response was brutal and she wanted to take it back. Picking up the car, and doing it warmly, told Bill, We can have differences, we can be angry at each other, we can even hate each other's guts and not want anything to do with one another, but I know you're not a demon, I know there's more complexity to this than meets my resentful eye, and underlying everything is still a caring connection that I'm struggling not to lose.

Perhaps the strongest evidence that Thérèse was making the transition toward a greater capacity for forgiveness lay in her ability to hate aspects of Bill without losing her feeling of love. She could say, in effect, "This person I love can be an awful prick at times," and this represented a huge shift toward love. She could want to kill him, and yet not kill him. This ability to live with ambivalence—with both love and hate but with the love predominating—is perhaps what most distinguishes the forgiving from the unforgiving personality.

Would a person be even more forgiving if there were no anger or hatred at all—if, for example, Thérèse adored Bill all the time and never found anything to fault him for? Not even a mother could have such unambivalent feelings. This is, again, the binary position, the positive side of a world split into black and white, with Bill enshrined in an idealized state where all his failings and the hurts they cause are preemptively forgiven. Idealization is just another aspect of enmeshment, and it is inherently unstable. When it dissolves, the unconscious, disavowed elements of envy and hatred come swarming forward like furies.

Like every resentful, indicting person, Thérèse was, in fact, quite prone to idealize and was always on the lookout for perfect figures to worship. There was frequently a golden calf in her life, often in the form of a male acquaintance who would have made the ideal husband. But as she moved toward monotheism and hence a more mature form of love, she slowly relinquished such false idols and her quest for them.

For Thérèse, particularly difficult aspects of Bill were his passivity, his boastfulness, and his name dropping, all of which filled her with a disrespect bordering on disgust. She would wipe him away and start dreaming about a perfect man (her "Robert Redfords," we used to say). Growing insight and the awakening of her caring for Bill helped her to keep both her disgust and her idealizing longings in check.

Disgust, like contempt and disdain, usually distances us from our true feelings. The hurt and rageful child becomes disgusted by the parent as a way of escaping his heartbreak. In adults, disgust may perform a similar task and usually bears the mark of an earlier, internalized drama. When Bill bragged about his achievements, Thérèse experienced him to be false and small and she wanted to flick him away—"like a piece of snot," she once confessed—much as she had seen her father flicked away by her mother. She hated her mother for doing it, and she hated her father acquiescing to that kind of treatment. She was furious at him for not being present in the strong way she needed him to be, so that he could preserve his own goodness for her and protect her as well, for she, too, could be flicked away by her mother. Eventually, her hurt, her disappointment, and her anger all turned to disgust, as she identified with her mom and gave up on her dad.

To make her internal drama conscious, to deal with it where it belongs, Thérèse needs to see that she is identifying Bill both with her father and with her own pathetic, flicked-away self, which she hated and didn't want to know about. Seeing all this would enable her to protect Bill from its contamination. It might free her eventually to say, "You're a wonderful guy, Bill, and a substantial guy, and it hurts me to hear you brag about yourself, because I know it comes out of not feeling good enough. And I feel pushed away by it, because I feel like the real you, the man I love, is not present." In this she could be kind and tolerant and still hold on to her point of view. That would represent an enormous achievement for her, as indeed it would for anyone.

No one is without inner goodness. Our hurts and resentments, our rageful withdrawals and revenge modes, are a part of a childlike protest, imbued with a sense of powerlessness, sometimes a kind of temper tantrum, sometimes experienced as a personal holocaust, which is often about feeling betrayed in love. The child in us is in a rage that the love that was supposed to be so plentiful has disappeared. The secure love still exists within us, but in our hurt we can no longer feel it. We achieve an outcast status; at least that's how we feel it to be.

Among the tasks of therapy is to help us both to take in caring and to recognize how we wipe away the good and hold on to the bad. That awareness can gradually build to a significant reassessment of oneself and one's behavior with others. So that one can begin to make a conscious choice not to be thrown into a bitter place by all the ways in which others inevitably hurt or disappoint us. One can be aware that feeling like a Have-not, always destined to be the last on line, is a psychological truth, not a literal one. Perhaps the most important thing is to know that the need to kill the other off—like the need to blame and search for scapegoats—is an aspect of our own psychology. "I've done all this to myself." Once we know that, love begins to have new possibilities.

THE DE-INHIBITION OF GRATITUDE

A patient has a dream. In the dream I make her favorite meal for her and she notes with surprise, while still dreaming, how much I am taking care of her. She doesn't really allow herself any feeling about it, she doesn't even quite acknowledge it, but she comes alive and turns derisive when I make a faulty move and spill some sauce. Relating the dream to me in session, her only comment is to marvel that she would dream of me cooking her a meal since she's not aware of feeling that I do much for her. I ask her how was it between us in group therapy the previous night. She gives a little shrug as if to say, Okay, not much, she can't remember one way or the other. But eventually she does remember that another group member said, "He has a special thing for you." She then glows and says, "Well, I feel like you do like me, that you do think I'm special." Why had she not held on to this? Why could she not digest it, live with it, be more fully nourished by it?

The zone of resentment is characterized by dependency (I need you to be a certain way, I need you to make things right), the zone of connection by *agency*—that is, the ability to be a power and an initiator in one's own right. Gratitude can only emerge from this second position, the position of strength. But we resist it. And in doing so, our lives and our relationships may come to feel more barren than they are. The stubborn, unconscious unwillingness to feel gratitude falls into the class of terrible things we do to ourselves. In rejecting it, we deny ourselves one of the fundamental pleasures of love.

There are so many reasons not to feel gratitude. It means letting go of resentment, that dependable source of power, that old friend, that symbol of loyalty to our childhood hurts and the people who inflicted them. Gratitude opens wounds. It reawakens us to our heartbreaks. We'd rather not love at all than face the truth about the past and abandon forever our unconscious dreams of a future made whole by perfection. We are unwilling to settle for anything less than mother-and-child reunion, a second coming of bliss. The patient's dream, in which she was reducing me from a gourmet giver to an annoying oaf, was a message that she was holding on to her resentment, that she was not allowing me to be worthy of her gratitude, that she did not want to release me from having to live up to her impossible expectations.

To keep gratitude a secret—to suppress our experience of it and to withhold its expression—may also be a function of envy. I don't want to give you my gratitude and make you into something good and beautiful when I feel so small and ugly. Fuck you and your goodness. Fuck you for being a Have when I'm a Have-not. And yet the irony is that allowing gratitude to flower, although it may stir a deep pain, makes the grateful one a Have as well.

This is true of every loving feeling. One can have a loving feeling and ignore it, let it fade, like a plant that isn't watered. Or one can beckon it into being, express it, make the most of it, and expand its presence—both in oneself and in the interpersonal field—in the process. A young man named Mike tells me that he is feeling anxious about his vacation plans; something bad will happen to him while he's away. He's begun to feel that way since the weekend when he and his girlfriend had a warm, connected time with each other. Before that, when they were feuding, which they have been doing for quite a while, he was looking forward to going away without her, flying off on wings of resentment and revenge. Now he's afraid his plane will fall. He's in the grip of separation anxiety, abandonment panic really.

I ask Mike if he would like to tell his girlfriend how good the weekend was and how much he'll miss her when he's gone. "Not really," he says. "She would like it, but it wouldn't do anything for me. It would just put me in a compromised position." Compromised, because now she will have the upper hand, she won't have to worry any more about losing him, and she can continue her mistreatment of him. I said, "Well don't do it if you're not doing it for you, but don't you see how you could be?" If he tells her about his loving feelings, he keeps the love alive, allows it to fill him up, augments it in all likelihood because of the response he'll get from her. And then he'll have that love to warm him and to take with him when he goes. Otherwise he's just left with an empty feeling and with the dread of separation.

Bill describes an incident in which his failure to maximize the good, which is to say make the best of his own loving impulses, led to a painful failure. He gave Thérèse a flower a few hours after an argument and was disappointed by her lack of response. After I question him, it becomes apparent what the gesture was supposed to convey: "This flower means that I would like you to come out to the garden and drink some tea and be near me while I work." His failure to be more explicit about his feelings caused him not to get the reaction he wanted.

Bill's reticence had a source many will appreciate: Speaking those feelings would make him too vulnerable; it would reveal a shameful longing for Thérèse that he wouldn't want to expose *(weak);* and, besides, it was more than he wanted to give at that moment. She didn't deserve it, she was too mean, she should just know to do what he wants and make that move on her own. So he remained a child, in effect, and lost an opportunity not only to have Thérèse the way he wanted her, but also to experience himself as an empowered man.

To make a move like this, from the zone of resentment to the zone of connection, takes some imagination. It means seeing beyond our sealed universe, beyond the Book of Mike or Bill, beyond the bitter stories we cling to—about ourselves, others, society, the gods. In this respect, the expression of gratitude and other ways of maximizing the good have a lot in common with forgiveness itself. It takes both creativity and courage to embrace something new, and there is an implicit element of mourning. We get security from our beliefs and attitudes, and giving them up entails a loss.

In so many marriages (like Bill and Thérèse's), resentment and fear bar the way to an expression of gratitude and other aspects of love that are actually there. Sometimes relationships go on and on like this, both people unaware of the goodness they share. A man who's been separated from his wife gets a call from her in which she tells him, "I don't think you're the cause of all my problems anymore. Because we've been separated for two years and I still have all my problems!" The call triggers memories of her sweet ability to own up, her cuteness when tickled, her generosity, her spirit. He is flooded with regret and remorse. These qualities of hers had meant so much to him, had lightened his burden, had made his married life much richer and more nourishing than his life before. But he had not allowed himself to enjoy, acknowledge, and celebrate them fully, and he had withheld from her and from himself the goodness that open feelings of gratitude and appreciation would have engendered. His criticisms had had validity, but he had lived in them too avidly, too afraid to take in love from an imperfect person who would use him and hurt him, too afraid to give love to someone who didn't yet deserve it. He felt a wish to make something up to her and began working on a poem that would evoke all those lost moments when he loved her and didn't say it. Mourning this loss filled him with sadness and helped make him a more sensitive man. It made a difference in his next relationship.

To mourn is to love again. This came to me vividly in a session with an older woman, an émigrée from Poland, where she had been part of an aristocratic family before the war. She is stunning, flirtatious, opinionated, sharp-tongued, and frequently indignant. She had not had a lasting relationship with a man since her husband left her when she was forty. She routinely vilified him as a womanizer, a ridiculous and inadequate husband, a terrible father. Today she was open to my questions about their relationship in a way she had not been before. She acknowledged that she felt loved by him. Suddenly, she burst into tears about the loss of this man she had not seen in thirty years. I thought (and said), *This is a woman a man could love.* All the rest is flirtation, adolescent cock-teasing, indignation over violations of propriety, narcissistic demands, and so forth. She acknowledged that it felt good to have my caring, my shoulder to cry on, and saw vividly how absent that quality was in all her other relationships. "But this hurts," she said.

I was reminded now of the final scene of Truffaut's movie *Mississippi Mermaid,* with Catherine Deneuve, a hardened, ruthless woman, raised in an orphanage, who has never been able to love and has gotten by using her looks to engage in exploitive relations with men. For two hours of screen time, she has employed all her cunning to cheat, ruin, exploit, and, finally, poison Jean-Paul Belmondo, even as he has fallen in love with her and made devastating and heroic sacrifices to save her life. But she has also gone through a gradual transformation, in which the capacity to love has begun to emerge in her. Swelling with gratitude and tears, she asks him repeatedly, with childlike simplicity, "Est-ce que l'amour fait mal? Est-ce que l'amour fait mal?" (Does love hurt?).

INCHING TOWARD EMPATHY

As we move away from the tendency to make other people players in our own internal dramas, we are freer to see them for who they are. "To understand all is to forgive all," the Buddha is believed to have said. But our hearts have to be open to understanding, which is not possible when in the victim mode.

Thérèse usually interpreted everything that Bill did or did not do extremely personally. He didn't do the hurtful things he did out of insecurity, or fear, or hopelessness of his own making. He did what he did because of her, because of her badness, because he wanted to reject her. Much of Bill's behavior that Thérèse interpreted as hurtful—his unwillingness to go to the beach with her or his dislike of certain things she loved—was not about her at all but a reflection of his own being that she could not tolerate and had to control out of her insecurity.

At one point during the treatment, they became estranged over his working late and the way things transpired on the phone when Thérèse got upset over it. She was particularly enraged when he became condescending. This really sets her off because it gets to that part of her that feels inferior. As we talked in session, she was still making disgust faces and attacking him, but she was showing more restraint than in the past. Bill, meanwhile, was like a dead man. I told him I couldn't feel his pulse. He spoke mechanically, and even when she told him in a nasty way, "You're putting me to sleep," he didn't respond. It is hard for him to acknowledge how frightened of her he is, let alone express his hurt and anger over being spoken to in this angry, rejecting, disgusted way. Instead he goes dead. But not so dead that he doesn't enjoy the frustration and pain his deadness is causing her.

When I asked Bill about all this, he acknowledged that he felt hurt and frightened. He spoke about his mother, how she hammered, intruded, made him cower, and the distancing, ironic defensive style he adopted in dealing with her. His face looked entirely different now. He was neither dead nor condescending. He looked boyish, open, vulnerable. Thérèse had been sitting with her arms folded, leaning the other way, looking pinched and askance. Now she was sitting forward, looking at him intently, warmly, a change reminiscent of Bill's shift toward her in one of our first sessions, when she had opened up about her tactics with Mona. Watching Bill, Thérèse seemed to be experiencing a revelation. Not just about who Bill was, but about who she was. She saw his fear, and she felt regret over how she intimidated him. She didn't know how intimidating she could be (a victim never does). She now felt both remorse and concern.

To gain a felt sense of another person's struggle is almost always affecting, even if one has been betrayed. Rachel and her friend, Larry, were part of a group that was toiling twelve to sixteen hours a day to get a new company off the ground. Suddenly, at the worst possible time, Larry disappeared, leaving them all high and dry, and very nearly destroying their dream. They heard he was drinking again and living down and out with a friend from his boozing days. Rachel wanted to kill him.

To keep the enterprise afloat, Rachel began helping Emma, who had been working most closely with Larry, to straighten out the mess he'd left behind. Rachel soon found Emma so demanding, fault-finding, and impossible, she wanted to throw up her hands and scream, "What do you want from me!" She found herself wondering what it had been like for Larry to work with her. Had he, too, felt cornered and overwhelmed? Was fleeing the only response he knew when the interpersonal pressure got that bad? Then she had a dream in which Larry appeared before her in terrible shape. He said he was sorry and pleaded to be forgiven. That morning, as she readied herself for work, she found her hate turning to sorrow, compassion, and a different kind of anger.

In the aftermath of catastrophic wounds, an obsessive, demonizing hatred may be mobilized to help us survive. And yet here, too, understanding eventually becomes a desirable thing, if for no other reason than we don't want to keep feeling like victims and living in hate. It rarely hurts us to be more generous. In many cases, even if the grievousness of the wrong is never acknowledged or atoned for, we may want to feel our way back to a caring place. It's the place we'd rather live.

EXTRAORDINARY
FORGIVENESS

WHEN A STRANGER MUGS YOU, TREATS YOU LIKE PREY, FORGIVENESS is often a less meaningful issue than for those who have previously had a place in your heart. With people who have never been important to us, recovery is more about undoing the chains of victimhood. We don't want to live in hate, we don't want to turn ourselves into the eternal prey of anyone. But moving on may not require much in the way of love or understanding. Hating the bad guy in a nonobsessive way may be enough. Eventually, as you repair, he's not someone you think about much anymore, one way or the other. The key thing is taking care of yourself.

But there are extraordinary exceptions in which people feel the need to connect with the stranger who harmed them. In 1995 Azim Khamisa's twenty-one-year-old son, Tariq, a student at San Diego State University, en route to deliver a pizza, was ambushed by four gang members and shot dead by a fourteen-year-old kid who had never met him. In the aftermath Khamisa needed to engage in some huge act of creativity on behalf of his own well-being. He found a kind of healing through an effort to connect with the murderer's guardian and grandfather, Plès Felix, who became his close friend and comrade, and to set up, with Felix's cooperation, a foundation to educate young people about violence.

Khamisa has told the world that whenever a crime like this is committed, two lives are destroyed, and he has emphasized that when young people get roped into gangs and senseless violence, society is betraying its youth. It was a point of view he came to almost immediately after the killing: "I left my body," he said, "because I couldn't withstand the shock, and, being a believer and meditating, I believed I went to the loving arms of my maker and maybe came back with this vision." The loss was also eased by the belief that people are reborn many times "in order to learn all the lessons to achieve enlightenment." He said he believes that "we come into life in self-chosen roles, which meant that I had selected my son and we had a contract that this is what would happen, and this put me closer to my mission this time around." But his faith has not meant he is able to adhere to this position easily. He told me that it has been a daily struggle to hold on to a sense of forgiveness and, I think, by implication, not to succumb to a bitter hate. "I could get up every morning and forgive my son's assailant, otherwise I can't get through the day, because the loss is there; there is an emptiness that will never be filled. This is a very, very deep-down pain. The pain scars the soul, and it scars it forever; and while there are good days and bad days, for every speech I give, it is tough not to cry. I cry, and I need recovery time." When we spoke, some three and a half years after the murder, he said, "One of the things I have not been able to do is meet my son's assailant, because emotionally I am not strong enough to withstand that. . . . But that is something I need to do for my own healing." (He has suggested that the young killer, Tony Hicks, who has done well in prison and expressed remorse for his crime, may have a job in the foundation some years from now when he comes out of jail.)

In his many talks around the country and the world, Khamisa has met people who have told him they don't understand how he could forgive such a crime, much less work for a reduction in the assailant's sentence, which he has also done, and that they themselves would be incapable of anything but an eye for an eye. I think most people would find it easier to understand them than him. And yet, although his actions have benefited Tony Hicks and his family beyond measure, offering Hicks a path to redemption that few people who have committed such crimes have access to, I don't think there can be any doubt that

Khamisa has done all this for himself. He has written (in his diary) that "losing an only son is devastating. It is spiritually ungodly, emotionally unloving and viscerally paralyzing. It is like a nuclear bomb detonating inside of you. However, if you survive the devastation, among the debris you see many new paths. I chose the path closer to my heart. As a result of this choice I am at a meaningful place. I am closer to my heart than I ever remember being. It is also the way I communicate with my son daily."

Khamisa has cleared his own path to redemption, one that people who get trapped in their bitterness cannot find. With the support of his faith, and also, he believes, through the good fortune of having had an extraordinarily loving childhood, he was able to find a way to move from the position of passive victim to active, engaged player in his own life. In the face of the most devastating of losses, he was able to employ two critical qualities, imagination and initiative, to move beyond whatever grim inner drama might have imprisoned him.

It is one of the horrors of violent crime, of course, that it not only causes terrible losses, but it often challenges the survivors beyond their psychological capacity to cope. Imagination fails. It is becoming more common, in the aftermath of childhood mayhem, like the mass killings in Littleton, Colorado, for parents to file a lawsuit against the parents of the child who killed their child. "Who else are we going to blame?" a devastated father asks a *New York Times* reporter. Sometimes revenge seems the only salvation. But whatever route one takes, the aftermath of violent crime is often catastrophic, with the victims left stuck in the worst internal realms.

In the more common, everyday experiences, where the losses are not so catastrophic, the ability to find one's inner strength, to remain a Have, and to deploy one's love creatively can also, as we've seen, be severely challenged. In established relationships, it's probably fair to say that we play a part in most of what befalls us, but there are, nevertheless, real and one-sided betrayals. People can be horribly brutal to one another. In some cases, the brutality is crushing and inexplicable, all the more so because we love the person who commits it.

COMPREHENDING THE
INCOMPREHENSIBLE

Susan suffered a traumatic and unexpected separation, in which her husband behaved in a heartless way, leaving her virtually destitute. She
found out that he had not only been having an affair, but had had a
whole series of them, probably from the day they were married nine
years earlier, that he had spent lavishly on the other women and had hidden his finances from her. When we spoke, as part of my work on this
book, she was looking back on things he had done since they first met,
some of them quite bizarre and disturbing—such as returning to the
parking lot and locking himself in the car with his dad for over an hour
when they were all out shopping and making preparations for the wedding, going to the wedding high on cocaine, or more recently beating his
head against the wall in the shower. There were so many things that she
had overlooked, that she had pushed aside, and that now came together
in this terrible new picture of him. It was a year and a half since he left,
and she was no longer in a state of collapse, although she was still taking
anti-depressants and sleep medication. She was wondering if she would
ever forgive him, which I considered an uncommon and perhaps valiant
question, given what she'd gone through. She said she found it impossible to imagine what it could be like from his point of view. We had the
following exchange:

> SUSAN: I just can't imagine why Alex would be so awful to
> me. What reasons could he have had?
>
> RK: He must have had them. Maybe they were things he
> could never get angry at you about because he felt so inferior,
> that there was something wrong with him for having his com-
> plaints. He may have felt that you were the perfect mama and
> that any dissatisfaction he had with you was neurotic or im-
> permissible. Maybe he felt powerless with women, so trauma-
> tized by a woman's anger or disappointment that he would lose
> his point of view. So that the only way he could get even and
> still be a man was to do things behind your back, including

seeing other women. But, of course, that meant you could never know what you did wrong, and everyone does wrong.

SUSAN: I think the biggest thing I did wrong was constantly turn the other way. Because, you know, this stuff happened before we got married, twice, and each time Alex begged and pleaded for me to take him back and forgive him. He said it was just an impulsive thing, and he had no feelings for the woman. One of them even called me! He had sworn up and down that he would never see her again, and she called and said, "I know you think Alex isn't seeing me anymore, but I just want you to know that he is, I want you to know the kind of man you're dealing with." And still I took him back.

RK: Why?

SUSAN: I guess I just wanted to believe. And, you know, he is down on his knees begging, and I thought, well, okay, I'll forgive him.

RK: In one way it's nice that you could forgive him; I think it does come out of the fact that you are really warmhearted. But you're also something of a sucker, because you do look the other way. You don't insist on getting to the bottom of things, and I think that's one of the ways in which you're implicated in the final disaster. You had tons of evidence all along of his being unstable, if not unfaithful, and you looked away. You have to take some responsibility for that. Also, by looking the other way, you were saying to him, I don't want to know who you really are. So that probably fed into his feelings of being deeply bad and unacceptable.

SUSAN: That is so true, but I still feel so good when I hear he is hurting. Ooh, I wish him pain!

RK: Well, I'm not surprised. How could you not? But I think at some point down the road, especially when you're not in such pain yourself anymore, when you have a new man in your life and you're doing okay . . .

SUSAN: Assuming all that happens!

RK: Right, assuming all that happens. If you stay miserable, you'll probably go on hating him and wish scorpions in his bed.

SUSAN: So you think I might be able to forgive him when I stop feeling like such a victim.

RK: Yes. I think, for you, moving on and feeling okay again is probably as important a part of forgiveness as understanding. And that has a lot to do with your ability to mourn.

SUSAN: Isn't that what I've been doing?

RK: Yes, although the question of how deeply and fully you'll do it and how long it will take is still open. Everyone has different requirements for dealing with loss. For some people, who have a lot of inner security, which is to say confidence in their ability to find love and be loved, mourning does not have to be prolonged. Others may need to have their lives change significantly for the better before they can get past the first stage, the victim stage. And some people can't even move on then. They can be remarried with a new family and still be actively bitter toward the person who jilted them.

SUSAN: Well, Alex really sent me back to a horrible place that—you know, I talked about this in therapy. A place where I feel doomed and unloved and like it's never going to be different, and I've spent all my life not wanting to know about that place.

RK: That's why you kept putting your head in the sand. You were afraid to find out what was really in Alex's heart, because it could send you back to that place. You were a little bit like Alex that way, you know.

SUSAN: Did I tell you that my father cheated on my mother? I always felt so terrible for her. She used to have to send me to go get him from his girlfriend's apartment. It was a nightmare. And now I feel like it's happened to me.

RK: It's amazing how the things we most fear we manage to make happen to ourselves.

SUSAN: You really think I made it happen?

RK: In some way, yeah. You certainly chose him. And you acted oblivious. It confirms my feeling about what you were doing back in the old days when you forgave him prematurely. It came about because you were reliving a family drama, acting out an identification with your mother that was unconscious and tremendously compelling for you.

SUSAN: Whew! It makes sense.

RK: What do you think it will take for you to move on?

SUSAN: Getting on my feet again. Not necessarily remarried, but maybe even that. Then I could feel that the curse is off. But I think I'll always wonder, why, why, why?

RK: You may never know the whole story. But if you did, I can imagine your saying that was a rough hand he got dealt, and even though what he did to you was horrible, what he got was worse. I think the more we know about what makes people the way they are and how hard it would be for them to be otherwise, the freer we are to be more generous.

Susan pointed out that there was another aspect to the situation with Alex, her current dealings with him. He was still being a prick about money, holding things up on the separation agreement, talking unflatteringly about her to their daughter. She said there was not going to be any forgiveness in that atmosphere. I agreed, but I did feel there was still room for communication, for protest, for letting him know that if they were going to have a satisfactory postmarital relationship he was going to have to clean up his act.

SUSAN: Well, that's interesting. What you're saying is that forgiveness does not require confession or repentance?

RK: You mean you would like him to acknowledge what he
did and how awful it was and show some contrition?

SUSAN: Right.

RK: I don't blame you. I'd want the same thing. It doesn't
look like you're going to get it, though; I don't know if Alex is
willing to look at himself that way. But it is possible to forgive
without that. It's a question of whether you want to live in a
grudge state or make the best of the way things are. I do think
separating is easier in a state of forgiveness. It leaves you in a
better place, and it frees you to move on in a way that bitterness does not.

SUSAN: Well, those feelings are hard to find right now.

We can see in Susan the wish to evolve beyond her bitter position
vis à vis Alex. Her forgiveness is a work in progress, a part of her general healing. With many people who have been hurt the way Susan was,
sometimes by a sibling or a close friend, they eventually reach a stage
where they no longer feel they are actively holding a grudge. They have
accepted the fact that they won't get an apology or any sort of caring response about what happened, and they know that if they try to get close
they will just get burned again. Abandoning any expectations of the person who hurt them, and eschewing all but perhaps the most formal contact, they move on, estranged but not actively hating, and they consider
themselves to have forgiven.

But there are degrees to which you let people back into your life and
degrees to which you let them back into your heart—which, of course,
are not the same thing—and there are all sorts of variations, some rep-
resenting a greater internal progress than others. The more evolved positions, in which the mourning and the letting go are more complete,
may be very hard to reach even if they are desired. The case of someone
who was deeply loved but is too abusive or too stubbornly, disappoint-
ingly hurtful, or too self-centered and irresponsible to be close to repre-

sents a special challenge. It is, however, possible to take such a person back into your heart, even if you do not let him get close to you in concrete terms. The inner attitude might be expressed something like this: "I love you, but I have to keep you at arm's length, because you're going to hurt me. I can't even express any of this to you because you're so insensitive, so defensive, so narcissistic, so hurtful, so immature you aren't able to open up the space inside yourself for my point of view. But I feel for you, I care about you—I smile when I think of you in some ways, and I am grateful for what you gave me when it was good."

I do not present this state of being as a prescription. We can't expect this or force it upon ourselves. We can only be where we are or just beyond it. For most of us, such a position can emerge only out of the complicated and unpredictable process of growth. But it is worth knowing about. To be there, and to be there solidly, is to be more fully a Have.

THE RENEWAL
OF PROTEST

STANLEY AND I WERE DEADLOCKED OVER HIS BILL. A MAN IN HIS thirties, Stanley was unattached, struggling to make it in a difficult field, and envious of my successes, real and imagined. He used his depression as a form of emotional blackmail. How could I say mean, critical things to him when he was clutching the edge of a cliff with his fingertips? When suicide or psychotic collapse might lie just around the corner? His envy betokened a hatred toward me ("You have and you won't share!" "I'm sinking and it's your fault!") that was never too far from surface.

Stan's envy also linked up with something in me—with my own readiness to feel guilty, in this case for not taking better care of him, for having more than him, for not being sympathetic enough—typical ways that therapists get enmeshed with their patients. As long as this remained unconscious in me, I colluded with him in my own imprisonment, keeping silent at times when I needed to be more assertive. I was, in effect, afraid of him and of his capacity to make me feel guilty.

To the extent that Stan had succeeded in controlling me, he was losing an important piece of me and what I could give him—in particular my protest and my freedom to be me. We had co-created a zone of deadness between us where he was allowed his infantile control and where I was cut off from him—rejecting, cold, silently resentful.

Despite this, our connection was a good one. It was dominated by warm feelings, and for the most part I was quite free to be myself and say what I wanted to, even if it offended him. And that is the way it is in relationships—zones of connection and disconnection, warmth and silent grudge, mixing like oil and water in a unique pattern of conscious and unconscious states of being.

Stan's insurance company had been holding up payments for several months, and Stan was doing the same to me. I asked him what his plans were for paying me. He said he was in bad shape financially, and so I had to wait. There was no concern in his voice. I told him, "I get the feeling you don't care much whether I get paid." He said, "Well . . . ," and shrugged as if this was a somewhat annoying and irrelevant line of inquiry. I asked him what the shrug meant. He said, "You know, it's not like my paying is going to make or break you." I said, "So, you really *don't* care if I get paid." He smiled sheepishly and shrugged again, as if to say, "Yeah, why would I?" I wanted to kill him.

The wish to hammer him, to nail him, to steel myself and ask "helpful" questions all welled up in me like an army in mobilization. I thought of saying, "If you don't pay, you can't stay," which would ultimately have made sense, but at this moment would have been nothing but a retaliation. I fought off these temptations to mobilize and tried to stay with my core feelings. I said, "That hurts."

This statement, so simple and unadorned, represented something of a departure for me in this relationship. I was breaking a taboo regarding what was allowed between us in the realm of his victim feelings. Looking back on that moment, I am reminded of a cartoon by William Steig in which a man steps, inadvertently, across a dotted line and, as he does so, he realizes, much to his own astonishment and apprehension, that the shackle which has been attached to his ankle since he knows not when has suddenly snapped and he is free.

I immediately heated up with a heightened sense of exposure and vulnerability. I knew I was risking a retaliatory tantrum. Stan could use what I said against me. He had done it before. But I also felt centered and strong. It was as if speaking plainly in my own behalf, without succumbing to his persecutory dramas or my own, had landed me in a surprisingly secure and empowered place. Strategic and retaliatory impulses shrank away. I waited.

Stanley was furious. He accused me of being obsessed with money. He said I was guilt-tripping him. He stormed and pouted for the rest of the session. And that was about as far as we got with it that day.

The next time we met, he looked remorseful. He told me that he had thought about it a lot and realized that, of course, he cared about whether I got paid. He brought a check that covered most of his balance and assured me he would have the rest the next month. He said he didn't feel good about the way he'd been treating me. When we moved on to why he'd been treating me this way, he eventually spoke reflectively about his envy and his wish to see me fall on my face. He wasn't saying he no longer had those feelings—far from it—but he was feeling them and talking about them, rather than unconsciously living through them.

I was interested to know more about his envy. He said he hated my office because it was too large, too nicely done, located in too prosperous a part of town. It bothered him that I had good taste and that I was dressing better in recent months than I had when we first met. "It's bad enough that you're a good therapist, why did you have to stop dressing like a schlemiel?" He hated when I occasionally wore a tie—it was too powerful. He didn't like that I played tennis, and he recalled once seeing me coming into the office with my racket, apparently fresh from a game. This, too, was an indication of my success, what he imagined of my status, and it aroused fantasies that I played with the sort of interesting, creative, and powerful people he wanted to associate with, who had their lives together, who conversed about important things, and had the money and the leisure to play on a weekday afternoon. (He himself played softball on weekday afternoons, but no matter.) He said he recently imagined my breaking my ankle on the court; it was a pleasurable fantasy.

None of this, of course, felt like an attack on me. It was, if anything, a warm moment between us. Here was all this aggression, and yet it did not feel mean; he was protecting me from it, addressing me from a different place from the thing he was describing. He would like me to break my ankle, lose my racket (and we can guess what else), stumble in the stock market (where he was sure I had funds), but that was not exactly the Stan who was speaking now. He was allowing himself his envy and his hatred, and, because he could allow it to himself, he could also have his very real caring. He was letting himself be a complex person, with feelings that could go in two different directions at the same time. It was a living example of an emergence into monotheism—love and hate existing together, but under the umbrella of love. And it came into being partly as the result of his initial expression of pure hatred ("Why should I care if a privileged, exploitive, miserly prick of a Have like you gets paid?") and what we ultimately did with it.

Stan also told me that he thought he reacted so fiercely in the previous session because he had felt me go cold on him, had felt the unspoken hatred that welled up in me in the seconds before I found my response, and this had been horrible for him. I remembered that moment well and acknowledged that I had turned cold and hateful before I spoke. He was grateful and relieved by that confirmation. As he got up to leave he said, "I don't mean to be giving you such a hard time." He thought about that and added, "Maybe I do."

My response to Stan the previous week ("That hurts"), which had been catalytic in much of this, had various therapeutic implications, but in personal terms I did what I did for myself. I said, in effect, I'm not going to treat you as so fragile that I am going to censor my feelings and let you walk on me; nor am I going to get drawn in by your envy such that I guiltily avoid confronting you; nor am I going to get hung up on *winning*, such that I act out my dependency (and enmeshment in my own past dramas) by bullying you—all of which was in me to do. I'm going to say what I need to say. In doing that, I emerged from my resentment and felt my own warmth for him return.

A few months later we had another encounter of the same sort. Stan called requesting an extra session. Without actually saying, "I'm desperate, you've got to come through on this," he sounded on the phone as if he would die if I did not comply, which felt to me like a threat and a manipulation; I was, in effect, being warned not to allow myself the freedom to say no. We had the extra session, which was on an issue about which he did feel desperate, but when we met again, I brought up the subject of his tone on the phone message. Doing so forced me to jump through the same internal hoops—he's going to attack me for finding fault with "every little tone in his voice," he's going to guilt-trip me for making him self-conscious and somehow wrong for having called and needed me, etc. And, indeed, this was what he did. But these were growth experiences for me. As my freedom grew, I hated Stan less. He could do what he does—all the games and dramas; the important thing was that in daring to protest and battling my own inner demons, I was not allowing his psychology to imprison me in mine. I could hate what he did, if that's how I felt, even hate certain aspects of him, without getting enmeshed in it and without having to hate him as a whole. These changes brought about a strengthening of our connection and, needless to say, of the value of our work.

DIGGING OUT THE SELF

We learn to disconnect as children when our protests don't get us what we need. That is our first encounter with hopelessness. And it is partly through that hopelessness that our ability to get what we need from others becomes impaired. That's when we sharpen our taste for revenge and all the other nasty, despairing, and perversely appealing alternatives to open, healthy, connected protest.

If we think of protest from an evolutionary perspective, it seems logical that it comes into play as an effort to restore a broken connection. The English analyst John Bowlby, the father of attachment theory, argued that just as the baby's cry is designed to elicit a caretaking response, its anger is designed to protest the absence or failure of that response. The parent's love and concern are activated and the hurt is relieved. A similar dynamic applies to later years.

But children who grow up with parents who have to be right, who meet protest and anger with defensiveness and counter-anger, come to think of every dissatisfaction or complaint that they have as reflecting back on them in some negative way. I'm always dissatisfied, I'm too selfish or too sensitive, I'm too hateful, too rageful. They become afraid of the kind of response their protests will be met with, and they become afraid of the fury that is lurking inside themselves, ready to pounce with a thousand years of hurt and frustration. They don't have a model of a happy endpoint, in which a statement like "I feel hurt by that" will elicit someone's concern. They don't have a model in which rage may be present but is contained, in which one struggles to give the other person the benefit of the doubt. They experience a humiliated fury that makes it impossible to reach out with anything but a club.

One result for many people is a tendency to think that power comes from cruelty or indifference. But, in reality, such things are not powerful, because cruelty and indifference emerge not from a self that's in possession of itself but from a self that is imprisoned in its inner drama. Authentic power comes from being able to speak your feelings, including protest and anger, from a nonenmeshed place.

Protest that is deformed by threats or indictments may tie someone's hands, induce compliance or capitulation, or achieve some other end, but it does not elicit caring. If we're lucky, the other person will hold onto his caring. He may even have the courage to protest what we're doing with him. But more likely we will activate his paranoia and rage, and he will be unable to recognize that there is still a hurt being in us that loves and wants to be loved.

Assertiveness training evolved in an effort to rid people of such destructive habits and teach them to ask direct questions, express a need or a point of view, state complaints and objections, and voice hurts—without manipulating, guilt-tripping, indicting, withdrawing, rejecting, and so on. But, as valuable as they can be, the skills of assertiveness are not enough to enable us to deal with the powerful ways in which our psychic life has been shaped by early experience. They cannot help me unravel what's mine from what's yours, see how I hold on to a black-and-white view of myself and others, liberate me from the compulsion to blame, help me to tolerate anger and criticism, or enable me to give others the freedom to be who they are and do what they need to do, even if, in so doing, they don't please me, arouse my envy, or activate my victim circuits.

The problem is not just that we get into victim states. In forming our protests we rely on defenses that are designed to keep us invulnerable and control the other person. Such defenses do not allow a simple directness. Operating through them, we do not convey, "This is what it feels like from here." We do not give the other person the benefit of the doubt. We do not invite him to consider and explore. We assume intents of all kinds—indeed, are utterly convinced of the truths that our paranoia and transference reactions convey to us—and, without the slightest awareness, we act superior or condemning, meanwhile utterly convinced that we are just speaking our feelings. We are then shocked when our good intentions are repaid with hostility.

Our psychology finds innumerable ways to undermine our words. If I speak with coldness, the underlying message—"I no longer consider you a friend," or "I warn you, you'd just better listen and not respond"—will be louder than any carefully thought-out words. And that message will become the agenda to which the other person reacts. If Susan tells Alex in the months before their marriage that she won't put up with any more affairs, or if she complains in later years that they don't have enough intimate emotional contact, her words may carry little weight with him. The extraordinary radar people have for the inner experience of others not only tells him that she has a fundamental lack of entitlement in this realm, but that she is, in subtle ways, inviting him to continue doing exactly what he does. Her identification with her cheated-on mother insures that.

In *Till We Have Faces,* Orual lived in a bitter fury at her sister for having left her and at the gods for having stolen her sister away. And was anyone ever more assertive? She was magnificently articulate in enumerating the ways she had been made to suffer. But the verbal skills of the courtroom are not applicable to matters of the heart. When Orual was at last willing and able to see into herself, she discovered a surprising set of feelings, including murderous envy and a history of having bitterly, by her own hand, kept herself a Have-not. And this completely altered her worldview. Who could deny that she had legitimate protests—Mommy, why did you have to die? Daddy, how could you treat me so cruelly? Why did you have to make me feel like a worthless, unfeminine *thing?* She had a right to her pain over the loss of Psyche. But her pain predated Psyche, and she had no right to make it Psyche's burden.

Orual is hardly alone in this. That's what makes the book's message so universal. We don't want to honor or even know the desperately alone and hungry parts of ourselves, we do not undertake the difficult journey that would enable us to care for, to mourn, our wounds, and then we make a child or a sibling, a friend or a spouse, responsible for keeping us out of our pain. The child must swear endless allegiance, never be angry or hating, and never truly separate, never (metaphorically) leave home, without being made to feel a traitor. The lover is monitored vigilantly for signs of infidelity. And so on. We've seen this displacement in many of our stories, going back to April and Roseanne, Norman and his sons, Thérèse and Mona.

Orual's protest would have had more legitimacy if she could have tempered her desperation with an acknowledgment of her ambivalence and her doubts. "Dearest Psyche, I know this is unfair to you, but I am angry, so angry at you for wanting to leave. I can't help taking it personally. I don't care what you say about your needs and your dreams. This feels like it's all about leaving *me*. You are leaving me, aren't you? And it doesn't seem to hurt you at all. I can't tell you what that does to me. I need you is the problem, and I fear I can't live without you. I'm torn, Psyche. I want to ask for your help, but if I do that, I can no longer control you. I'd be admitting I have a problem, and that would spoil everything. Especially since you're so perfect and I'm so awful. How can I tell you I have a problem? I'd be humiliated, I'd be groveling. Do I have a problem? Is it so wrong to feel so wronged by this? I feel so in the grip of enviousness, of possessiveness, I can't find a way out. I'm willing to do anything, to pressure you, blackmail you, make you forsake your destiny if it will serve my happiness—my only hope for happiness! But I feel bad about this, Psyche, I hate that I'm this way, because I don't want to hurt you. Oh, God, what am I to do?"

Such an acknowledgment, such a degree of awareness was, of course, beyond Orual's capacity. Lewis wouldn't have written his book and I wouldn't be writing mine if, caught in our deepest wounds, we could easily manage such a speech. Orual was too hampered by her emotional scar tissue to find anything in herself but a bitter response. She did have choices, and she saw them later, but the impulse toward resentment and revenge was like a torrent inside her she could not resist leaping into.

And yet it is worth considering what another choice would have looked like and where it might have taken her. A statement like the one above, however jumbled and confused, certainly would have given her sister more room to move. And since Psyche was a loving person, it could only have moved her to embrace Orual. "Oh, Orual, I love you with all my heart, and I feel your pain. I never knew you felt so alone and so desperate. This is a part of you I have only glimpsed. I remember those times, now, when I found you alone, looking so sad. Maybe I didn't want to see it. I loved so much the goodness of what we had." This was exactly the sort of embrace Orual had never had, an embrace in the place of her greatest pain, and an invitation to tell more, to feel and to share that forbidden anguished self. This is what anyone might need in order to embrace himself and eventually to move on.

Having abandoned her poisonous efforts at possession and control, Orual could perhaps have accepted Psyche's loving concern, and this could have begun her own mourning process. It might have given her the courage to move away from her envy, to let her sister go, and to face herself. It might have pointed the way toward the stronger, more self-loving parts of herself, and ultimately toward a healing that would have enabled her to love others and to have love in her life. Such a parting exchange between her and Psyche would have been a parting worth having, in which she had Psyche as never before, had her in a way she never could in the midst of her possessiveness, had her even as she lost her.

But regardless of Psyche's response and whatever might have followed, acknowledging the complexity of the feelings that swarmed inside of her would have been a positive step for Orual. It would have been affirming for her, fair to her sister, and respectful of the gods; and eventually she found it. In this place, she could know and assert herself fully. But until she found it, her lifelong lament—that her sister had been stolen; that she, because of her looks, was locked out of love and joy and the goodness of life; that the gods had tricked her into believing the wrong things, and so on—false, yet horribly well articulated—left her isolated, hostile, and stripped of the legitimacy that all the while dwelt unseen within her.

The habits we develop for operating in the zone of resentment are difficult to see and difficult to break even when we begin to see them. They represent the survival strategies of a child who dares not open his heart. They are not meant to reach the other person and initiate a meaningful exchange. They come from a part of the self that already feels rejected or worse and does not believe a meaningful exchange is possible; the other person's ears are shut. To make demands in an open, nonmanipulative way, to ask a probing question, to protest, to be warmly, noncontrollingly angry, to inquire openly about something that feels hurt-ful—to check it out—to reveal one's ambivalence and self-doubts along the way, is worse than pissing in the wind; it is to put oneself in the po-sition of being condemned, refused, shut out, abandoned; it is to have one's unloved status confirmed. This is a huge impediment to forgive-ness. The most important things do not get said and people allow their unconscious fantasies to take over. They never have a chance to hear an apology, an explanation that may enable them to take the offense less personally, or simply to see that the person who hurt them cares about the hurt they caused. But absent the opportunity for such valuable ex-changes, what possible legitimacy can there be to our feelings of perse-cution or blame?

The unspoken acts as a powerful pull toward paranoid fantasy life. The need to speak our hearts fully and with passion cannot be escaped. Even an apology doesn't obviate this need. Unless it is fulfilled, the undertow of resentment, pulling us toward a wounded place, remains strong. The relationship may resume, but something is lost—the trust, the warmth, the intimacy do not feel quite the same. The injured person may think, "I've forgiven all that. I'm a forgiving person." But he hasn't and he's not. Scarring has occurred, there's a new subject to avoid, a topic he knows will make him feel hateful and that will disrupt his marriage or friendship, and a formerly healthy part of the relationship has suc-cumbed to the fibrous tissue of resentment.

The skills of assertiveness are important. But I want to stress here not so much the skills as the emotional struggle to reach the full com-plexity of one's truth, the right to own it without shame or guilt, and the courage to speak it. From that place, a great deal of clarity and vitality will find its way into one's voice.

PROTEST AND THE FREEDOM TO BE

Successful protest is but one aspect of healthy self-assertion, and it is by no means the only one related to forgiveness. If we can't say no or can't ask for help, if we connect to others mainly through some compulsive activity like serving, if we are always making excuses for others and seeing the bad in ourselves, we will become bitter and grudging as surely as if we can't speak up when offended. But protest is perhaps especially critical because it is the last fork in the road toward resentment, the last chance to express dissatisfaction before succumbing to one's persecutory dramas and losing the feeling of connection.

Like most successful assertiveness, healthy protest grows out of a healthy entitlement and strong boundaries. One feels that one deserves good things from others, feels empowered to speak up when one doesn't get them, does not lose one's agenda in the face of someone else's. Healthy entitlement gives us the confidence to know what we feel and to express it. It enables a wife to say to her husband, "You're not making enough time for me; all your energy goes into the job, the gym, and the car. What about me!" It enables a husband to say to his wife, "How come you give me that lousy half-smile when I come in the door. I want a better greeting, I want the good smile!" And, in each case, to say these things from an essentially caring heart: I love you and believe you love me, even if I don't think you're acting that way right now.

Implicit in both of these spousal protests is a good relationship with the self: I have a right to be loved, I have a right to be treated well, and if I'm not, I'm going to say something and get things fixed. I also have positive expectations of others: They will care, they will respond, I will get what I want. (I may not get it, but my basic expectation is that I will.) On the other hand, if we feel too ashamed of having needs, if we feel too undeserving to ask or to protest when we don't get, or if we get caught in the narcissistic trap of believing we shouldn't have to ask, we are likely to say nothing and become resentful. We drift into the inevitable paranoid fantasy, and the other person doesn't find out what we need or what we're not getting until we're hammering him for it.

Entitlement also enables us to feel free to test parts of ourselves that aren't officially sanctioned, aren't by the book, parts of ourselves that may seem bad or irrational. Ken, a man in group therapy finds himself feeling angered and jealous about all the attention another man, Charles, is getting. He cannot contain himself. He blurts out, "I don't want Charles getting any more of the group's attention; I think he gets too much as it is!"

Ken is leaping into the unknown with this. But the group enjoys his

honesty and lack of rancor. The protest doesn't feel anything like an attack. He is talking about what *he* feels, with the full knowledge that it
could come from God-knows-where in his own psychology and may
have nothing to do with Charles's doing anything wrong. Supported by
the group's delight, he repeats his "selfish" outburst in various ways in
the coming weeks—"Charles is getting too much again! I can't stand
it!"—and this becomes a surprising passageway to a more satisfying presence for himself in the group, where he feels enlivened and able to take
more.

The freedom to speak a broad range of feelings, not just the safe pro-
scribed ones, is a vital part of our upbringing. The secure child, speaking from his monotheism, can say, "I'm so angry at you, Mommy, I want
to hurt you now," with no thought of acting it out and no thought that
he is in any danger for speaking it. We don't all have this upbringing, but
we can develop that secure element by speaking more openly about
what's inside of us and having positive experiences. We open up to ourselves when we speak our feelings, and, often, the world opens up to us,
too.

The capacity to listen to protest and listen to anger, to take them in,
is as important in its way as the capacity to protest well in the first place.
The problem is not just that we blame back or counterattack in other
ways. We have to correct, to prove it isn't true, so that the felt experience
of the other person is pushed away. Are we able to take in a contrary
point of view? Are we able to listen even if it hurts, even if we're sure it's
wrong, even if the protest is not nicely done? Tolerating hurt is part of
effective listening. It's an important contribution to repair. But it is not
always easy to come by.

There is no question that we make it difficult for one another to
protest. We inhibit one another with implicit threats: Don't criticize me.
Don't disapprove of me. Don't get angry with me. Don't make demands
on me. To say to a friend, "When you talk to me like that, I feel like I
don't want to know you," can be an extraordinarily powerful positive,
connecting thing to say. But we fear the response. (Go fuck yourself,
you're always complaining.) This fear gets in the way of many of our
most dynamic communications. "You're being condescending, and I
hate it when you get that way." (You're too sensitive, you don't even

know when I'm kidding.) "I hate your depression. It feels selfish and self-absorbed and like you don't really care that I'm left out in the cold." (Wow, that makes me feel just great.) "I was crushed by what you wrote. It felt like a stab in the back." (That's because you can't take criticism.) "Why didn't you back me up at the meeting? Did you not like what I was saying?" (Oh, no, I just didn't see what I could add.)

The controlling response, or even just the fear of it, has the power to hold us hostage, especially when we're dealing with people who mean a lot to us. It activates our shame. It activates our guilt. And so we rush back into prison—we apologize, we hold our tongue, we get into bitter efforts to prove ourselves right or place the blame on the other.

This is, of course, just another way of describing a continuing pre-occupation with a punitive inner parent who did not welcome our protests and demands as children. So we become overly dependent on the receptivity of others (whom we inevitably confuse with that parent). We don't have our own entitlement—it has to come from them. This places too much power and responsibility in the hands of the people for whom our protest is meant. Under such conditions, protest is either in-hibited ("I'm going to be assertive now if it is all right with you") or overly armored ("I'll kill you if you disagree"). It can't come out right. It comes soaked in dependency and a clinging animosity that often mani-fests itself in the horrible need to convince.

Freeing ourselves from such enmeshment can take years of hard work, because it means extricating ourselves from the psychological structure that got laid down for us as children. But people are right, I think, to feel that this is a fight worth fighting, even if it never gets fin-ished.

In the end, protest is something we do for ourselves. A receptive cli-mate makes the job much easier. That's always true, and no one is im-mune to the need for that. But, all the same, if we don't protest, or if we do it poorly, the failure is ours and so is the loss.

When protest comes from a healthy, entitled place, it is strong, clear, and catalytic. Even if, concretely, you get nothing for it, you've gotten a lot, because you've performed a vital function. You've spoken what you needed to speak. In doing so you've moved away from your persecutory dramas and toward self-love: I'm okay and I want to take care of myself.

In this way, good protest is related to both separation and mourning. You're not clinging to the ungiving parent, waiting earnestly, eternally, bitterly, for his approval or affection or his finally owning up. You are connected, symbolically, to the love of the loving parent and other loving figures in your life and to your own lovingness. So that even if you get met with coldness, incredulity, argumentativeness, or anger, neither your point of view, your feeling of entitlement, nor your sense of okayness is lost. You may feel hurt, you may feel sad, very sad; but you live in a world where you are cared for, even if not by this person at this moment. It is, in effect, a shift toward secure attachment, toward relocating the realm of security that exists within you, and acting creatively from that place. In all this, protest is fundamentally different from and antithetical to blame.

OPENNESS TO COMPLEXTY

Constructive protest is not about having a row. It is about talking about what matters. Ideally, in many cases, it is a beginning, an opening to a larger communication in which everyone gets to have his say and find out more. People are not convicted in advance; there is a spirit of inquiry. "I'm concerned that you haven't called; is there something to it?" as opposed to, "I can't believe you haven't called, and it's obvious that you're playing games with me." There is an openness about our interior processes: "When you don't call, I start to feel you don't care; it arouses all my anxieties about being dumped." Leaving things open this way gives the other person freedom. It allows for the possibility that we may have co-created whatever it is we don't like. It gives us our best chance to find out what the real story is, and the real story may put our minds at rest.

If I am protesting from a caring, connected place, if I haven't already turned resentful, I am not afraid to hear another point of view. There might be some reason why my friend or lover hasn't called, and I might be part of that reason. There might be some reason why my husband wants to avoid me or my wife is giving me a sour puss. Their point of view doesn't alter my right to be cared about, nor does it make me bad, but it may show me something that I haven't seen before, that I have some responsibility, some changing of my own to do.

The freedom to look inward with an accepting attitude toward ourselves and our processes makes it easier to appreciate the full complexity of our feelings when dealing with a person we care about in conflict. I was encouraged during one of our couples sessions when Bill was able to say, "Part of me feels that I am a bad person when Thérèse comes down on me like that, and I'm tempted to start confessing and making amends. But part of me is resentful for being made to feel that I'm a bad person, and I want to just blow her away for being so ready to see things I do in the worst light. And then there's part of me that feels really sorry that she is so hurt—regardless of who's right and who's wrong—and I want to make her feel better. But that part kind of loses out, I think." Once he has that clarity, which comes in part from letting himself be who he is, he can bring it to Thérèse or anyone else in a creative way.

The complex interweaving of past and present is evident in almost every interpersonal complaint, and it takes a special effort to sort out what's mine from what's yours. Another example comes to mind from my work. Richard, a somewhat formal man who has a managerial job in a government agency, tells me that he is angry at his friend Jason, who is about to become a father. Jason never said a word to Richard about his and his wife's plans for a baby or his doubts about having one, and then announced the pregnancy to Richard at the same time he told the rest of the world, at the beginning of the fourth month. Richard tells me that he feels shut out and finds himself losing interest in the friendship. This benign-sounding "losing interest" is Richard's polite, well-mannered form of murderousness. Jason is already convicted of being a false and rejecting friend. There is no way Richard feels able to say, "Jason, I feel bad that you didn't tell me. All those months. We talked all the time. Why did you treat me like everyone else? I thought I was special. Was there some reason you didn't want me to know?" He can't speak this way, he says, because the pain of being rejected is too potent; it makes his stomach double up.

As we talk it becomes evident that Richard is envious that Jason is having a baby when Richard, who has always felt more strongly about children, is struggling with a fertility problem; and he is envious that Jason has a Wall Street job and that his son will have more than any future son that Richard might have. It eats at him to think about Jason's kid in private school, his room brimming with toys and advantages, while his kid lives on brown rice and hand-me-downs. This is his inner drama, his history of deprivation, very real psychologically if not so real anymore in concrete terms. He tells me, "I don't want to talk to Jason right now, I don't like him, and I don't know why." But, unconsciously, he seems to be feeling, "Jason is a hateful persecutor, he's the Have who makes me a Have-not, and I want to get rid of him." It's an extraordinary transformation of who Jason is, which ignores all the goodness in Jason which Richard has come to value.

When Richard separates out what is his—his envy, his competitiveness, his agony of Have-notness—he is able to see the real Jason again and to focus on a realm of hurt and legitimate protest—namely Jason's inclination to withhold when it comes to those things that are most personal. And this is something he does with everyone, not just Richard. When that becomes clear, the whole constellation of feelings changes: "Jason, you're so damn secretive it hurts—because I love you and want more of you." Jason may not change if he were to hear such a protest, may not be ready to change, may not want to change, and that would be a source of sadness for Richard; but it is a sadness that he can deal with.

Being clearer about what he brings to the table might cause Richard to consider another possibility as well—that Jason knows about Richard's envy, is wary of it, and cautious about bringing up anything that might excite it. This could lead to a new sort of communication between the two men, and, if need be, a different kind of protest: "Don't shut me out, Jason, because of my envy. Don't start thinking that's all there is to me. I'd rather you get mad at me than shut me out."

Not every protest is fair or kind. Not every protest is legitimate. We may find that our whole perspective was skewed ("I guess I went off half-cocked," "I guess this has more to do with me than with you," "You're right, that was unfair"). But in a monotheistic mind-set we can live with that, because being wrong or being bad, getting caught up in our own inner dramas, seeing how we are drawn to envy or cruelty, does not invalidate our goodness and worth.

ANGER
WITHOUT
BITTERNESS

LIFE IS SWEET, DIRECTED BY MIKE LEIGH, IS A FILM ABOUT A working-class English family in the early 1980s. The husband, Andy (Jim Broadbent), a sweet, offbeat guy, ekes out a modest living as a chef and has recently been snookered into buying a decrepit old snack wagon—a "caravan"—in the hopes of fixing it up and starting his own business. His wife, Wendy (Alison Steadman), a funny and spirited woman with a sometimes annoying laugh, teaches dance to small schoolgirls. They have grown twin girls, somewhere around twenty years old, living at home. One of them, Nat, seems well-adjusted, if a bit dry and subdued. The other, Nicola, is a negative, alienated brat. She is disdainful in her attitudes toward the other family members, eats separately from them if she eats at all, and is both anorexic and bulimic (we see her gorge on chocolate and vomit). Her room is a pigsty. She looks a mess, and she exudes a separatist, nihilistic stance toward the world.

Nicola (Jane Horrocks) is not hard, even though she talks as if she were. Beneath her scowling contemptuousness, the vulnerable kid is still evident. Toward the end of the film, two people have confrontations with her. The first is the unnamed guy (David Thewlis) she's been having sex with, who can match her sneer for sneer and has an extraordinarily fleshy and insolent mouth. He comes over, as usual, when her parents and sister are at work. They start necking, and she immediately asks him if he wants to do it. He says no, he doesn't want "it," he wants her.

> BOYFRIEND: "I come in, we go straight upstairs, we do it—bingo, you're a pain in the ass. I don't want that. I want to see you nice."

Nicola looks suspicious: "What's nice? It's just a boring cliché."

"No, no, nice. Showing a bit of civility, a bit of respect."

Nicola doesn't like this. She snarls, "You don't show me no respect!"

> BOYFRIEND: "I'm trying to respect you now, I'm trying to treat you like a real person, instead of some fucking shag bag. Come on, talk to me."

She acts like the whole thing is ridiculous. "What *about?*" she says dismissively.

"Anything you think, anything you know, what you care about."

NICOLA, snarling: "Ey?"

"You have all these fucking books upstairs, *Women Who Love Men Too Much, Men Who Hate Women, Women Who Love, Women in Love, Women's Room, Female Eunuch*—have you read any of that crap?"

"What's it to you?"

"Have you?"

NICOLA: " 'Course."

"So what have you learned from it?"

NICOLA: "I'm a *feminist.*"

The boyfriend makes a face. "What's a *feminist?*"

Nicola tries to re-engage him in smooching. "Come on," she implores.

But he won't let go: "No, no, what's it mean?"

NICOLA: "Stop being *antagonistic.*"

The boyfriend, getting heated up and more provocative: "I'm not being antagonistic. I'm trying to have an intelligent conversation with you. Are you capable of that? Ey? . . . I don't think you are, are you? A bit vacant inside, a bit of an airhead, nothing going on, a bit dumb, a bit dizzy, dimbo, bimbo, dumb blonde stuff, ain't ya, ey?" He whacks her on the head a few times. " 'Ello? Anyone at home? Anyone at home? 'Ello? 'Ello?" They're both silent. He shakes his head. "You're a fake."

Nicola lowers her head and makes a pouting face. "I am *intelligent.*" There's a pause. "Are you coming upstairs?"

The boyfriend, manipulating his big, fleshy lips into something of a mock, sadistic snarl: "No."

"Well, piss off then."

He makes another face and proclaims his agreement: "All right!"

Nicola is alone. She looks distressed. This wasn't supposed to happen. Her mother comes home and starts straightening up the house. She arrives at Nicola's doorway. Nicola is lying on her messy bed, clutching her pillow.

WENDY: "How many days, Nicola, look at the state of ya. You sit in there like there's a grey cloud over ya, it's like the sun's falling. You got no energy, 'cause you don't eat your dinners. You've got no joy in your soul."

NICOLA (disdainfully): "How do *you* know?"

WENDY: "I know because you've given up. You're unhappy, that's how I know."

NICOLA: "I *am* happy."

WENDY: You've lost all your friends, I don't see them knocking on the door anymore."

Nicola: "I don't want any friends. They disappoint ya."

Wendy tries to tell her that she is apathetic as well. "You say you want to change the world, you're supposed to be political, but I don't see you doing anything about it. . . . All you do is sit here looking at the four walls and twinking and twitching." She begins closing the door.

Nicola calls after her plaintively, "You sound *perfect.*"

Wendy: "No, I'm not perfect. But I haven't given up. I'm still out there fighting. And I'll tell you what, Nicola, every time I look out that window and see that rusty old caravan sitting there, do you know what it says to me? It says that there's a man who hasn't given up either, who's still out there fighting, looking for his dream."

Nicola: "It says to me, there's a man who's getting greedy."

Wendy (disbelieving): "Greedy? Your dad? He's the most un-selfish man I've ever met. Do you know he's up at six o'clock every morning, slogging his guts out at a job that he hates, which is more than you do. And he still comes home at the end of the week with sod-all."

Nicola: "I just don't want to be exploited."

Wendy: "Exploited? You're not prepared to work. Full stop."

Nicola: "You've accepted Nat as a plumber and you didn't like that at first."

Wendy: "No, I didn't like it. But I can see now that I was wrong, because she's happy."

Nicola (plaintively): "I don't know what I want to do yet!"

Wendy: "Oh, don't you? Well, you had your chance, Nicola, when you were seventeen, when you were at college doing your three A-levels. You were going great, and suddenly you stopped. You stopped eating, you stopped everything. You ended up eight weeks at the hospital."

NICOLA (whimpering, abused): "You *put* me there. I didn't want to go."

WENDY: "Oh, for God's sake Nicola, you were at death's door."

NICOLA (crying, abused): "You were trying to control my life."

WENDY: "You were dying!"

NICOLA: "No, I wasn't."

WENDY: "Yes, you were."

NICOLA: "I would know if I were dying!"

WENDY: "Doctor Harris told us you had two weeks to live!"

Nicola looks jolted. Her expression sobers; her chin trembles. Wendy looks at her warmly, considering what to say next. She picks up where she left off: "You didn't know that, did ya?"

Nicola shakes her head. Her mother continues, telling her about her own struggles when she was young, doing her A-levels, pregnant with twins at seventeen, no money, she and Andy coming through it all happily.

Nicola responds through bitter tears, "Well, don't blame me! I didn't ask to be born!"

WENDY (pained, exasperated): "I'm not blaming you, Nicola, I just want you to be happy, that's all. And you're not! I wouldn't care what crummy job you did, I wouldn't care how scruffy you looked, as long as you were happy, but you're not. Something inside you has died. You've given up." She sniffs back a tear. "Ain't one day I could walk through that door and you could look at me and you could say, Look, Mom, help me, please, I don't know what I'm doing, I don't know where I'm going. Then, I would say, Great, because now we can be honest with each other, now we can start talking . . ."

NICOLA: "But I'm not in a mess."

WENDY: "Aren't ya?"

NICOLA: "You're giving me a problem when I haven't got one."

Wendy throws her head up, sniffles, exclaims something under her breath, along the lines of "God help me," sniffles some more, looks thoughtful.

NICOLA: "If you hate me so much, why don't you throw me out?"

WENDY: "We don't hate you! We love you, right? Stupid girl."

Wendy leaves. Nicola cries. Wendy, alone, also cries lightly, reflects.

Here we have two people who are angry at Nicola, each trying to reach out to her in his own way. The boyfriend is provocative and a bit cruel, but he really is, as he says, treating her with respect. As aggressive as he is, he is coming from a caring place. He is confronting her in a way that most people won't. And, more important, he is doing it with the door open; he wants to connect. He's angry because he wants her and she won't put out, except in the conventional sense. It's easy to imagine Nicola being grateful to him one day.

The confrontation between Wendy and Nicola revolves around standard parent-child stuff. The child is behaving badly, harming herself in the process, and the parent is pained and angry. This case is complicated by the fact that Nicola is an adult and, therefore, beyond the reach of certain forms of discipline, and that she seems to be literally destroying her life. But the core feeling for the parent in most such cases is one of pain for the child and simultaneously of powerful temptation: to get sucked into an inner drama in which the parent feels responsible, guilty, worthless, etc., and thus massively enraged at the child and determined to control her by any means possible. This, of course, only encourages the self-destructive behavior, which, if it wasn't before, now becomes a weapon in the child's struggle against the parent.

None of this comes into play with Wendy. No matter what she says, no matter how upset or angry she feels, you never get the sense that she is losing touch with the love she feels for her child. It is her love, in a sense, that gives her the authority to be angry and that keeps the conflict from getting out of hand. Wendy could wring Nicola's neck, but she doesn't. There is not a moment of bitterness, of "Look what you've done to me," or the heavy-handedness that might service the bitterness: "As long as you live under this roof. . . ." At one point in the film Wendy and her other daughter are joking about the possibility of having a pet alligator, and Wendy, who is always joking, says with a laugh, "It could eat Nicola!" Her daughter responds in a way that suggests she would really like an alligator to eat her sister. Suddenly, the exchange is not funny to Wendy anymore, and a look of distress crosses her face.

Wendy is not enmeshed with Nicola, which makes true hatefulness foreign to her. She is not desperately trying to save her, needing Nicola to be all right so that she, Wendy, can experience herself as all right. Nor does she blame herself for Nicola's problems, and, therefore, become overly solicitous and unable to say anything that might offend. It's not that she isn't open to seeing where she may have done harm. But she recognizes and accepts Nicola's separateness. She doesn't derive her own worth from her. She is able to love from a healthy distance.

Wendy is in pain over Nicola, but she's not going down with her. She is not the kind of person who would throw herself into the grave if her child died. Nicola's death would be horrible, and it would stay with her forever. She might want to die at first, but we sense that she would come through somehow. She is sustained by a sense of goodness inside of her, and it is partly for this reason that her love never falters throughout the encounter. You never feel bad for Nicola to have to be on the receiving end of her mother's protest or her anger. Just the opposite.

GOOD FIGHTS

Anger is our most controversial emotion, and we all need to be on better terms with it. Some people believe it is bad all the time and may even fool themselves into thinking they don't feel it. Some are addicted to it and too familiar with both the satisfaction and the sickening emptiness of victory. Few get it right. We saw in our discussion of revenge what a vicious and destructive addiction anger can be for some. Others dread it because it is the doorway to their hurt. And yet if we are not free to be angry, if we don't allow ourselves our aggression, we are not free to *be,* and we are certainly not free to love. How can you love someone when you're seething with inhibited rage? Unexpressed anger colonizes the emotional life. It's like a cancer, sapping our vitality, aggravating our feelings of shame, weighing us down with depression, and secreting a steady stream of bitterness throughout our being.

Much can and has been said about the expression of anger and what gives it legitimacy. I'm going to limit myself to this: The hardest thing about anger is to have the freedom to feel it and express it and to still hold on to your caring. In a speech before a black audience some forty years ago, Malcolm X said:

> I for one, as a Muslim, believe that the white man is intelligent enough that if he were made to realize how black people feel and how fed up we are, without that old compromise and sweet talk . . . Why you're the one that makes it hard for yourself! The white man believes you when you go to him with that old sweet talk because you've been sweet-talking him ever since he brought you here. Stop sweet-talking him. Tell him how you feel. Tell him what kind of hell you been catchin'. And let him know that if he is not ready to clean up his house, if he is *not* ready to clean up his house, he shouldn't have a house. It should catch on fire. And burn down.*

This kind of talk was (understandably) considered incendiary. But what is Malcolm saying? Stop being afraid to speak your truth, stop pretending, let the whites know you're hurting, let them know you're mad. And although he ends with a threat, he begins with the hopeful implication of his unfinished thought—that the straight truth, even if angry, will be heard and responded to.

---

* From the documentary *Malcolm X: Make It Plain,* produced and directed by Orlando Bagwell for *The American Experience* on PBS.

From his point of view, how could this truth be spoken in anything but an angry way? After his trip to Mecca, Malcolm came to believe that he had gone overboard in his attacks on whites—defining them as devils and blaming them for all the evil in the world (the black-and-white version of black and white). But I don't think he ever meant to retract his anger. That anger needed to be expressed and still needs to be expressed. And one of the special qualities about Malcolm's anger, especially after Mecca, but, I think, even before, was that, as hard as it was for a white person to hear him, he did want to communicate, not just indict. Toward the end of his life Malcolm was seeking to express his anger while holding to the view that we are all human. He could say, "You are oppressing us, damaging us, humiliating us" without turning that powerful truth and the huge hurt and anger that accompanies it into demonization, rejection of the white world, or violence.

People need to be fully expressed, in all their feelings, positive and negative, even if they go overboard at times. Somewhere in their rage is an important message that needs to be heard and made sense of, by themselves as well as others. Once, during my work with Thérèse and Bill, I showed up late at my office, several minutes after the session was scheduled to begin, and Bill was there, waiting in the hall, looking tight and miserable. He said nothing, but I could feel his coldness.

When the session started, I asked him if he had any feelings about my being late. "Sort of." I questioned him more and the feelings started to emerge: The pain of having to worry whether I would show up at all. The humiliation of being in the hall, waiting. The sense that his time and his schedule didn't matter to me. The childhood feelings it aroused of not being cared about or good enough. I asked him why he didn't say anything to me. He said he didn't want to sound like a baby, he didn't feel his anger was okay. As we spoke, it also became clear that this baby was burning hot with rage and was already having fantasies of replacing me. But his rage had nowhere to go. If he got angry, if he threatened me, I might say, "To hell with you." He would lose me. So he shut himself down, telling himself over and over, as he stood in the hall seething, that he should be able to handle a small thing like this, and if he felt bad about it, there was probably something wrong with him, not me, and meanwhile, insidiously, wondering about another couples therapist a friend had told him about.

I could not get near him. I had my first taste of what drove Thérèse insane. The feeling of being annihilated with a controlled, somewhat depressive, but nevertheless steely propriety. "Nothing's wrong. There's nothing to talk about." As if I were engaging in a silly exercise to even ask him about it, this stupid thing therapists feel they need to do. His unspoken hostility froze the space between us. "This is much worse than open anger," I said. "This is like death."

"You're making too much of it," he said. "How can I get bent out of shape by something so petty? It's not as if you do this every time."

I said, "Thanks for the defense, but you still have your feelings. Why not enjoy them? Who cares if they're right or wrong?"

The idea that his aggression was something he could enjoy, that it did not have to wipe me out and that he did not have to be wiped out if it turned out he was "wrong," was new to him. He had had the sadistic enjoyment of blowing off someone he didn't care about with his righteous indignation; but the idea of a positive enjoyment, just from letting me know I could go fuck myself the next time I left him standing in the hall, was strange. "Even if I said, Well, fuck you, too!, and we ended up staring at the walls for the next five minutes, would it all be over?" I asked him. I thought I saw a glimmer of interest in this concept, although it was still some time before he thawed out.

Anger, like any other form of protest, can be expressed with an openness to the other person's point of view, in combination with other feelings, in various intensities, with an acknowledgment of one's uncertainty. It's possible to say "I'm angry" and say why without acting angry. The important thing is to be able to allow ourselves the full complexity of who we are.

A woman has an accident with her father-in-law's car, and, afterwards, her husband is obsessed about the condition of the car and the cost of the repairs. He keeps jumping at her to review the details of the accident and paces in anxious anticipation of his father's reaction. She is hurt and seething. She tells him that he is being a prick, that he isn't caring about her, that all he can think about is the fucking money and how pissed his father is going to be. She says she is furious at him for getting that way, that he doesn't even seem to notice that she is just back from the emergency room and is still rattled and hurt. She then runs off and bursts into tears. Such anger is a necessary self-assertion, vitally important to be expressed, even if it doesn't immediately engender a change of heart.

The intensity of the anger, the presence or absence of a "fuck you," is not always the most important issue. It's more a matter of where it comes from and what it's trying to do. In the movie *Private Parts,* about the infamous disk jockey Howard Stern, Stern's wife, Allison, goes into a ballistic rage at him for telling a joke on the air about her miscarriage. She spits, "Shut up! Shut up!" when he tries to explain and "Fuck you! Fuck you! Fuck you!" when she's done, but we never feel that she's trying to destroy him. She doesn't sound like a victim who's been crushed by a monster. She may want him to crawl off and feel very guilty, she may want to put him in the doghouse and make him suffer, but there is no sense of grudge about her. We know she will eventually accept an apology and a promise of better behavior and that it will be over. She may want to kill him but she is not murderous.

A patient once teased me that "murderous" is my favorite word, as if to say that I loved flamboyant language. But I don't think the word is flamboyant. We do want to kill and we do act annihilating. Certain hurts make us feel like a wild animal inside, all claws and fangs, who wants to rip to shreds the person who is hurting us. The more we deny it, the more likely we are to act it out. That's where we get denunciation and indictment, cold withdrawal, the relentless cross-examination by which the other person is painted into a horrible corner. That's where we get such horrible parental statements as, "I'm doing this for your own good," or "I'm not angry, I'm disappointed," and all the other guilt-tripping deceits that make children and others feel reduced to worthlessness.

I had a patient who found it extremely difficult to express anger. She often felt broken and humiliated by the anger of others to the point where she lost her grip on her thoughts. And yet when anger came out of her it was very much like the poisonous stream of reproaches to which she had been subjected by her mother. She told me once, a few minutes after laying waste to my character, "I feel ugly and disgusting when I'm doing it, but I feel like I don't have any other option." She is convinced—and with good reason, given her early experience—that if she expresses her anger in a more open, nondemolishing fashion, she will be savaged in just the way she savaged me. Indeed, in her fantasy, in her anticipation, I am already savaging her that way. So her attack on me is partly a counterattack, partly an effort to destroy me while my planes are still on the ground.

This is a fundamentally different use of anger than what we witnessed earlier in *Life Is Sweet*. If either Wendy or Nicola's lover experienced a wish at any point to wipe out Nicola—and it's hard to believe they didn't—neither one of them acted on it.

I've described Wendy as free of certain enmeshing elements in her relationship with her daughter that might otherwise have made her more threatened and violent. But one doesn't have to be free of enmeshments in order to express anger well. The inner drama and the delusions and fears associated with it are what make us murderous; the inner drama is what makes the clean expression of anger so difficult; but it doesn't make it impossible. Indeed, since the inner drama is an inevitable part of our most important relationships, there is little point in discussing anger in its absence. The important thing is to know that certain actions hurt or threaten us terribly, throw us into a blind, primitive state, and make us want to kill. That knowledge can be the beginning of a different kind of struggle—to restrain ourselves, to give more benefit of the doubt, to be more generous and still to locate our hurt and our protest. Where there's enough trust, we can even acknowledge what we're going through ("I'm feeling really threatened by this," or "I'm feeling like I want to kill you"), and this may be enough to begin turning the interaction in a new direction.

In the end it is probably impossible to ever codify the manner in which people manage their repairs or the extraordinarily creative ways in which they come to know each other, extract vengeance, hide their love, or play it out. Even bad fights can turn out well if people don't get so frozen in their resentments that they lose all knowledge of their love. In some relationships the inner dramas have such a profound grip and each person is so caught up in vengefulness that it is only after a period of rage and destruction—as portrayed, for instance, in Edward Albee's *Who's Afraid of Virginia Woolf*—that one is able to reach a state of repair. One recognizes with sorrow all the pain one has caused, lets go of all the hurt one has endured, and reconnects with all the love one feels, deep, deep love, for this person whose flaws are so terribly like one's own and whom one had to annihilate partly for that reason. The road there isn't pretty, but it is redeemed by the outcome and perhaps, in the process, something is learned about the need to protect the other from the demons in oneself. I sometimes thought of Thérèse and Bill in this context.

LOVE AND RAGE

Both Thérèse and Bill were severely handicapped in the expression of protest. Thérèse protested loud and hard, but usually with overtones of disgust, contempt, and dismissiveness, which made her scary and controlling, but ultimately got her little. Bill was just the opposite but no less impotent and equally rageful. Rather than protest, which scared him, he drifted away from her and began to feel that she didn't matter to him. In Thérèse's words, he became "a well-mannered stranger."

In one session Thérèse started to cry. She whimpered about her horrible feelings about herself and her fear that she had ruined everything with Bill and that he didn't love her. I looked at Bill. He was blank. He seemed to have left the room. Finally, I asked him what he was feeling. "I don't know, I feel bad." I persisted until Bill acknowledged, first, that actually he didn't feel much, second, that he had tuned out, and, finally, that her crying turned him off. He managed to squeeze out that he didn't feel it was real, that he felt manipulated, and he hung his head, as if he had no right to say this, as if saying this made him a bad person who would be ejected from the human community (i.e., rejected by his authoritarian, moralistic father).

Bill's response gave Thérèse the opportunity to go into a self-righteous, blaming attack. How can I ever be open? How can I ever ask him for anything? Aren't I allowed to cry? And so on.

"Why can't you permit yourself to be angry at that hateful, manipulative cry?" I asked Bill. "Why couldn't you say, 'Don't do that to me!'?" He had reasons every bit as good as hers. But by not protesting, by cutting his own anger off at the legs, he made himself her victim and, in doing so, he deprived her, first of himself, but also of valuable feedback that could help her to see what she was doing. Unless she could really feel him, she would stay caught in the stronger orbit of her mesmerizing, internal relationships with her parents.

Bill objected that he didn't see the point of getting angry at her, didn't see how it would change anything. "What am I supposed to do? Say, 'Fuck you!'?" I replied that a "Fuck you!" from him would be a gift, but I asked if there were any more affirmative way he could put it. "I could tell her to stop breaking my friggin' balls," he said in a low, miserable tone.

I said, "That would be great, but there's a tone in your voice. Do you hear it?"

Bill was silent.

"Yeah," Thérèse said, "he sounds like he wants to rub me out! He sounds like his father, actually, the long-suffering victim. And, believe me, Bill, I should know. Every person in my family is a victim."

"But I *am* a victim! I'm a victim of your ball-breaking!"

I asked Thérèse how he sounded now. She sheepishly admitted that she liked the way he sounded now, but added that he wasn't *right*.

Bill could not see the difference between how he sounded now and how he sounded before. I said, "There was something in your tone before that's akin to the whimper you hate in Thérèse. She may be breaking your balls with her drama-queen routine, but you sound as if she's *got* you by the balls, as if you're a prisoner and she's the jailer, as if you're not a free man and not a player in all this. Maybe that's why you have to rub her out. The second time sounded much warmer, more alive and free."

BILL: "This is why I don't get angry. It's just too hard. It's easier to withdraw."

"Yeah, but that's just as bad, worse. If you could say, 'Stop breaking my balls!' and still feel the warmth you have for her, then you'd be in business."

This was hard for Bill to grasp, because as soon as Thérèse became absorbed in her inner drama—"Look what you're doing to me, you heartless man; I'm drowning and it's your fault"—it sent him directly into his own inner drama. He began to feel his lifelong guilt about not being what his parents needed him to be, his dread that they would die if he were not the perfect son, the perfect eldest child, and that then he would be left alone, orphaned because of his own badness and inadequacy and forever crushed. Having such feelings stirred up makes him go into a mountainous internal rage that quickly disintegrates into depression. In the grip of his inner drama, he not only can't protest effectively; he can only shut himself down or lunge for her throat.

What he does with his daughter at times is quite different. When Julie acts regally with him, gives him orders in her obnoxiously entitled, teenagery way, he can say, "Yes, your majesty!" in a grandiloquent manner and then accede to her demand if it doesn't really bother him. Or he can say, "Begging your majesty's pardon, but the valet is already booked for the time you requested," which might lead to a bantering exchange that he actually enjoys, in which she skirts the edge of insolence and he gently indulges his aggression without ever really getting emotionally involved with the bitchy side of her.

With Thérèse he finds this impossible. He can't respond to her heart-clutching histrionics. He can't say something like: "Can I do anything to comfort you in your final days?" He can't tease her out of her victim state or at least take a stance firmly outside of it: "This is between you and your therapist, don't get me involved!" He cannot say this straight, and he cannot say it laughing, with his fingers crossed in front of him as if he were warding off a demon. He doesn't have enough distance to enjoy himself (and her) that way.

Indeed, even if he tried to be playful it would come out laced with poison. She too readily engages his own early trauma, which is still largely unmourned and unconscious—he hasn't worked with it enough. To him his parents are still simple, good folk, hardworking immigrants who had high standards for him and loved him to death. So he has no idea of how his inner reality of a tormented, intruded-upon boy who had to be his family's savior could color and transform his external reality. In some crazy place inside himself he really believes when Thérèse clutches her heart and sniffles in despair that she is dying and it's his fault. He panics with guilt and the need to save her, even as he simultaneously hates her for stirring him up this way.

I said to him, "So, she's going crazy, as we all can do, but that doesn't mean you have to go with her." But this was foreign to Bill, the idea that there are separate realities and that she didn't have control over his unless he allowed it.

The exchange with Bill made Thérèse think about her whimper, and in the next session she raised the subject herself. She was troubled because she couldn't see what was wrong with her crying. But she asked the question as if she were interested in an answer, not as if Bill and I were culprits, who were, sniff, sniff, "taking away my right to cry!" Being able to ask this way was an important development for her. She was really opening herself up to feedback, and about something in her that was not so pleasant, rather than setting us up for the next attack. What we got to was that she didn't believe she would be heard or taken care of if she didn't do her manipulative drama-queen whimper. "I guess my credo has always been, If you can't make a person feel guilty, you'll never get anything from him." Once again, her self-deprecating forthrightness disarmed me and endeared her to me.

I asked her if she knew how Bill would respond if she cried in an ordinary way, just cried, because she was hurting, because she felt bad about herself, because she felt alone, whatever. "Yeah, he'd be sweet, I know he would."

"So your credo is not really applicable to Bill."

"I really have to let go of that."

IT TOOK A LONG TIME and much coaching from me before Bill finally told Thérèse in a powerful way how he felt about having to live under the gun with her. He was telling her she needed to back off in some conflict she was having with their daughter. "Here he goes again," Thérèse said. "Whatever Julie does is good, whatever I do is bad." Bill blurted out: "It drives me nuts when she does this!"

"Tell her," I said.

"This drives me nuts! You can't hear a criticism without turning it into two against one. The truth is you just don't want to listen. You turn everything around, and I *hate* that." At one point I asked him what he thought Thérèse felt toward him. "Like I don't really have a point of view, like I'm just out to get her. It's as if you think I don't care about you—and I do, damn it!"

Thérèse's response to this was one of victimization. "I feel like he hates me and thinks I'm an awful person," she said. I said, "Yeah, he hates you when you behave like this. But he hates you because he loves you. Why would he care otherwise?" She smirked and said she did not hear it that way, absolutely not, and she thought the thing he said about caring was just tacked on. Bill, I was pleased to see, did not back down in the face of this; he stayed angry and told her that he found it infuriating that she took what he'd said in that way. He muttered something. I said, "Say it." He said, "This is emotional blackmail!"

This commitment to his own anger was for Bill an essential building block of forgiveness. As long as anger was not an option for him, or only an option that he could exercise in a dissociated way, through a cold withdrawal or occasional bouts of temper, he could not stay connected. For him to protest in this way was to stay connected, stay vulnerable, demonstrate a determination to get something better for himself and for the relationship. If he were ever to put an end to this tendency toward vacant, dissociated grudge and embrace Thérèse more fully, this act of standing up for himself, of being there for himself, of self-actualization would be an essential prerequisite.

Thérèse wore an expression of pinched persecution. She looked as if she might walk out. I told her, "Hey, this is a lot better than what you normally get from him. He's coming out, he's not being a wimp or withdrawn, those are the things that you always complain about." But Thérèse was stuck in her negative zone, and it was some time before she was able to hear Bill's anger—or anyone's anger—without feeling abused, and without leaning on a feeling of abuse as a weapon in her struggle for control.

Like many people, Thérèse was allergic to criticism or anger directed at her. Their expression immediately suffused her with shame and guilt, brought her back to a place of humiliation, and caused her to respond with fury, defeat, or counter-blaming. She may not have liked Bill's withdrawal, but she did a lot to encourage it.

Bill, meanwhile, had trouble standing up to her in a strong, direct way, so that months passed before he worked himself up to a similarly powerful expression of anger. I remember this session, because Thérèse came back at him full bore with a passionate expression of her own anger that was not a guilt trip or a wipeout but gave voice to her legitimate hurts. She was furious at him for avoiding conflict, for drifting away rather than dealing with her. "I feel like I'm living half the time with someone who's not even there!" Thérèse cried after she said this. "I feel so *lonely*. It's awful living with someone who's not there."

The room was silent for a few moments while Thérèse dabbed her eyes. Neither one of them said anything to acknowledge the other or to advance the dialogue in any way. But soon Thérèse was beaming sheepishly toward Bill and he was glowing back.

Later in the session, I asked Thérèse if this feeling of being abandoned, of living with someone who's not there was familiar to her. "Yeah, of course, my dad," she said. As we worked with this, she felt how deeply her father's emotional abandonment affected her, how very important it was, how she obscured it with contempt, so that Bill never knew the hurt that lay behind her nasty dismissals. Bill was the target of a lot of stored up childhood rage, and he was getting it in the same way both she and her father got it from her mother. This realization softened her toward him. Recognizing what she was bringing from the past, the unmourned losses that still had her in their grip, enabled her to be more forgiving.

Meanwhile, there was no doubt in my mind that both Thérèse and Bill each felt enlivened, engaged, and optimistic after having aired their anger in a good way. They had gotten in touch with their passion and vitality, and that had made them feel good about themselves and each other. Bill was touched by Thérèse's sadness and her need for him. This was a new experience for him, as he was always ready to believe he didn't matter to her, a belief that had its own childhood roots. Certainly neither one felt downtrodden. Bill said that being nailed in a clean way also felt good.

This session became a kind of beacon for them. They realized that they did, indeed, love each other but that the love had suffered and been obscured by a multitude of grudges, only made worse by the deadly ways they used their aggression. They hadn't known how to have a good fight.

They were also coming to another recognition: Their problems were an "us" issue. "I always thought, right up to today," Thérèse said around this time, "that our marriage would be fixed when Bill got better. For so many years in therapy, working on myself, I never really saw myself as part of the problem. This goes back before Bill. I've done things to men—and they've accused me of being horrible and insensitive—and I never got it. Like, what are they talking about? I never understood that my rages and denunciations were any kind of problem. It didn't matter what I said or how brutal it was. Because *I* was hurt and *I* had a right. What worries me is I still feel that way! I don't know if I can change it. But I do see it. I see how awful I can be and I see how that feeds into everything that goes on between us."

At the same time, Thérèse was also beginning to appreciate the good that she brought to the relationship—her efforts to change, her honesty, her energy, her genuine caring, her sense of humor about herself—something that, for all her self-serving protests, she had never really believed in before. As she inched away from being the wounded victim, she was becoming freer to see herself in all her dimensions.

TWELVE

OWNING
UP

MANY YEARS AGO I READ A VERY BRIEF STORY IN A MAGAZINE BY A writer who had inadvertently observed a small drama on a city street. It was a scene between a boyfriend and girlfriend, perhaps seniors in high school. The boy was a deaf mute. I don't remember exactly what happened, but I see them lounging about together outside school when a disturbing event took place related to the boy's disability. Either he did something oafish or became confused, or perhaps some other youths insulted him. In any case, his girlfriend, exasperated and embarrassed before her peers, lost patience with him, dismissed him, called him an idiot—"Like, why do I waste my time with you?" His face fell. He looked crushed. The girl was immediately horrified by what she had done. She took him in her arms and kissed him, kissed him tenderly, over and over, on his ears, on his mouth, as if to say, again and again, I'm sorry, I love you, I love all of you, including the ears that can't hear, including the mouth that can't speak.

Apology (and, when necessary, the redress of grievances) is an act of giving that can be as powerful and transforming as forgiveness. Certainly we crave it as much. We want a release from our own worst feelings about ourselves; we want to feel cared about and connected again. Apology and forgiveness are indistinguishable at times, and the two can become entwined and merged in the general atmosphere of intimacy and repair. Often to apologize one must go through some kind of forgiveness first. They represent a similar letting go.

In public life, when a political or religious leader apologizes, the emotional impact can be profound. I think President Clinton in 1997 deeply affected some of the black men who had been intentionally left untreated for syphilis by the U.S. Public Health Service in the 1930s— the infamous Tuskegee experiment—by publicly apologizing for this atrocious betrayal. The health service had wanted to track the effects of syphilis in blacks and had told the ailing men, most of them illiterate sharecroppers from rural Alabama, that they merely suffered from "bad blood." They were left untreated for decades, some of them passing the disease on to their wives and, through them, to their children. Millions of dollars in reparations had already been paid by the time Clinton spoke. But the apology offered something else. In addition to being an expression of remorse for what we did, or failed to stop, or what was done in our name, it says, in effect, You are human, you are part of us, you were wronged, we see that, we care, our hearts are heavy. Armenians all over the world have been waiting for a similar statement of contrition from the government of Turkey for the genocidal slaughters of 1915. The heart needs such confirmations.

Pope John Paul II has had a similar effect on many Jews for his "confession of sins against the people of Israel" in April 2000. Unfortunately, his decision to keep the Church pristine by conceding only misdeeds by its erring "sons and daughters," his unwillingness to own up more fully and acknowledge specifically at least some of the many appalling things that were done by the Church itself, have left many others, understandably, dissatisfied. What he was up against politically in making his apology—the fears of church leaders that the good image of the Church would be besmirched—is not unlike the internal conflicts individuals face when considering whether and how much to own up regarding their personal behavior. It often takes great faith and courage to do it fully. And yet even a partial apology can represent a meaningful step.

The wish to repair by facing and acknowledging one's misdeeds has many aspects to it. There is what we want to do for those we've harmed, but there is also what we want to do for ourselves—to experience ourselves as whole again, as loving beings again, to expiate guilt, to retake our place in the human family. It represents a kind of purification. One can be at one with oneself again. In this sense, apology is related to both confession and atonement. I am reminded of an incident in the film *Gandhi,* which takes place during the riots that convulsed India around the time of independence. Hindus and Muslims were fighting each other in the streets, terrible atrocities were committed on both sides, and Gandhi was protesting with a hunger strike. A man with crazed eyes bursts in on Gandhi and throws a piece of bread on his prone body. "Here, eat, eat!" he cries. "I'm going to hell but not with your death on my soul!"

Gandhi: "Only God decides who goes to hell."

"I killed a child! I smashed his head against a wall!"

"Why?"

The man looks as if he will cry: "They killed my son, my boy." He holds his hand at the height of about a five-year-old child. "The Muslims killed my son!"

"I know a way out of hell," Gandhi says. "Find a child. A child whose mother and father have been killed. A little boy, about this high, and raise him as your own. Only be sure that he is a Muslim and that you raise him as one."

The man looks at Gandhi in stunned silence, moving quickly through disturbance, awe, and gratitude. The first part of the prescription, to adopt a boy, might have been easy enough; but it would not have coped with the man's guilt. The second part, the humbling part, the hard part—this was a Hindu fanatic, after all—would redeem him and allow him to experience himself as human again. His devotion to his adopted Muslim son and his Islamic upbringing would be a daily penance for his crime and a daily refutation of his sectarian passions, of his having succumbed to a primitive splitting between good Hindus and evil Moslems; it would be a dedication to healing a split he had helped to foster.

Archbishop Desmond Tutu of South Africa, in discussing that country's Truth and Reconciliation Commission, has said that there are two kinds of justice, retributive and restorative, and his country, initially under the leadership of Nelson Mandela, is seeking the latter. South Africa is granting amnesty to those on both sides of the struggle that brought down apartheid, who come forward to fully and publicly confess the crimes they committed under the old regime, including the most dreadful, politically motivated murders. People whose spouses or children were killed do not necessarily forgive those who show remorse—although some of them do. More important, this significant act of national communication has given people a chance to express themselves as never before, to express contrition and rage, as well as to hear apologies, to know who harmed them and why, to voice one's hatred toward those who lack remorse and even toward those who don't, and to put a more human face on those who could be conceived of before only as monsters. Regardless of how one feels about murderers and torturers going free, or other aspects of life in South Africa today, there is in this process some public movement toward healing, toward community, toward monotheism.

Needless to say, similar factors come into play in our personal lives as well. We do bad things and we don't want to fess up. But bad things have a way of turning into good things. They can be opportunities for a repair that reaffirms our love or connection and even takes it to a stronger place. But the fear of guilt and the fear of shame, not to mention the fear of retribution, can make us flee and lose that opportunity. We don't expect to meet a forgiving self in the other person.

"I Wanted to Hurt You"

Two weeks after Bill refused to accompany Thérèse for the ovarian cancer screening, they came into treatment with that event weighing on each of them. "I told her I was sorry," Bill said, sounding like a bad boy who couldn't get anywhere with his stubborn mother. His words did not convey much caring, just a kind of peevishness that his apology hadn't gotten her off his back. Thérèse started getting worked up. I interrupted.

I said, "Well, let me ask you, Bill, why didn't you go with her?" Bill gave the official line about the nightmare week he was having. I said, "If Julie said, 'Daddy, I'm scared, they think I might have cancer, they want me to come in for a cancer test,' would you have found a way?" He said "Yes" without hesitation.

"So what's it about?" More guilty silence. "How did she ask you?"

"Well, it wasn't anything like what you just said."

"What was it like?"

"She didn't make it sound that important."

"So you think you might have responded better if she let you know how much she needed you?"

"Absolutely. If she had said she was scared and really needed me there, it would have been different. But that wasn't the only thing." He shook his head as if he didn't know what the other thing could be, although I guessed from his expression he was coming into contact with one of his indicting inner voices.

"Do you think maybe you wanted to hurt Thérèse?" Bill looked confused. "Well, what was going on between you that week?"

Thérèse recalled that they had had a fight a few days earlier and that it hadn't been resolved. Bill awakened now and angrily corrected Thérèse's interpretation of what had happened. They went at it for a while. Then Bill fell silent. We established what his silence meant: that he felt hurt by her style of confrontation and was simmering. I said to him, "So you think you were hurt by her then, too?"

"Yeah."

"And you were simmering and wanting to get back at her?"

"Yeah, you're right, I was. There was no way to get through to her."

"So you think maybe you wanted to hurt her?" Bill looked at Thérèse and nodded. "Yeah, I did want to hurt you." He turned to me: "I wanted to hurt her." He looked at her again, warmly. They stared at each other for several moments. "I'm sorry, sweetheart," he said. "That was mean. I'm sorry. I really wasn't thinking at all about what you were going through."

Thérèse broke into sobs, and Bill embraced her. She pounded him on the shoulder, even as she folded into him, crying, "Why do you have to be so mean! Why do you have to be such an insensitive fuck!" while he held her and repeated gently, "I'm sorry, I'm sorry." I thought to myself, for all his limitations, he can reach her like no one else. Later on, when we returned to the subject of the take-no-prisoners quality of her aggression as well as the distant, uninviting way she'd asked him to come with her to the clinic (I don't really need you, but you can come if you like), she owned up more readily than usual. Regarding the latter, she was able to see that the offhand way in which she spoke was partly to protect herself against rejection but also, partly, a setup in which Bill would be given a new opportunity to be bad and keep the old story alive. I was certain she would not have been so receptive to this view if she had not first felt validated.

APOLOGY'S COMPLEXITIES

In his apology to Thérèse, Bill abandoned all the arguments he could have made about how it was she who really caused him to do it. He got out of his inner drama with his blaming and indicting voices and simply gave. He relinquished any effort to prove himself the more aggrieved partner or hold on to the moral high ground in their ongoing struggles. He saw the pain he had caused and went with his caring.

The effect on Thérèse was like the bursting of a dam. It was as if she had suddenly been liberated from both the hurt of how he had treated her and the punishing places that had taken over inside herself ("I'm a monster who doesn't deserve to be loved"). Guilt, self-blame, self-hatred, shame, regret may all come into play when we have been wounded, because the wounding links up with the parts of us that always stand ready to accuse. They set up a vicious internal debate, in which Thérèse, in this case, tries to fend off the badness by trying to stick it to Bill. Bill's apology freed her from all that.

We often feel, and say, that certain things are unforgivable. We doubt that we can ever get over a wrong that someone has done us. We may even define it as "unforgivable" and proclaim the unforgivableness of it far and wide. And yet a well-done apology, with a full opening of the heart—This is where I was, this is why I was there, I know I hurt you, and I feel terrible about it—melts all that, overwhelming and amazing the logic of our resentment.

A similar transformation can take hold of us regarding the person whom we do not consciously hold a grudge against but have, rather, "lost interest in." We've seen this happen when children seal themselves off from parents. It can happen with a spouse. It can happen with a friend. It's hard to imagine ever wanting to be close to him again. But let him openly speak his heart, reveal his pain, discuss the troubles or limitations that may have caused him to act as he did, show sorrow for the hurt he has caused, and our attitude is transformed. We are surprised to discover that we do care, have always cared, but that the caring switch was turned off.

Like forgiveness, apology can take many forms. It can be perfunctory and without feeling and therefore hardly an apology at all; it can be partial but still real; it can be full-hearted and transforming, bringing about a fundamental reconnection and rekindling of love. But like forgiveness, apologies born of guilty fear, a compulsive wish to please, or compliance (like Bill's original efforts) are not worth much. Apology is not about submitting or eating crow. It's not necessarily about seeking forgiveness or wanting anything from the other person—that's really a separate issue. It's about wanting to give. It's an expression of one's being and often of one's love. It is something we feel we owe to the other, but we do it as much for ourselves, out of our own desire to give.

People feel guilty and apologize all the time, but often it results from shame (what I did to you makes me look bad and I can't tolerate that), or what might be called superego guilt, which is more like fear of a higher authority (those inner voices) than genuine remorse. Apology that comes mainly from this part of ourselves is not a form of giving; it is more a form of pleading. We want to get the sense of *wrongness* off of us and so we petition the person to let us off the hook: If you forgive me, I'll get out of this state. If you forgive me, I can stop worrying that you hate me and will reject me. If I apologize, maybe you'll get off my back. "Come on, I *apologized!*" we say, getting angry that we're not getting the results we want. There is no warmth in these apologies.

As long as Bill was unconsciously and obsessively caught up in his own shame and guilt, neither one of those feelings could serve their legitimate purpose of motivating him toward a creative act of change or restitution or amends. He felt too oppressed and threatened, too caught up in an inner drama in which he was the victim to let go of the ongoing blaming match that so soured his marriage. He was like a child, head lowered, reciting what had to be recited, and taking whatever medicine was his due. Needless to say, this gave little if anything to Thérèse.

When apologies emerge from an obsessive sense of guilt or shame, there is no real change in the quality of one's inner life. The blaming and murderousness remain, only now they are being used in a different way, with ourselves at the head of the target list. The wronged person may feel lobbied, or threatened, or forced to witness a ritual self-immolation, any of which may end up feeling more like a demand or a punishment than an act of giving. To stab yourself with horrible remorse is not giving; it's just another way of withdrawing, withholding, not being there. Authentic apology is not like this. It emerges from concern. And the same concern that is aroused in us for the person we have harmed is hopefully available on our own behalf as well; there is a turn toward a more caring state.

Unfortunately, we tend to be overly sensitive to anger, or to any expression of dissatisfaction, and thus quick to feel indicted and become defensive about the very thing we need to apologize for. This may place a strong, giving apology beyond our reach. Or we are too dependent on the other person to hold on to the connectedness, so that anything less than a perfect protest—and maybe even that—throws us into a resentful state. ("You don't have to be so angry!") Either way, we don't really take in the complaint, it doesn't reach us in the caring place that needs to be activated, with the result that repair becomes impossible. The failure to reach this caring place is what accounts for so many grudging apologies. "Well, my therapist said to me that I was caring more about what everyone thought than I was about you, and he thinks I should apologize for that." This is thin.

A patient tells me that she became peevish at her husband when she came home late from work, because he hadn't washed the accumulation of dishes. Now she would have to do them, because he was helping their son with his homework and would be done too late to start another chore. When she finished in the kitchen, she was still in a snit and behaved badly toward him. We had talked many times in the past about how warmly and uncomplainingly she reacts to every act of nastiness or disregard from the men at work but that she readily loses her temper with her husband and son. She tells me that in this particular case her behavior was especially unfair because her husband had had good reasons for not doing the dishes and that he was probably catching the hell that should have gone to others. I ask if she apologized. Yes. How well? About seventy-five percent, she says. But when she repeats what she said, it sounds like a lot less. It has no warmth in it. It's a legal acknowledgment of wrongdoing: Yeah, you're right, *touché,* I give, you win this one—but no tenderness about what she had just put him through. So how is he supposed to let go and move on?

She offers a grudging apology because she's afraid that to really apologize will be an act of surrender. She can't give to him, because at such times she is too caught up in experiencing him as a parent; she is back in the perpetual family courtroom. She will be finally proved the wrong one in all of their previous battles. He will now be able to dance on her head. That is the template she brings, the imprint from a blaming family. But, in reality, to be tender and caring is to be strong—there's nothing in the nature of surrender or lowering oneself about it.

What made Bill's apology especially moving was his ability to own up. That is something people so long for from each other and find so hard to get. Owning up means getting past one's defensiveness. It means stepping out of the blaming system where one person has to be not only wrong, but the bad one, the unforgiven. When a patient says that he picks me apart in his mind and doesn't feel good about that, it is a valuable owning up that helps explain an important aspect of our relationship. Perhaps, most important, the aggression is no longer dissociated. It is owned, it is acknowledged, and, as a result, it becomes less overwhelming and controlling to the person who feels it. This is infinitely better, because when aggression is disavowed or dissociated it cannot be modulated by one's caring. It lies outside the (monotheistic) envelope. It operates on its own primitive rules of kill or be killed.

The need for owning up is a pervasive aspect of close relationships. We do things that are thoughtless, inconsiderate, selfish, mean, and we do them often in disguised ways. In almost every conflict, one or both people are covering something up, presenting themselves as cleaner than they really are, all the more so if blaming has been an important factor in their upbringing. This kind of behavior is very threatening—someone is going to be *it,* is going to get nailed to his own self-hatred and shame and feel deeply and unforgivably bad. To say, "First I made a dumb mistake and then I blamed you for it," and to say it with caring, gives a lot, even if there is no formal apology, because it frees the other person from that badness. It is also a way of stepping out of the blaming system. It suggests the security of self-love, the ability to forgive *oneself:* I can admit this; it's not pretty, but it doesn't make me an awful person; I may be nervous about rejection or punishment but still have enough faith in my own okayness and in our connection that I can reach out and take care of you.

"Maybe I don't sound so congratulatory about your achievement because I'm envious. I wish it were me." Such owning up can be more than a release for the other person. Assuming it comes from a caring place, a place where one would at least like to congratulate, it has the capacity to trigger a complementary warmth, which would imply an acceptance, a forgiveness.

Different offenses, not to mention different psychologies and different relationships, make it impossible to generalize about the essential ingredients of repair. Owning up is not always the critical thing. In some situations it may be the easy part. In 1992 a seminary newsletter reported an extraordinary confrontation, reminiscent of Corby and Nigel in Chapter 2. It is the account of a mother who met the driver who killed her daughter in a car accident: "Her eyes were red. She reached out for me. As I hugged her, I heard her saying over and over, 'I'm sorry, I'm so sorry.' I heard myself saying, 'It's okay' . . . But it wasn't okay. This woman was responsible for the death of my daughter. . . . It wasn't what Sharon, the driver, said that day that made me realize that I would never hold it against her. It was the suffering in her voice. No vindictiveness on my part could punish her more, nor give me peace, nor bring Kris back."* One can imagine how unmoved this mother would have been had Sharon apologized and acknowledged her fault but been too paranoid and self-protective to display her feelings spontaneously.

Ideally, we do not want forgiveness to be held hostage to apology. We need to forgive as much for our own sake as for the other's, and we do not want to be dependent on another person's state of mind or psy-

---

*S. Overdorf, "A Sprint to the Sunshine," *St. Mary's College Courier.* Cited by F. Clark Power in "Commentary," *Human Development,* 37 (1994): 81–85.

chological development. But contrition or remorse can help us greatly in moving forward, and without it, in certain circumstances, forgiveness may be difficult, impossible, or even pointless. In *Dead Man Walking* a nun takes it upon herself to work with a death-row inmate who has been convicted of killing two teenagers who were necking in a car near the woods. She knows he has a soul, that he suffers, that at some level he deserves to be loved. But it is only as he gives up some of his sneering tough-guy denial and reveals himself and some of his anguish that her heart (and ours) warms to him.

I've been emphasizing the importance of caring in apology, that it emerges from the connected place in us, that it often requires a letting go of the resentments and inner entanglements that might otherwise keep us locked in a bitter, adversarial state. But not every apology needs to be deeply felt. There is something to be said for apology that is done honestly, not as a submission to guilt or shame, but just because it is right. There can be something of the experimental in it. Sometimes the act of apology comes first, and then the feelings follow. Sometimes they only follow because of the goodness of what one gets back.

Just as forgiveness cannot be coerced, neither can apology or the admission of wrongdoing, at least not an apology worth having. It is hard to apologize or feel our concern when backed against the wall. A patient storms into the session furious at me for starting five minutes late. I'm selfish, only care about my needs, everything is on my schedule, I take off whenever I want to and he has to comply. Unlike Bill, who in a similar circumstance wiped me out with silence and avoidance, this patient wipes me out with denunciation. I ask if there was anyone else who he felt was selfish, only interested in what he wanted, never really there for him. His mother. He immediately sees that 80 percent of his anger relates to her, and this awareness translates into a renewed warmth toward me, a warmth that clearly has a reparative quality to it. I may have done wrong, but I'm not a demon, I don't deserve trashing. I am at once hit with a wave of relief, as if my back is no longer against the wall. And for the first time since the session began, I want to tell him how sorry I am that he felt uncared for or disrespected by me and that I truly do want to be there for him.

Dependency vs.
Doing the Right Thing

What happens when two brothers fight and each one not only expects an apology from the other but is dependent upon it? "I'm not going to apologize! Let him apologize!" Sibling relations can be very hot because of the power of the transferences going in both directions, the lifetime of failed expectations and remembered hurts, the inherent rivalry, the intimate knowledge, which provides ample opportunity to hurt in just the right way for maximum effect. They may each have some of the same bad parent in them and they are each quick to see it in the other. Often both are stuck in the same family blaming, disparaging, or retaliatory systems, out of which neither can help the other to exit. They may each have a dream of what the other should have been that they cannot let go of.

Joel runs a small but successful business with his younger brother, Tony. Joel is the nuts-and-bolts man. He gets things done, and he gets them done when they're supposed to be done. When he leaves, there's nothing left over for others to clean up. Joel resents the fact that he does more of the grunt work. He worries whenever he goes away that the business will die in Tony's hands. He also envies Tony's easy-goingness and wishes he had his charm.

Tony does the selling. He is fun, but he is disorganized and doesn't mind if others pick up after him. For his part, Tony feels as if he lives under the gun of his older brother's criticism. And he deals with it by denying that there is any truth to Joel's protests and by doing just the opposite of what he knows Joel would want. So it was not untypical that on this particular Friday evening Joel immediately started cleaning up after the last client had left, while Tony lay on the couch scrutinizing a magazine.

Joel asked Tony, in a controlled voice, if he would give him a hand clearing up. Tony said, "Sure," but didn't move. A few minutes later, Joel said more tightly, "I thought you were going to help." Tony looked up with a "Here he goes again" grimace and said, "I *will.*"

Joel was losing the battle to control his rage. "When?" he said.

Tony replied as if addressing someone with a serious characterological disorder. "Get off my back," he said. But when he got up, he merely looked at his watch and poured himself a cup of coffee. Joel was now a living mass of hatred. "What the *fuck* are you doing?"

Tony: "Will you lay off? My God, you're a crazy man."

Joel picked up a pad and hurled it at Tony, then a pencil, then anything within his reach. Tony cleared his few remaining things off the coffee table and left.

Joel was crushed and humiliated and determined to end the partnership. He knew he had behaved horribly but fought off that knowledge by keeping the blame on Tony. His wife thought he should apologize to Tony, which further infuriated him. They had the following exchange:

"So I'm the bad guy? I'm the monster?"

"You were a monster, so just apologize and get it over with."

But this only made matters worse. The sense of badness in Joel was so ferocious, had taken him to such an inner hell, that he could not allow any admission of badness. That ended the conversation till later in the weekend, when he was in a more mellow place with her and could admit that he himself hates when he behaves that way. "But he provokes it!" Joel added.

"You provoke each other," she said.

"I can't do that! I can't bear letting him think I was the problem. He's got to know what he did. I'm supposed to apologize and let him think that *I'm* the problem! I can't bear that. He provokes it! And he never owns up."

"So you're going to wait till he owns up?"

Joel imagined what this would mean. Tension, silence, a hostile coldness between him and his brother for days, and then perhaps a tortured effort to talk about what happened that would quickly lead to a mutual blaming session.

"You know what I do when I get into one of these things with my sister?" his wife said. "I imagine how I would feel if one of us died before we made up. You know, would I really want it to end like that, holding a grudge? I think, Why should we have to spend any time in that place? It just isn't worth it. I don't need to be so right. I'd rather be enjoying her."

"Enjoy Tony? I don't know."

"Oh, come on, you get a big kick out of each other."

Joel replied as if he were thinking aloud: "On the one hand, I could make up and start enjoying him again, on the other I could whack his eyeballs out. Which would be more fun?" The implication was that he would much prefer the latter. He was getting to a place where he was beginning to see what he ought to do but was still too caught up in resentment to want to give it to Tony.

"Why can't you be different, even if he's not?" Joel's wife asked.

Joel was taken by surprise and inspired by this idea. It made him realize what his struggle was all about—being who he wanted to be. His resentment, his holding out, was a child's dependency. It's like a temper tantrum: I'm never going to play with you again! I'm going to hold on forever until you make it right! But why should he let Tony's stubbornness define him this way? He saw now the infantile quality in his protest. Why couldn't he have said, "I'm pissed that you're not helping," and left it at that? This line of thinking represented a breakthrough for him.

On Monday, he apologized to Tony for going berserk. He apologized even though he felt that he had been wronged, indeed that he had been *more* wronged. It was a peace offering, and, therefore, a genuine act of caring, even though he was not fully in touch with how much he may have hurt Tony with his murderous behavior. (He still wasn't ready to admit to himself that he'd truly been awful.) But he took responsibility, didn't insist on sharing the blame, and, as a result, Tony didn't feel under the gun. He felt grateful and softened. "Hey, I'm sorry, too," he said— even though he would have been even more hard-pressed than Joel to identify anything he'd done wrong. Joel's apology liberated Tony from his badness and his blaming voices, so that he could apologize, too. Later that day they were joking and having a good time again, and Joel felt he had accomplished something important for himself.

Joel's struggle has a number of universal characteristics, some of which should perhaps be made more explicit. He is trying to come to terms with what he did. He feels thoroughly ashamed of his assault—and did from the very first moment, but not because of any feeling for Tony and the emotional pain it may have caused him. Rather, he doesn't like the way it makes him look—out of control, hysterical, weak, unmasculine. Even now, he hasn't quite achieved a healthy level of guilt: I did something really bad to Tony and I want to make things whole with him. Part of what gets in the way, of course, is the shame itself. He doesn't want to look at what he did; he just wants to forget it; and he certainly doesn't want to unwrap it, like a deformed body part, for Tony to sneer at. He is also afraid of where a confession will leave him in the perennial sibling blaming system. Having had a father who was an emotional Stalinist in the realm of repair—confess your badness and I'll retract my rage—it's easy for him to imagine his apology being a form of submission, where he will play masochist to Tony's sadist.

Now it's true that Tony could reject Joel's efforts: "I don't want your apologies, just don't do it again. Got it?" And this, again, raises the question, where does apology come from inside us? Rarely is it from just one place. We are always operating out of a mixture of motives. But does apology have to feel weak—"I was bad, I'm in your hands, don't crush me"? Could it not feel strong: "I am taking initiative, this is coming from my caring, I have something I want to give"? It strengthens us when we are able to locate—or at least to imagine—this creative, proactive self within us. That not only enhances our courage and the quality of what we do, but also helps us to stay in repair mode when we don't get the response we want. It might enable Joel, for instance, to withstand Tony's coolness and give him the space to be that way, rather than slip back into victimhood and revenge, in which case all his work is lost.

The relationship between Joel and Tony is still laced with resentment and may always be to some extent. Their forgiveness work, should they choose to pursue it, could go a long way further. This is true of virtually all relationships. There's never one reparative event that ties it all together and makes two people right with each other for all thereafter. At the moment, they are happy to have gotten over a hurdle, they are feeling good about themselves and each other and preferring to push aside remaining dissatisfactions and bitterness. If they can keep things on an even keel that way, they may decide that's good enough. It all depends on what their goals are for the relationship, how much closeness and depth they want, and whether they can accommodate each other's limits in this regard. Can Joel, for instance, tolerate Tony's resistance to knowing himself better and his allergy to talking things out?

Joel can, in any case, move forward on his own. An example of where he might go next would be to allow himself to know in a deeper way that his temper tantrums are brutal and unacceptable. Right now he still feels entitled to them. He doesn't like what he looks like all the time, but feels that blowing up and lashing out are his rightful responses to certain kinds of provocations. It will represent another level of growth for him when he can observe such behavior and be appalled, not so much by how it makes him look, but by the fact that he would let himself treat someone that way. It will be a significant development in his relationship with his brother when he can tell Tony he's sorry for having treated him in such a nasty way, that he knows it's not right and doesn't want to do it anymore. When he can further overcome his defensiveness and narcissism to the point where he can be genuinely interested in Tony's experience—What has it been like to be on the receiving end of Mr. Together, the judgmental older brother?—he will be going even further in overcoming the resentments that divide them.

THE THEFT

To find the secure place from which a potent apology can emerge is not always an easy thing. It certainly was not easy for Joel who was only able to accomplish it with his brother for the first time in his late thirties. It can be an excruciating task whenever there is so much shame that one cannot face the implications of what one has done, or where the trust is not strong enough to allow a full owning up, or, more commonly, some combination of the two. That is why apology is so often incomplete or compromised. Sheldon, a human resources manager for a Boston-area firm, relates the story of an apology that did not quite do the job it was intended to do.

> This is about a friend of mine who I felt was stealing from me, because, four or five years ago, when he was in my apartment there were certain things missing. I actually said something to him about it, and he was just like, "Sheldon, what are you saying, are you accusing me of stealing from you?" And I just backed off; I said, "I don't know, there are just things missing," and I let it drop.

His response was so vehement, I thought, This *is* ridiculous. What am I thinking? But one day, maybe six months later, I was at his home on the Cape. It was a very hot day, and I was in a sweat, and I asked him if I could borrow a T-shirt. I went upstairs. I guess I opened the wrong drawer. Because when I opened this drawer I saw all of my stuff there—shirts and sweaters that belonged to me. I can't tell you how I felt. It was a feeling that went down to my knees. All this stuff that was missing. I had had no idea what happened to it, and it was all there. Including, when I looked in another closet, the boots, the slippers. It wasn't just one thing that he might have loved; it was like a wholesale burglary.

Well, I still didn't believe it. Because I couldn't imagine that Ted would do this. He had been a lifelong friend. He was my son's godfather. I didn't even tell him what I had seen. I made an excuse to leave early, I went back to Boston, and went to my bedroom just to make *sure* that these things weren't there, or that these weren't duplicates, that he hadn't bought similar clothes. And sure enough, they were missing. I felt so awful, I felt so hurt, so betrayed, so violated. Who was I to him, anyway, if this was the way he treated me—like someone to be preyed upon? And for all these years! But I think what I minded most was his giving me the feeling that there was something wrong with me for suspecting this. That was the worst. It makes you feel that you're crazy, that your cognitive abilities have somehow failed you, when, in fact, it's just the reverse.

I still didn't know what to do. But the next week we were driving somewhere in town together and I said that I knew he had been stealing from me. And he looked at me like I was completely out of my mind. He said, "How could you *say* that, you're so paranoid when it comes to material things, how could you *dream* I could take anything from you." He had pulled this before, this *act,* and I had believed him. He had made me feel like I was really crazy. So now I was in a kind of frenzy.

So I said, "Look, I know that you've been stealing, because I opened the drawer of your bureau and I saw all my stuff there."

He said, "You opened *my* drawers!" I said, "Look, don't change the subject, and don't fuck around with me, because if you want to stay friends with me, *ever*, you're going to have to admit this to me, because otherwise there's no room for friendship at all, if you keep on lying about this. I saw all my stuff in your drawer! And I'm doubly furious because you've been mind-fucking me about this all along!"

Well, at that point he just kind of collapsed emotionally; he looked really humiliated. Finally, he admitted that he did take it, he didn't know why, he felt really humiliated about it, and couldn't discuss it with me any more that day. And I was driving, and I thought, God, I just hope I don't have an accident, because I felt so upset. Anyway, I said, "I can't drive any further." So we aborted whatever we were doing, and I said, "We've got to talk about this another time."

I really didn't know what to do. I discussed it with a few people, because this was a really valuable friendship to me. We'd been friends about twenty years. And I decided to talk about it with him. And he said that it was his envy that prompted the stealing, that he'd been very envious of me, that it was like I had so much and he had so little—which was a complete distortion, but that's how he felt. And I still didn't know quite what to do, because it was such a betrayal. Whenever I thought what he must have been feeling toward me, the hate, whatever, when he took that stuff, I wondered whether I could go on being friends. And our friendship was in jeopardy for some time after that, but I decided that if I was going to keep the friendship, which I wanted to do, that I was going to just have to put it aside and have him promise that he would never do it again, which he did. I don't think it's ever happened again, I haven't really given it much opportunity for it to happen again. But I've forgiven him for it and we've stayed friends.

I assumed from the way he spoke that much remained unresolved in Sheldon about the theft and the friendship. I asked him if he felt there was something more he needed from Ted:

I wanted him to talk more, to admit it, to tell me more about his feelings toward me, why he did it, to show some regret. And he never has. Whenever I bring it up, he gives me the feeling that I'm taunting him or hurting him. I tried to bring it up humorously, which didn't work, and seriously, which didn't work. So I think we've just put it aside.

Ownership—what were his feelings toward me that made him do it? And regret—a sorrow for having done it, a caring for the hurt that was caused. These are often the things that an injured person needs most. I asked Sheldon if he could have moved on more fully if he had felt Ted's regret.

Yes. Absolutely. But I don't think he ever felt the regret. He just didn't want to deal with it. It was too humiliating. And it was such a shock, because it's something you don't expect from someone with intelligence and professionalism and a certain station in life. I don't hold this against him; I don't hold a grudge, it's just made me wary in certain situations. I'm still not completely trusting. It still always enters my mind. But he's a wonderful friend, he would do anything for me, he loves me, I'm very, very fond of him, and we have a good friendship, but I guess this thing has never been fully resolved.

Ted's theft has to be seen as a retaliation for some perceived wrong, real or imagined; it is a primitive protest, the protest of a very young child who is imprisoned by envy and hatred and not allowed his voice. Until Ted can find his voice, speak the hatred that made him steal, but speak it in a way that protects Sheldon from the murderous, infantile wrath that is obviously at work here, he will not be able to find his own legitimacy, and he will not be able to forgive, let alone apologize. He will keep seeing his crime as too awful to contemplate and himself as too ugly to look at, much like a child who's been told to stand in the corner by a furious parent. And this will keep him feeling like Sheldon's victim.

Since this prescription is in all likelihood way beyond Ted's capacity, it is not surprising that the unhappy encounters between the two men ended in a stalemate. Unconsciously, Ted must have known that if he even got close to speaking what motivated him, he would turn into a frenzied ball of rage, and that if he got beyond that rage, he would encounter losses beyond his ability to revisit or endure.

But if we assume that what has been said of forgiveness, that it is a communication from one sinner to another, is also true of apology, and that in relationships no one is ever entirely clean, we can try to imagine an unspoken aspect of their friendship, which might help explain Ted's resentment—not just in terms of his own childhood trauma. In his perfunctory apology, Ted said he felt envious of Sheldon. Envy implies not only that I feel you have more but also a bitterness that you won't share, that you're at fault in some way for my not having. The unshared thing could be love, *joie de vivre,* self-confidence, or anything else. In other words, Ted, although he seemed to experience his envy in material terms, may feel inferior to Sheldon, may feel like an *emotional* or *characterological* Have-not alongside him, and feel all this at least in part because Sheldon is withholding something that would enable Ted to partake of the goodness and feel his equal.

We've all seen friendships like this, in which one person feels less talented, less formidable, less admired by the opposite sex, and in which the other person feeds off these feelings in some way, perhaps unconsciously, in order to bolster himself. Sheldon may, therefore, have participated in Ted's feelings of inferiority and used them to his advantage by playing the senior partner, the more together guy, the hero to Ted's sidekick. He may have acted like Ted's therapist, listening to Ted's self-doubts and encouraging him, but never giving Ted what he really needed, the inner Sheldon who had much in common with him. In this retelling of the story, the envy still emerges from Ted's inner drama. Envy—and the need to harm the object of envy—is almost certainly an issue for him that goes way beyond his relationship with Sheldon. But it is hard to imagine two men so deeply engaged for so many years without the envy of one or both of them entering into the coin of their relationship. Somehow they needed to get to this dynamic between them.

Ted did something very destructive, and with a less caring man than Sheldon it might have ended the friendship. If they can begin to speak about whatever it is that still lies unspoken between them, there may be an opportunity for a deeper repair. It would require that Ted go to a place that he doesn't want to go, may not be ready to go. For example: "I am tormented by envy and inferiority. I was never good enough for my father. I sometimes feel as if you play on that. I don't know if it's true, but when you tease me, I feel as if you're lording it over me." If Ted can hear Sheldon say, "I'm sorry, I didn't realize. Maybe I have liked being the more together one," or words to that effect, he may be able to find some relief from his torments and some legitimacy in the relationship— "It's not just me." This may free him to give Sheldon the fuller owning up, the real caring, the real regret, that Sheldon so wants. In the end, each will have had his say, and each will have had to confront himself more deeply. The friendship will be enriched by gratitude, empathy, and a new sense of equality.

Understanding and empathy are not only a critical element in forgiving others but in forgiving oneself as well. Empathy for oneself doesn't make bad behavior good, but it helps for Ted to know where it came from in him so that he doesn't feel so crippled by shame, as if he were subhuman. Sometimes this kind of knowledge precedes and helps make an apology possible (as long as it is not used as a justification). At other times it only comes after, perhaps with the help of the person to whom the apology is addressed.

As it turned out, Sheldon gave up trying to press Ted for an explanation. He could see he was getting nowhere, and, if we knew all the details, we might conclude it was the wisest thing to do. He worked on his own to try to restore his feelings for Ted; he truly wanted to forgive. But his love for Ted was compromised; he needed more than Ted could give.

THE OBSESSIVE NEED

The need for others to own up exists in everyone. We are not saints, and except for our children, to whom we may extend a special level of understanding ("That's the best he can do right now, but my love is undiminished"), we do tend to depend on mutuality in repair. But this need can be extreme in some people. It is the hook that defines their enmeshment. Growing up with a parent who could never own up can make a child preoccupied with digging out the truth of the other person's motives and feelings. "Admit it!" becomes his obsession. It's the bucking bronco that he rides through one relationship after another, and it has the capacity to keep him up at night in dialogue with the offending person: "Own up to how horrible you are. Own up! Own up!" (Because if you don't, then I am left being the horrible one. Then I cannot locate my own goodness.) A man like this may be able to forgive almost anything—genuinely, sweetly—in part because he is so grateful for the truth that frees him. The same kind of obsession can get embedded in a need for apology, regret, displays of caring.

Such obsessions need to be respected. They verge on being a fundamental need, a part of what defines the person. Not everything can be grown out of entirely or therapized away. "I need to know people deeply, especially their bad parts; that's part of who I am." But to honor an aspect of our psychology fully, we not only need to respect it, but also to work with it, to *know* it fully, to recognize how it may limit us. In that way, we can have more control over it, as opposed to the other way around. And this means that at certain junctures in our relationships with others, especially those who are not ready to own up or can't see that far into themselves or are not close enough to us to want to engage in such a trusting exchange, we need to back up and recognize that the more important need at this moment is not for the other to own up but for us to face the fact that they can't or won't own up, to deal with our dependency and try to be less trapped by it.

What Can We Expect in Return for Contrition?

Nothing is more ruinous to apology than the insistence on a quid pro quo. We sometimes expect that when we apologize, everything should then be taken care of. The person should stop being angry and stop being hurt. But apology is not always a cure. And sometimes the effect of what you did is not so easy to erase. It doesn't mean you have to be craven. But you may have to suffer the apartness longer than you might like. You may have to remember that the caring still needs to be flowing toward the person you harmed. And if you need relief from your own inner voices denouncing you for being bad, you may not find it in the person you've apologized to.

In November 1998, in Lubbock, Texas, the local police arrested Patricia Bibbs, the Hampton University women's basketball coach, her assistant, and her husband at a local Wal-Mart. The three, all black, were handcuffed and taken away in a police van after a shopper falsely accused them of trying to engage her in an illegal scam. For Bibbs, who, over fifteen years, had built up a reputation as a respected coach, this was all about dignity and humiliation. "All I could think of was having my team see me like this," she told the *New York Times*. "I saw [another] one of my assistant coaches come out to the parking lot. I just yelled at him: 'Please don't let them see me like this. Keep them away.'" On the way to the police station, her assistant, who was five months' pregnant, vomited in the squad car. The three were booked and placed in a dingy cell.

Several days later the Lubbock mayor flew to Hampton, Virginia, to apologize. But Bibbs, who according to the *Times* report listened graciously to the apology, did not feel that the matter was settled for her. Weeping, she said that the apology may have removed the nail, but the hole was still there. "I've been in education for twenty-six years. I deal with young ladies. Everybody knows that I'm a professional person. I'm a lady. I carry myself like that. . . . I have one of the best-dressed teams. Look what they've done to me. How can you get that back?" In these words, in this anguish, we hear the power this event had for her.

Nothing in the newspaper report, which included a photograph of Bibbs in tears, at a news conference, two days after the event, suggested that she was wallowing for effect or milking the situation for political purposes or enjoying an opportunity to get even. This was the pain of someone who felt disgraced. Such was the humiliation of the handcuffs, the squad car, the jail cell. Bibbs's pain may not have been comfortable for Lubbock officials who felt guilty, who tried to atone, who were worried about their town's image. It is easy to imagine that they would have liked to hug and make up, so they could forget about this travesty and move on. Bibbs's pain may not even be understandable, because they may not have the same sensitivities. But her pain needed to be respected. Which is to say sometimes even the best apology doesn't yield the desired results, at least not right away.

I think this case is a good example of the importance of not linking apology with forgiveness. No one can entirely ignore politics and image, but, ideally, the mayor flies in as an act of contrition. It is something he feels he needs to do, which he hopes will aid in Bibbs's healing, and he is pleased just to be given an audience and to be heard, so that he can perform this essential function. He doesn't expect a quid pro quo, he is not going there to beg forgiveness.

"I'm sorry, please forgive me" usually yields the desired response. The other person recognizes our humanity. But sometimes, for any number of reasons, some more legitimate than others, the person we've hurt cannot or will not let go. This can be painful for the apologizer. Some people can hold on to things interminably, so that, even if you're married and things are going fairly well, you may feel that your spouse always has you in the doghouse to some degree. In such circumstances you have to find your forgiveness elsewhere; you can't let yourself be defined by the other person's bitterness.

"My wife has never let go of the fact," Bill told me, "that twenty-five years ago, before we got married, I left her briefly for another girl. The worst part of it was that when Thérèse asked me what I liked about that girl, I told her. So here we are, three decades later, and I'm amazed, every couple of years, there it is again: 'Well, I guess I'm not as good as *Laura*.'"

Bill needed to find a way to live with that quality in Thérèse without forming complementary scar tissue of his own. Otherwise he would accede not only to her definition of him, but to the limits her resentment might place on their ability to be close and enjoy each other. Fortunately for both of them, Bill was able to do this.

Can you ever insist on being forgiven? It may seem odd, but I would say yes, especially in intimate relationships. In everyday connections, where hurting and getting hurt are a part of the way things are, and where love and repair are part of the picture, people have a right to expect forgiveness eventually and to protest if they don't get it. Bill had many times demanded that Thérèse let go of his ancient rejection of her when she brought up Laura in some peevish way. Sometimes he was peevish in response, which did nothing to bring her around and was really a way of joining her in the disconnected place. At other times he was warm, charming, teasing, which bespoke a good feeling about himself and a loving, forgiving attitude toward Thérèse in the midst of her unforgivingness. She never, officially, let go of her resentment, but at such moments it hardly mattered.

Such a situation makes a confusion of all our categories. Is Thérèse really holding a grudge if Bill can tickle her and make her come around? Is she really holding a grudge if she loves him and lives that love much of the time? Perhaps we could say that there is an island of unforgiveness in her about his leaving her long ago, and if they were to get stranded on that island, and she were to live through the self that inhabits that island, she would feel no sense of caring for him whatever, only hatred and the desire for revenge.

The question is: Which aspects of the self predominate? Is it an oil-in-water pattern or water-in-oil? When we hole up on an island of resentment and disconnection, so that the whole configuration of consciousness shifts accordingly, how willing and able are we to emerge? Do we get stuck in our bitterness, feeling that we've arrived at the true and fitting place? Or do we know that this is for now and, however strongly we feel it, it is not the last word? Do we recognize that love and hate can merge into and out of one another in astonishing ways, that there is always a more enveloping pattern and that the most enveloping pattern is love? For much of her life, Thérèse was not open to such thinking. Resentment had been her closest friend.

The fact that Bill could, for the most part, forgive himself for his affair was helpful to Thérèse. His lack of submission on that score made it harder for her to live comfortably with her wounded logic. More difficult for Bill would have been Thérèse's unwillingness to accept his apology over the clinic appointment; he needed her forgiveness much more in that case because he did feel so guilty and at risk of being overrun by his own indicting voices.

It's hard to be sure when forgiveness is psychologically feasible or warranted. We don't usually know what people are struggling with or why they cannot—or even should not—allow themselves to let go. But given what we know of Thérèse's tendency to nurse her bitterness, it would make sense for us to want to tell her, "You're wrong to hold on to your anger over the clinic. Why live this way? It's time to move on." It would certainly be wrong for Bill to keep himself in the doghouse even if she did. At a certain point, we would want him to forgive himself. He's human, which means he's going to have hateful feelings and occasionally do hateful things. Even when we've been hurtful or damaging, there has to be a limit to how long we make ourselves suffer. Turning oneself into a perpetually guilty and reduced person is no gift to anyone. For Bill, in this marriage, it would be another way of disappearing.

It would be good for Bill to challenge Thérèse: "Why don't I have any money in the bank with you? Why can't you hold on to the good things we've been to each other? Why does this have to be the defining moment?" Thérèse does need to hear this sort of thing from time to time. Who knows what might have happened if she had heard it from Mona?

THIRTEEN

CAN WE FORGIVE OUR PARENTS?

THERE IS A JOKE IN WHICH ONE ANALYST TELLS ANOTHER, "YOU know, I made the most extraordinary Freudian slip the other day. We were at my mother's for dinner and I meant to say, 'Would you please pass the salt.' But what came out was, 'Boy, did you mess up my life, you hideous old bag!' "

It is, of course, delightful to think that analysts are as ensnared in the aftereffects of childhood misery as the next person, or even more so. But it is not so much the past that haunts the analyst in the joke but the way he holds on to it. Acting out one's rage with a parent is a way of staying enmeshed. If a man repeatedly sticks the knife of rage into his mother for what she did to him when he was little, it's not the past that's killing him but the knifings themselves, whether they come out in actual encounters with the mother, in bitter complaints to others, in restaging his mother dramas with his wife, or only in his fantasies. It doesn't matter that he is the one who is holding the knife; it still wounds him. His chronic hatred is part of his pattern of enmeshment. The analyst's gross verbal slip (the impossible grossness of it is more than half the laugh) reveals not so much what he feels about his mother but that he is still living with her and controlled by her—indeed, still enthralled with her in some way.

Equally debilitating might be the various ways in which he lives with himself—judging, blaming, finding fault. If he tries to write a professional article, he may find that his imaginary reader is a disapproving female presence whom he is always trying to please. He may suffer from writer's block, have a hard time finding his voice, or agonize miserably over every word he drafts, as the witch sits on his shoulder shaking her head. This quality of wanting to please the reproachful loved one, of being controlled by her and wanting to kill her has been portrayed recently in the TV show *The Sopranos,* in the relationship between Tony, the mafioso, and the mother who torments him. Like Tony, the analyst is still in love with his mother, still holding on, still waiting for her to drop her demonic disguise and revert to the angel she must truly be.

Much of this book has been about how we hold on to our parents in this way, although, as we've seen, it can take many different forms. It raises the question: Can there be meaningful communication with a parent about the past? In many cases, yes. Especially if one has moved beyond one's own family's liabilities in communication style—to be able to differentiate, for instance, between sniping, condemning, manipulating, bullying, denouncing, etc. and reaching out. You hurt me, I want to *say* it, I want you to *hear* it, I want you to *hurt* perhaps, I want you to *care,* I want you to let me *know* you care.

I think some people are lucky to have a parent who is able to live up to this need, who is willing to reflect on how he behaved as a parent, who can hear, "You really hurt me with your temper when I was little" without becoming defensive, who can show a satisfying and believable caring now about the pain inflicted then. A very unusual parent might even be able to withstand and respond creatively to the adult child who cannot separate himself enough from his inner drama to deliver his protest in a mature way. The parent is mature enough himself to tolerate the infantile rage he could not tolerate when his child was little. Such growth, such responsiveness, such sorrow can be a gift. It can be liberating. Because part of the grown child's holding on consists of a wish for the parent to own up and for his reality to finally be acknowledged. But this kind of repair is rare and one holds out for it at the risk of one's own growth.

For the fact is there are many people who are not going to change in the face of protest. They're too locked in to whatever they are. And especially if those people are not the ones we choose but the ones we get dealt, then there has to be another approach. Of course, with parents things are always operating on more than one level. There's the solution for me and my father. But there's also what I do with the father inside me, the relationship between little me and Dad, whether it's going to remain dissociated—in which case I am going to be stuck there forever, vacillating between a bitter disconnect and naïve pursuit—or whether I'm going to enable that to evolve.

We all have to come to terms with our parents, both the good in them and the bad. It may be helpful in this respect to recognize that we are dealing with two different sets of parents—the parent we grew up with, whom we struggle with internally, and the living parent of today. The internal parents have mythic dimensions. They are the ones who adored us and wounded us, whom we idealize and demonize, and from whom we need to separate in order to be more whole. The parents of to-day, by contrast, are other people, like us, with their own feelings and struggles. We sometimes need to try as hard with them as we do with others not to see them through the prisms of the past. This does not mean that the present-day parents are any nicer than they were in the past. They may be difficult and hard to take. But they are not in charge now. The control they have is only what our psyches grant them. One aspect of separation, and of growing up, is the recognition that parents are, indeed, separate people. Another is that they may never live up to our deep wish that they do better.

Peter tells me that he doesn't believe his father will ever change. But his father has already changed, is reaching out to him and getting nowhere. Regina knows that if she tells her father, "I need a hug from you, Dad," she'll get it and it will be authentic and full of warmth. But she doesn't ask for the hug. She hates the fact that she has to ask. So in-stead of hugging her dad, she hugs her resentments. Ralph is troubled by the pathetic way his dad worships Ralph's success and wants to ride his financial coattails, but aside from being repelled by his father and want-ing to smash him, he does not consider that he has options; that he could talk to his father about his discomfort. David knows that if he in-sists that his father listen to him, his father will put aside his self-absorption and listen. But this awareness only seems to deepen David's morose feeling that his relationship with his father is hopeless. If he has to become a fuller person and bring himself and his father to a better place, then he has finally surrendered all hope that his father will become the nurturant, attentive, dynamic dad he was always supposed to be.

We see in these patterns a hesitation to grow up, to be an agent, an empowered person, a refusal not only to forgive our parents for what they're not and move on, but also a reluctance to get more for ourselves, to be a Have. It is so hard to finally abandon the dreams of the child. And, of course, as we've seen, the same applies to other relationships. The childhood stubbornness we hold on to with parents can replicate itself in almost any domain of our lives.

A child does not have the intellectual and emotional resources to step outside the orbit of his parents and tell himself: "This is not about me. My father is simply too disturbed at times to love me properly." Or: "My mother is a very troubled woman. She's bitter, she's envious, she sometimes has evil wishes toward those she loves, but I don't have to take it personally. I still know she loves me, even though she hurts me." In discussing mourning earlier in the book, I asked, What child can possibly say such things? To that I would now add, What adult can afford not to?

A man reports a dream. The dream is about his mother's face, just her face, looking at him without expression. "She seemed to have asked me a question, if things could be different between us, or was I still involved with the two wounded children. In other words, was I too caught up in the past to let myself love her? I initially assumed her face was her current face, but it was really much younger, maybe the way she looked when she was forty. It was also very plain, none of the manipulation or the hysteria or the threatening stuff she often does. It was as if I were seeing her, just her. Yesterday I had spoken to her on the phone and she was doing her hysterical thing, and I got so irritable. I do this all the time. I either start going after her in some way that I don't really want to do, or I just have to get away from her. And I feel bad about that; I'm tired of it. I guess I feel she's not going to be around that much longer, and I feel bad that I keep rejecting her. I don't want to let those things I hate about her define the relationship anymore. *I* want to define the relationship. I don't want to be so reactive. It *is* living in the past. Even though she can certainly be quite awful in the present. I want to get closer to my good feelings for her, not wanting to hurt her. That's where I want to live."

The Love That Was Always There

It is easy to be confused about one's parents. Nicola in *Life Is Sweet* gives her father the bum rap "greedy" because it is the only way she can rationalize the hole she's in. Parents and children get ripped apart by religious issues, by failed enterprises, by betrayals that stir up so much bitterness that the love and longing they have for one another are wiped from consciousness.

Sometimes we idealize one parent and demonize the other. Only when we see the faults of the one, can we appreciate the goodness of the other. When the parents are in conflict with each other and the child's loyalties are strained, unhappy divisions may result. "I always subscribed to my father's story that he was the wounded party," a friend relates. "That's the single thing that always got in the way of my relationship with my mother. Realizing that and telling her about it opened up a whole area of communication with Mom that I didn't know I could have."

My friend Anna, now in her early fifties, held a grudge against her mother that grew out of a family tragedy that had pushed her mother to the edge. Anna describes her struggle to forgive her mother and to emerge from the grip of her resentments:

> It's a slow process [she says], and I guess the way I'm forgiving her is to feel compassion for her and to be able to feel her love for me, really for the first time. It's come about partly because our [teenage] son, Adam, has been rejecting us so much. He's not able to feel our love, or so it seems. That's been awful for me, and it's really made me think.
>
> My feelings toward my mother were always so convoluted. I think I've been judging her very harshly all these years, and a lot of that had to do with my brother being mentally ill and taking up so much of her attention.
>
> Also, I didn't feel like she saw me. I felt like my father saw me, and my mother I felt like, well, I'm sorry, I mean, the thing was she was a phony about my brother! She couldn't face that there was something wrong. On the other hand, she did face it

constantly by taking him to doctors all the time. She dedicated her whole life to him and I was very jealous, and my jealousy warped however I really felt about her, and there was also my judgment that she was doing the wrong thing, that I could do a better job, and she really was missing the boat with him. She was so stupid not to understand that this was the wrong way to treat him!

I must have been so resentful. But now I really see she did the best she could, and it was valiant of her to make the effort. It was a rough time in terms of psychiatry and mental health issues, nobody even knew what to call these things. And my father was a terrible father to my brother, terrible. He had this war going on with my mother about how to treat him—to my father a military academy would have been the right solution, and that she wanted to use the psychological approach was disgusting to him. I don't remember my father ever being warm to my brother. It was terrible, it was really terrible, and so naturally my mother gravitated toward him.

But I felt robbed. I think that's what it really comes down to. And also, her idea of what a girl should be, what I should be, was so, so different from my conception of myself. I guess I do resent her. All these years of craving her love and approval. But I think what's different now is that I'm seeing that there are things to be grateful for, too, because, as I say, I realize that the love I was craving, it wasn't everything I needed it to be, but it was there, she did love me. She does love me. And that means a lot to me now.

We can hear in Anna's struggle to forgive her mother not just an effort to be fair and good, but also an effort toward reclamation, toward having a loving mother, toward being a more loving person, toward being a person who is a Have, whose resentments will not be allowed to cloud the goodness of her life. As she spoke about herself and her mother, she spontaneously elaborated to include other relationships:

Realizing that about my mother is helping me to realize that about other people, that everyone has their blind spots and their shortcomings, and it's not personal to me.

JEREMY'S FATHER was a severe alcoholic. Insensitive, irresponsible, he paid little attention to Jeremy and his brother after he and their mother divorced, he evaded child support, and he let their stepfather adopt them. Jeremy saw him rarely, idealized him, and only realized how hurtful and neglectful he had been after he got into therapy in his twenties. He recalled the painful disappointment of his father's refusal to lend him his car for the senior prom or help him out financially at a critical time in college. "It was things like that that built up a deep, angry bitterness." In his mid-twenties, Jeremy says, "I wrote him a letter, telling him what a first-class son of a bitch I thought he was and really let out all the rage. He wrote back a very defensive letter, and then we were alienated for many years." Some twenty years later, when visiting home, he tried to contact his father, but "he didn't want to see me, which hurt deeply." Jeremy finally saw his father when he was in an old-age home after a stroke. His father was affectionate and thrilled to see him. But they didn't see each other again until his father was on his deathbed many years later.

He had had another stroke and was entirely incapacitated. He was immobilized in bed, an old man, and all he could do was make this desperate guttural sound, "Auch! Auch! Auch!" like a wounded animal. I was there with my brother and my mother and my half-sister, and you could see, in this end-point of his life, where all his faculties had been taken away and he was barely able to breathe, that he knew who we were and that he was trying to say something very loving. And I think at that point I was able to let go of the anger. I just let it go. I realized that he had a variety of struggles and conflicts, not too dissimilar from myself, I suppose, and that he lived a long life, had brought four children into the world and did a half-assed job with the first two, and probably wasn't much better with the second two, only took care of them because he had this strong woman behind him. But I felt a great sense of relief and a sense of forgiveness and a sense of compassion.

Jeremy sounded as if he were choking up, and I said he must have felt a lot of love for his father.

I did. I think I did all my life feel a lot of love for him, and that's where the anger was coming from, because I felt rejected. And I also felt he loved me a lot. It was something that got badly out of whack, probably because of my ego and because of his ego.

I think that people are better able to forgive the more they have in their life, and Jeremy had a lot. Unlike his brother, whose life turned out disastrously—and who never even got to the point of getting angry at his parents, let alone forgiving them—Jeremy struggled hard to get an education, to work on himself in therapy for many years, to seek new role models, to try new things, to have exciting experiences. He emerged out of the alcoholic, violent, unschooled environment in which he had been raised to become a professional man. He married once and well, and raised two children who are adults now. He's proud of them and has good relationships with them. He is still not without his struggles, but he has a good life, and most of all, he feels loved. I asked him whether he thought that having all that he had made a difference in his capacity to forgive his father. He considered this. "If my life had turned out badly," he said, "I don't know how it would be."

ANGER SOMETIMES COMES FIRST

Attachment studies of adults have found some people who talk glowingly about parents whom they are barely connected to. Although they voice a lack of interest in intimate relationships and act as if love does not matter much to them, when talking about their parents, many of them speak in superlatives ("My mother was a saint"). But, when interviewed more closely, they not only fail to substantiate such evaluations but blithely reveal details of their upbringings that make the listener or the reader cringe. Reporting these studies in *Becoming Attached,* I wrote that one man

> called his mother "nice" but eventually revealed that she was often drunk and swore at him. When asked if that bothered him, he replied, "Not at all. That's what made me the strong person I am today. I'm not like those people at work who have to hold [each other's] hands before making a decision." Another . . . described his mother as "loving," "caring," "the world's most affectionate person," "invariably available to her children," "an institution." But pressed for details, he could not recall a single instance of his mother's warmth or nurturance. A third . . . described his mother as "excellent" and his relationship with her as "fine." Yet when probed on the point, he eventually recalled having broken his hand as a child and being too afraid to tell her.

These are dramatic examples of dissociated experience. It is the dissociation of the person who, as a child, experienced his protest as useless and his pain and frustration as too overwhelming to tolerate the continued pursuit of parental love, understanding, or reform. And so the parent was made unimportant. Contempt, hatred, self-hatred, solitary rituals, obsessions move in to seal up the wound. But the official position is one of adoration. My father used to have this quality when he talked about his mother. "Oh, she was a saint," he would say as if he were speaking about one of his heroes. "She did great deeds for the community." But he had little interest in her as an adult. What was left unspoken, unrepresented by these words—which I know my father believed—was his own little self, hidden away inside him all these years, bruised and embittered about "never getting a push," who could not understand why the passionate caring she offered the downtrodden of the Lower East Side was not directed toward him, except perhaps that he just wasn't worth it. He was left dumbfounded by the whole depriving atmosphere of his childhood, without even the words to speak it.

To be dissociated in this way from one's hatred and fury, not to mention the tenderness and hurt that lie beneath it, is to live as far away from another person—and oneself—as one can possibly get. At least the rageful child, although no more resolved, is still engaged in some way, still expressing his love and disappointment and wish for repair. So we are presented with the irony that for some people to forgive their parents, they must first hate them, even if it is not acted out, for it is in their fury that they may relocate their hurt and their love. Then, as the mourning process progresses, the grown child may come to some understanding, some empathy for the parents themselves, what their struggles were all about, the horrible distractions and limitations they labored under, inner and outer, and why, in a certain sense, they could not have been otherwise.

When one is dealing with an oppressive or insidious parent, especially one who remains so, the relationship may even be lost for some time. If and when one is able to build a bridge back to that parent, from a position of strength and clarity, and from a love that is no longer the love of a dependent and wounded child, whatever forgiveness one brings to the renewed relationship will not be a gift-shop forgiveness, but a forgiveness worth having. And even then the forgiveness might not look like something that would win a ribbon at a forgiveness fair or have the dramatic satisfaction of *King Lear*. Because it is unlikely to be complete. The grown child of an emotionally battering or depriving parent may not have the essential intactness that is so apparent in Cordelia. And he may not be dealing with a parent who has seen his sins, who feels the remorse that helps build a bridge from the other direction. So the work will be incomplete, and islands of resentment will coexist with islands of warmth and caring. The parent may be disappointed that the child still keeps his distance, that he doesn't trust, that he still harbors a bitter anger, that "there's no statute of limitations." But the child may nevertheless be exhibiting growth and courage; if he is lucky, his work will bring him back to a felt knowledge of his essential love for the parent, and this will be a great gift to both of them. Even if this love is not reclaimed until after the parent's death, it is a love worth having.

My friend Melanie was raised by parents who had survived the Nazi camps. Her childhood was suffocating. She had only one role, to heal everybody in the family and bring joy into their lives. She was like a possession, and any form of resistance to her enslavement was met with indictments. "We were like three people squeezed into a burning telephone booth, and anyone who tried to get out was the Nazi." She became the good, selfless, unquestioning caretaker of these two damaged, hungry, controlling parents. It was only in her middle adulthood, when she saw how stingy and depriving her parents had been and continued to be, saw how niggling and depriving she herself had been—toward herself, her husband, her son—that she had an awakening and pulled away.

In order to protect herself from her guilt (for refusing to continue to service her parents) and from the magnetic tug of the psychological home that formed her, in order to keep herself from sliding back into her false, compliant, sleepwalking self in which she spent much of her life, Melanie built a wall. The wall could be seen as the antithesis of forgiveness, but she needed it, and it was an important accomplishment for her, especially given the death-camp guilt she was struggling against. Without it she could never evolve into the true self from which a true forgiveness might emerge. Behind her wall she has been able to develop. She sees something unforgiving in the wall but also believes it has saved her.

Her parents, aggrieved and wounded, incapable of separation or of tolerating separation, burdened by losses that were beyond their capacity to process, could not forgive Melanie for breaking out of their orbit, for denying their story of their blameless selves, for refusing to be what they needed her to be—grateful, subservient, adoring, self-sacrificing. They denied everything, insisted they had given her a wonderful life, fought back with guilt: "After all we did for you, how could you be such an ingrate? After all we've been through, this is the child we got."

> I could not allow myself [she says] to get lulled back into that space where it was just the three of us. Remember that movie many years ago with Michael Caine, *The Ipcress File,* where they're brainwashing him and he knows that he has to not allow it to happen? He sneaks a pin to somewhere on his body, and he sticks the pin in as they're doing the brainwashing, and the pin keeps him from succumbing. For me the not-forgiveness when it comes to their lies—I can forgive for other things—

keeps me myself. It's not filled with hate, because I am still a good daughter, but I'm also good to me.

I asked her if she thought she would cry at their funerals. "I hope I can cry, because it would mean that I have enough of myself that I can give something to them."

This question would soon have immediate personal meaning to me.

KADDISH

One night my son began asking questions about my father's experience in the war. I said, "Rafe, we're going to be seeing Grandpa in a couple of days, why don't we write down all your questions and ask him." Before long we had something like thirty questions ranging from how many ships were in Dad's convoy when he sailed to the war, to whether he had friends in the service, and how many guys worked with him on his civilian job as a railway mail clerk and whether he was disappointed when the railway mail service was phased out. I thought, My dad is going to love this! I had no idea that I was flying into disappointment, although it might have been obvious to others, like my sister or stepbrother. I was the little boy all over again, rushing to my dad with the gift of Rafie's and my enthusiasm.

Before we started, I took my father aside, because he abhorred violence and warfare, and warned him that he might not like all the questions. There, in retrospect, was all the evidence I needed that, unconsciously, I knew what I was dealing with—namely, a man who would find something to disapprove of no matter how well hidden it was by goodness. I kept this awareness of who my dad was unconscious—at least in the context of my reaching out to him; I saw it clearly at other times—because I could not accept that it applied to me. It couldn't be true, mustn't be true, that this character trait was so strong it could make him rejecting of me. I would not accept that, despite a lifetime of evidence and a lifetime of my own bitter complaints against him. I would not let it interfere with my futile pursuit of him. And the pursuit, too, was unconscious. I never talked to myself about it. It was a perfect example of how unprocessed trauma leaves us captive to a repetitive and virtually doomed pattern of behavior.

Looking back now it is obvious that I have remembered every slight I have felt from my father, as well as every compliment he ever gave me. And yet I had never said to myself, "Look at how much he means to you, how hurt you are, and how starved you feel for his approval." In this regard, I was still a child. I had never let myself focus on how much it hurt that my dad didn't respond to me with enthusiasm, that he criticized me, that he brushed me off. All that was buried, buried without funeral, without grieving, just buried. Which means, of course, not buried. It lived in me through my contempt, my explosions, my turning the tables on him—"I don't want you, you don't mean that much to me, it's of no particular consequence what does or doesn't happen between us." It lived on through my identification with him. And it lived on in the way I relived it in repetition with others. Meanwhile, I kept making advances, struggling to find the perfect gift for the man who rejects every gift, and then being bitterly disappointed by his indifference or growls of displeasure. Never did I remotely think of myself as a man who was still trying to please his father. Nor did I let myself know the other truth: that I loved him despite his rejections. I became focused on his inadequacies: "What was there to love?" This was the form my rage and disappointment took, especially as a young person. It reduced my capacity to recognize myself as a loving person.

Once, years ago, I gave him a book I found on a remainder table. I told him it only cost fifty cents. He was delighted by the book and read the whole thing. Afterwards, when I wanted to buy him a book, I would tell him I bought it for myself but didn't have time to read it now, and would he be interested in borrowing it? That worked, too. But in all this, I never acknowledged to myself the feelings behind the reaching out. That I was still in love and still courting.

In the years before he died I could see that I had made some gains in my inner relationship with him. I had a dream in which he showed his caring for me. I felt grateful. I found myself able to gain something through identifying with positive qualities in him that I never before focused on, even though in some dim way I had seen them. I pulled back further from my overreacting with him and found, at times, that we could connect in ways that surprised and gratified me.

The day came, and Rafie asked his questions, and Dad responded, and it was good enough. My father was in a good mood that day and my sister commented later on how ungrumpy he was. When the questions came, he answered them as best he could, but he was not delighted or brimming with enthusiasm or appreciation. I felt some unconscious disappointment, but I counted it a success anyway.

I called him a few days later to make contact and to ask how he enjoyed Rafie's interview. I was the naïve supplicant again: "Let's *kvell**, Dad. Let's talk about how nice that was!" But I heard in his voice that he didn't think it was so nice. Why? All those questions about violence. I said, "Dad, if you check out a thousand six-year-old boys you'll find that 950 of them have the same interests. That's what they want to talk about—guns, tanks, soldiers, Indians, pirates, explosions." "But I feel you encourage it," he said. He said it nicely, no trace of the dismissing tone I was accustomed to, and we had an unusually positive exchange. I said, "Dad, the only reason I encouraged him to ask these questions is because I want him to have a connection with you." He told me he felt it was impossible for him to be connected to Rafie. He was too old. He couldn't do any of the things a grandfather should be able to do with a grandson, have a catch, etc. "You know how old I was when he was born? *Eighty years old,* Bobby." This was a reprimand to me. "This should have happened ten, twenty years ago." I had no idea he was so disappointed. I said, "Yeah, that's the way it should have been, but let's make the best of what we have." He said, "Okay." It was the furthest we'd ever gone. He then bitterly reminded me that the day before was my stepmother Evelyn's birthday and I hadn't called.

It wasn't long after this incident with Rafie that my father took ill. I called him in the hospital and told him I would be coming down the next day. "Don't bother, Bobby." I said, "Well, I'd like to." "What do you need to come for?" he growled. I started tumbling into the small self I often experienced with him. I forged forward with an explanation. I said

---

*Yiddish: Let's embrace and indulge ourselves in the enjoyment of this goodness.

I wanted to see him, wanted to see how he was. . . . "If you want to know anything about how I am, you can call Evelyn," he said. "You don't have to . . ." and so it went.

I arrived at the hospital on a Wednesday afternoon. He was feeling good, totally relieved of the symptoms that had brought him in, and in unusually high spirits. He told every staff person about my previous books and how good they were, something he had not done before in my presence. Later on, we were alone in the room and he asked me to roll his table closer to the bed. A wheel hit one of his slippers and the table momentarily lurched. He snapped at me as if I were an annoying incompetent, and I felt myself begin to feel as if it were so. Later yet, sitting on the side of his bed I told him that when he talked to me that way, I felt hurt and unloved. He was surprised—why should love enter into it? I talked a little bit about love, a word that never came up much in our family when I was growing up, and how it shows up in everything. He became defensive and reminded me of the money he lent me years before when I was a young man working on my second book, speaking in a tone that a father might use with a son who was a total fuck-up, which, amazingly, is what I instantly felt like. In his own, indicting, internal court of law, he was on trial for not being a good father, and was angrily bringing forth evidence, even though all I wanted was his love at that moment. I was able to stay an adult and turn the conversation elsewhere. Twice, I told him emphatically that I loved him. He didn't say much in return but he beamed and kissed me twice when I left, a rare display of exuberance.

A month later he was in the hospital again. Speaking with Evelyn on the phone, I asked her if he had said anything to her about the conversation he and I had had about love. "No," she said, "but that night, he told me that he loved me, which he never does." I thought at once, I want him to say it to *me!* I told Ev how much it had hurt never to have heard that from him, how much I wanted that all my life. This alone, this wanting, was a breakthrough. I really felt it now. I was choked up. I told her I never even knew how much I wanted it. I said, "You don't want to feel it. It's easier just to be angry." She reassured me of how much he loved me, of recently finding a treasure trove of stuff related to me going back to day one. "And he is so proud of you." She spoke about what a good heart he has, "if only he didn't have that personality!" All my life I had heard this about his love for me and it meant little because it was not conveyed in the way he spoke to me. We talked about his father who never spoke to him, about his saintly mother who somehow managed to raise five incredibly depressed or disturbed children, stuff I had always known, always used to explain why my father was the way he was, but now I felt it in a different way, in a caring way, caring for him.

After talking to Ev, I called him. I asked him if he had enough to read. I wanted to know if he'd be interested in the Klemperer diary (of a free Jew's life in Nazi Germany). He snarled, No, no books, don't get him any books. It was not a charming snarl, not curmudgeonly, there was nothing endearing about it, no hidden tone of "I love you but can't admit it." It felt cold, irritable, and rejecting.

Again, I felt my connection to him slipping away; or, maybe, to more exact, I felt my connection to my mature self, my loving self, slipping away. I could feel myself morphing into the resentful, wounded boy. I was losing the desire to visit him, the feeling that it mattered at all.

I told him I would be coming down in the afternoon. Again, he gruffly told me not to come. There's no need, I could find out whatever I needed to know about his platelet count, etc., by calling and speaking to him or Ev. There was an incensed quality to his voice, as if the thought of my coming angered him, like a new book or another gift. Recalling now that he'd only accept a book if it was something I possessed already, not a new purchase, not a real gift, I told him, It's no big problem to come, I take the train, I do work, I entertain myself that way, and he responded, "Well, take the train to Philadelphia and back, get your work done, and don't bother stopping here." It was everything I could do not to want to kill him myself—"Fine! Forget it!" as my son might say—not to get derailed by his perpetual sourness, which, in fact, had very little, if anything to do with me. I told him I would come. He accepted it with a resigned tone.

I sat with him and Evelyn in the hospital room for part of the afternoon, talking casually. My father could not lift his head and participated only fitfully. There was no trace of displeasure over my being there; that would not have been like him. Now that I was there, he was pleased. As time went on, I got into a tormented struggle with myself. He might be close to death. I could leave well enough alone—accept as final memories the way he beamed at me the previous time, the two kisses he gave me, telling Ev he loved her; it all had a poetic fullness to it. If he died now, I could feel satisfied that we had come to a good place. Besides, he was weak, and I didn't want to push him. On the other hand, I wanted to hear him say "I love you."

I went out in the hall and started pacing. I wasn't sure I even knew what I wanted or why I wanted it or whether it mattered. At last, I waved to Evelyn and asked her to leave me alone with him.

Sitting beside his bed again, I asked my father if he remembered our conversation about love from the previous visit. No, he said, he remembered nothing, nothing. I said, "Well, I thought afterwards that I would like to hear you tell me that you love me."

"I never told you?"

"No."

"Not even when you were little?"

"No."

"What about your mother?"

"Well, I don't remember, but she didn't say it that much either."

He became indignant. "Imagine that! And from a mother!"

Before I knew it, he was on a roll. I stopped him by saying, "Let's not talk about Mom." And then, when he stopped, I said, "I still want to hear it."

He reached out his hand to me and cradled my chin. I let him have it, and he held it like that while he spoke. He said, very tenderly, "I love you, you're my little boy"—then he caught himself—"Look at you! A little boy!"—I was crying—"And I love your little boy, too." He looked directly into my eyes as he spoke, and there was no doubt that he meant and felt every word. After a bit, I stopped weeping, and he took his hand from my face and put it on the railing. I rested my hand on top, holding his. We kept it like that for some time.

He could see how much his words meant to me. I told him I was happy he loved Rafie, too. He smiled. Before long, he wanted to get back to my mother and her purported sins. I said, "Let's not." Later, he started defending himself again, more softly this time, by citing his past deeds as a father. I felt sad that he had to enumerate and told him I knew he had been a good father.

Walking back to the station, choked up, I was struck by the thought that his love had always been there, perhaps for the asking. I thought, How sad, all these years without this. "Why did he have to be so awful!" And how sad for him. When you're the child, you feel so full of hurt and anger, and you don't think how much the parent may be hurting, too. But as I thought about this more in the coming weeks, I realized it was not the same for him. He was too cut off. He did not suffer over these things in the same way I did.

Of course, he loved me. But that love had not been there for the asking. I was lucky at the end, with much effort on my part and the shadow of death hanging over him, that he was able to get access to it. But if he bragged about me to others, the me he bragged about didn't exist when I was present. The me he spoke to, like so much else in his life, was, much of the time, an annoyance and a disappointment. I don't think he ever asked himself, How can I express the loving side of me, rather than the constant grumpiness and disapproval?

Despite this, I loved him and always had. I saw that now. I had spent a lifetime reaching out. I worked so hard with him and gave him so much and never credited myself because he didn't credit me. His gift to me in the end was helping me to see the truth of that lovingness in me. That love and my ability to feel it was my forgiveness. It was not complete, it is still a work in progress, but it has remained of huge and lasting importance to me.

To mourn is to love again, even if it only happens in pieces. I think it is one of the primary goals of psychotherapy, to help us get past our defenses and reexperience the world of feeling we have left behind. But to reexperience the love is also to reexperience the agony of hurt and loss. These threads of feeling are bound together.

In the months after my father's death I noticed how frequently my thoughts turned to him. Something in the news about World War II, political turmoil in the former U.S.S.R., the death of Joe DiMaggio—it seemed that almost every day a topic arose that made me think, Oh, here's something to talk to Dad about, something that will please him to talk about, make it possible to share and enjoy each other. Now that he was dead, I realized that these thoughts had been coming to me like this, almost daily, for much of my adult life, followed by efforts that typically got me little. "Why did he have to be so awful?" I thought again, but with barely any bitterness, mostly sadness and love.

FOURTEEN

LETTING
GO

IN PEDRO ALMODOVAR'S FILM *ALL ABOUT MY MOTHER*, MANUELA loses her teenage son in a car accident. A former actress living on the margins, now with a respectable, middle-class life, she had come to Madrid pregnant with him, seventeen years earlier, fleeing Barcelona and her outrageously self-centered lover, Antonio, who had become a transvestite. During her time in Madrid she had not communicated with Antonio, who never learned he had a son.

The bulk of the story takes place in Barcelona, to which Manuela now returns. She seeks out and, by a curious twist of fate, ends up working for—and becoming very close to—the famous actress whose car had hit and killed her son. She also renews her friendship with Agrada, a transvestite prostitute, who is still a friend of Antonio's. Agrada introduces Manuela to a pretty young nun who works with the down and out. The nun turns out to be pregnant. Manuela takes her in because she cannot tolerate living with her parents in her current state. Manuela soon discovers, much to her horror and fury, that the father of the unborn child is none other than Antonio himself, now dying of AIDS but with his narcissistic charm intact. He has passed along the virus to the mother, who soon dies in childbirth, and to the baby. Manuela becomes the mother of this baby.

In a memorable scene, Manuela meets Antonio in a café in order to introduce him to his new son. He is immensely grateful and tenderly takes the baby from her. She hands it to him lovingly. Given what she's been through and what he's done, it is surprising and affecting to see her filled with pleasure at the opportunity to give Antonio what she had withheld before.

The mother of the dead girl happens to pass by and witnesses this loving moment. She is filled with horror and disgust that this drag-queen monster who killed her daughter is touching her grandchild who carries his virus. We recognize ourselves in the grandmother's grim gaze. She represents hurt, rage, the wish for revenge—all legitimate, all justi-fied. As I watched the film, I identified more easily with the grand-mother's reaction than Manuela's. I think most people would.

And yet we would not forswear that loving moment. As Manuela gently hands Antonio this new baby she loves, *their* baby strangely, she shines with affection for baby and father, as Antonio delicately, adoringly receives him. This is at least as right, this capacity of Manuela to locate the goodness and to live in it.

All About My Mother is a broadly forgiving film. No one is a pariah, even if he's a son of a bitch, no one is judged, no matter how neurotic or self-destructive, no one lies outside the film's embrace. Everyone is hu-man, everyone has a right to be. We repeatedly find Manuela connect-ing deeply and satisfyingly with people she might just as easily hold a grudge against or look down upon. The film seems to say, as does for-giveness itself, that we can have each other; that we can feel good instead of bad; that bad things, even very bad things, do not have to entomb us in a resentful place. More broadly, we can be a Have, we can let ourselves have. Life can be full despite its imperfections, despite our losses and wounds, despite all the ways in which people and events disappoint us.

But sometimes in order to have, we also have to let go. What exactly we may need to let go of will differ at different junctures in our lives. It may be related to our wish that the world live up to our expectations, our resentments about what we don't have, the urge to blame, the crazy idea that we have to get even and of the lust to do so, our insistence on the primacy of our inner drama and of fitting others into it, our need to have things only one way or no way at all.

Letting go is Orual on the mountainside as she climbs to find her sister in *Till We Have Faces,* shocking her bitter, deprived self with the thought, "Why should your heart not dance?" It is Thérèse seeing that her struggles with Bill are a "we" issue, not a "him" issue. It is Bill letting go of his dread of being labeled bad in order to see the pain he caused Thérèse and apologize to her. It's Joel's willingness to relinquish his life-long grievances against his brother, Tony, and his conviction that Tony was more in the wrong in order to do the good, reparative thing (apologize) and, in the process, become more of a Have ("I want to enjoy my brother").

In his decision to apologize to Tony, Joel presents a portrait of separation in progress. We don't have to like everything about the person we love. We don't have to have perfect mutuality in repair. We don't have to be there for each other every minute or in just the right way. We don't always have to like the same things as the people we love. We don't have to be so thrown off by the qualities in them we dislike. We can give them the space to be. And we, too, can have the space to be. This theme of separation without detachment is a fundamental aspect of letting go, and it runs through all our relationships, especially our closest ones. It was a big feature of my work with Bill—helping him to see that he could stand back from Thérèse's drama-queen routine without having to stand back from Thérèse herself and drift out of the relationship. If Thérèse cannot separate in some way, if she is harping that Bill loves golf more than her and that he's a selfish monster for going out to play when she wants him to go antiquing with her, he can still go play, still enjoy himself, know it's Thérèse being Thérèse, be angry at her without joining her in the drama, and, most important, retain his warmth, not have to kill her off inside himself in order to have his freedom.

Daniel, an unmarried man in his seventies, has a dream. The main thing he remembers is that cords are reaching out from himself into the world and connecting to various people in his life, and, with this image, the feeling that somehow all his longings will be taken care of and he will be filled up. I suggest that they sound like umbilical cords. You are a man of great passions and great appetites, I say, tremendous emotional longings, you want so much from people, and yet people might think, Oh, there's Daniel the hermit.

When Daniel enters the world of relationships, he finds the atmosphere teeming with shoulds, like a swarm of locusts. All he can think about is what he should do with this person or that person—show concern, take care of, don't hurt. This was the swarm of locusts he grew up in that emanated from his adolescent, self-involved mother—Please me, Don't embarrass me, Always serve me—and his reproachful, drill-sergeant father. He needs desperately to connect with people. But facing those locusts is exhausting and debilitating. To be connected means to be intruded upon and controlled, to have no way out if he wants to leave, to have no right to ever put himself first. It is so much easier to retreat into his world of dreams, of brilliant intellectual visions, of painful longings for the one person who will be so attuned to him and so caring that she will wave the locusts away, like Moses parting the waters, and make it all come out right.

For Daniel, there's no letting go, no possibility of connection, if he does not respect that swarm and the barrier to intimacy it creates. Who can blame him for his solitary solutions or his utopian dreams? And yet there is some action that he is able to take that he doesn't take. There is some way in which he colludes in his imprisonment, often I think by waving away the possibility of a small connection, something less than umbilical, that would give him a little chunk of gratification.

Daniel confessed to me once that, at times, he feels something stirring in him, a feeling that might connect him to me or the other people he carefully keeps at bay. But the feelings don't feel strong enough; they feel diffuse and vague, and he dismisses them. To allow himself such imperfect little feelings and to act on them would be to let go, at least for the moment, of his wish that every affectional event be transcendent. It would represent a move away from the angry baby in him—determined to have the resplendent breast or nothing at all—and toward his empowered self. I refer to his treating me like a functionary with whom there can be no shared feelings, no moments of connectedness, no intimacies. What good am I when what he needs is a perfect connection with a perfect woman?

Daniel chews this over. "Is it like saying," he asks, "that the more ordinary food you eat, the less you crave vodka and chocolate?" I thought that a poignant prescription, especially coming from a former alcoholic, for how to grow beyond, to gradually let go of, those nearly impossible to fulfill, leftover longings from our traumatic past.

FERRETING OUT THE GOOD

Joyce and I are in the final months of our work together. She is moving to another city. We are trying to get to her feelings about parting. She doesn't want to be a fool and get all weepy and sentimental about me. She knows that an inner voice will tell her after she is gone that I never cared and that she'll feel ridiculous. She describes for the first time how vigilant she is with friends. If they come to town and don't call, if they don't call in general, if they don't reach out, they're not good friends. Joyce attributes this to insecurity, but I say it's more than that, it's active paranoia, ferreting out opportunities for disconnection and resentment. I tell her she needs to be more active in ferreting out the positive. For instance: She says she has a hard time holding on to my caring partly because I don't use the words, I never tell her flat out how much she means to me, it comes through only in nonverbal ways. I say, Well, maybe in that case, she needs to get better at holding on to the nonverbal.

I have feelings about Joyce's negativity—her distance, her emotional stinginess at such moments. I ask her how she perceives my feelings toward her: Am I embracing? A lot of powerful things have happened between us in the last two months. Has she been there? I've been there. There's passion and protest in my voice. She hears it and says I sound upset. Yes, I say, I guess I am. She's crying now: Of course, she knows I care, and she admits for the first time that she has a mantra she says to herself between sessions when we're apart: "No, you must remember, he doesn't care, he doesn't care, he doesn't care."

It's ironic that the very thing that would enable us to feel better about the ways in which our parents failed us—namely, getting more gratification as adults—is often barred by the resentments that bind us to our losses. Besides, as we've said, love hurts, and the mantra protects us from it.

Ferreting out the good can be quite difficult to come to, at least in regard to those frightened, resentful, enmeshed spaces within us where the habit of seeking and building on goodness does not already exist. Some people, dimly aware of their own negativity and unable to tolerate it, put on a mask of kindness and generosity that is loaded with denial. But to ferret out the good with full feeling of the inner forces one is struggling against, that is a true push toward growth.

That is also, in a way, the essence of agency, of recognizing that we have power, that we make our lives happen, that we can be a force for bringing a relationship to a better place. It is not just up to the other person—to change, to stop being bad—even if he is a parent, even if he is a boss, even if he is unreasonable, even if the merest gleam in his eye ignites our inner drama with all its feelings of persecution, shame, hatred, rage, and helplessness. We don't have to enter the equation from any of those places, like prisoners bracing ourselves for how the warden is going to behave and making plans to get even. We have alternatives.

Ferreting out the good can be applied to our assessment of ourselves. Daniel has spent a lifetime searching for perfection in love and has been disappointed. He can't tolerate his girlfriend's not being attuned to him in just the right way. He is tormented by this side of himself, that he can't let a woman be imperfect, and doesn't know if he'll ever get beyond it. Over time, I pose a series of questions to him:

Daniel, what about you? Is there room for you to be imperfect? Are you able to say, This is me, I'm nuts, I want to soar, I need perfection? Not in an entitled way, like the world has to bend to your will, but can you accept that that's who you are? You're a man who wants too much. You're always reaching for the paradise of merger experience. When you're with Susan, you want to be like a baby at the breast. But can you also add this: that you can survive not getting it all the time, that even if you can't tolerate Susan's not responding to your joke the way you want her to, that you'll eventually come around and the relationship will continue. That you can have your protest: Darn it, Susan, I want you to pay more attention to me! Or, I want you to go into treatment and do something about your depression. That you can have your rage: The bitch didn't get my joke! She dropped me on the floor again! Right in the middle of my feed! That you can even have your hopelessness: Life is awful and this will never work out! But can you also have another part, that remains attached, that knows you're not only a baby, that you will find a way to stay alive and stay connected?

I was feeling strongly that if Daniel were able to be on better terms with his narcissism this way—if he could grant himself some toleration, the right to be who he is—he would not be so controlled by it.

I once asked Daniel what kind of parent he was to himself. There is something dry about him, his clothes often look as if they were grabbed off the rack, I imagine his apartment to be very utilitarian, piled high with books, and few amenities, little to cherish or to please the eye. Is he a good parent to himself? "Sure," he says. "I take good care of myself, I dress myself, I eat—that's all there is." I say, "Well, that's all there was to what you got." He knows what I'm referring to: "Oh, right!" he says. "Except also, Behave! Do as you're told! Don't make a fuss! Button that button!" He could have added, "And be what I need you to be rather than what you need to be in order to become who you are."

I remind him of his six-year-old nephew, the one unencumbered love in his life. With this boy, uniquely with this boy, he is tolerant, encouraging, hugely empathic, demonstrative. He glows now and tells me a touching story about the two of them. I ask if he could imagine being that kind of parent to himself. He finds this a shocking thought. To be so tolerant, so warm, so allowing for mistakes. To not send himself to Siberia for the first wrong move. In the gulag of the unforgiven, it is often we ourselves who suffer the harshest sentences.

SHAMEFUL AND DISLIKED ASPECTS OF THE SELF

Earlier, in discussing mourning, I referred to the child's need for another point of view. It is critical for him, when dealing with his hurts and losses, to be wrapped in the caring presence of another person, which enables him to overcome his sense of badness and replace it with compassion. The same is true for adults. We need a warm embrace to help us deal with our hurts, including those we inflict on ourselves.

Every time we go to someone we trust with an obsessive feeling of shame, guilt, or regret and get it worked out, or at least worked on, so that it loses some of its tyrannical grip, we are engaged in a healing intimacy. It takes courage to do this. It runs counter to our defensive impulses. It represents the ultimate collapse of the need to justify, to blame, to get even. For we are letting another part of us speak, the part that is in doubt, the part that believes we may be wrong, so wrong that our very worth is thrown into question. But unless that part can be allowed to speak, there can be no healing.

In processing our immediate sadness and hurts by opening ourselves to another, we are inevitably processing at a deeper level as well; we are mourning an aspect of our relationship with a parental figure—in which we felt bad or inadequate and desperately needed him to reaffirm our goodness. It is an aspect of separation, a way of letting go, for the disapproving internalized parent is no longer the arbiter of how we see ourselves. We are allowing another voice to matter.

The caring presence and the other point of view are equally important in dealing with what I've been calling paranoia. It helps us assess: How much have I been wronged? And how much is my inner drama coloring my perceptions? Our paranoia is so compelling that even the smartest person finds it hard to stand back and evaluate it accurately on his own. We need help. People have always needed help. Therapy can certainly help. I think of it as perhaps an essential nutrient of modern life. But help of this sort is, ideally, something we want to make a part of our civilian lives as well. So that Thérèse can go to Bill and say, "I feel like a horrible mother," and know that she will get a caring, honest perspective, one that will not whitewash her failings, that will indeed help her see where she's gone astray, but do so in a loving context. In Bill's embrace, Thérèse learns again that to err, even in horrible ways, is human, that there is almost always room for repair, that the bad things we do do not wipe out our goodness or—in most cases—cause us to lose irretrievably the love of those who care about us.

To take a more forgiving stance toward ourselves is to let go of the idea of erasing the old or becoming a completely different sort of person. It's about managing and using who we are in a different way. The paranoia doesn't go away, certainly not all at once, but we learn to take it into account, to contain it better, to put it on the table, at times, in a more open manner. As we come to a place where we are able to respect our paranoia but not indulge it, we begin to have different experiences, experiences that are less likely to reinforce our sense of victimhood. We feel our way toward new boundaries, toward using our anger and hurts in different ways, with the added ingredients of awareness and concern. "I see what I do, I see how it can hurt myself and others, and I care about it. I don't like being that way." Such awareness, such concern, creates its own mutation. It is central to the forgiving self.

Change that is not allied with a caring for disliked aspects of the self cannot be trusted. In our day, with our awareness of psychology, with our intense attention to relationships, and a utopian assumption that people are perfectible and that we strivers after mental health can overcome all our deficits, the truth that to be human is to have to struggle to some extent with our infantileness and primitivity is easily obscured and forgotten. But it doesn't make us feel better about ourselves.

Religion can help motivate a genuine forgiveness of oneself and others. The relationship to a forgiving God can help carry on the work of a relationship with a forgiving parent as well as make up for some of its lapses. But religion can also, at times, reinforce a split view of the moral universe. One of the problems for some people who experience a sudden religious conversion is that their negativity may be forcefully suppressed. It is not transformed, it is not mitigated. It is not processed. They do not move from a black-and-white universe to monotheism. Rather there is a move from black to white, from paranoia and hatred, to idealization. The radiant self faces a radiant world. Rancor is eradicated, leaving behind a goodness and toleration that cannot be sustained because it is strained through denial. This psychic state is inherently unstable. Denial is not only infuriating to others, it leaves one with the sense of harboring a horrible person within. The approved behavior, the sanctified self, eventually comes to feel false and burdensome, even explosive.

Some people cope with their disavowed negativity by making relationships in general less important. They don't allow themselves to be touched; they are communing exclusively with the divine. In extreme cases the radiant universe can only be sustained by the dictatorial control of others or isolation within a like-minded group. The bad stuff may now be projected outward, onto the unenlightened, who lose their status as similar human beings and may even be seen as evil.

The pressure to suppress negative emotions is an inevitable aspect of social and family life. There's no way around that. People come into therapy who are suffering from being too "good," falsely good, unable to be selfish, aggressive, envious, greedy, angry, or hating. They desperately need to get on better terms with this side of themselves, even if their wish is to sever it.

CAN WE FORGIVE OURSELVES?

A sense of shame and doubts about our own goodness are common threads of our lives. We are ready to believe that our negative emotions invalidate everything else. We test ourselves with difficult choices. Which door would we choose: the lady or the tiger? Well, there is probably a part of us that on a bad day would rather see our lover devoured than safe in another's arms. What if we were dying? Would we urge our young spouse to continue on, to have a happy life, to find someone new to love? Maybe not. Perhaps the only thing we can imagine—at least for now—is the wish that our spouse join us in death or wear black forever. Both of these tormented choices, the tiger and the tomb, say something about our unhealed sense of loss and deprivation. But does having that in us make us so bad? Is it really all there is? And, as we get more and feel less deprived, are we not more generous as well?

My patient, Stan, who envies and resents what he believes I have and he doesn't, still wishes I would break my ankle playing tennis. But he's come to know that that wish is a part of a bigger picture in which he cares about me—a great deal really—and can be quite tender and protective at times. He sees the ups and downs of his envy and his negative wishes toward me as a barometer of how well he is doing in his own life. Being able to let me in on the places his envy goes has brought us closer together and given him a greater sense of stability about himself. "I feel like I'm hating you today" does not have to be a barrier; it can be a source of connection. Stan is becoming more comfortable with the awareness that to be in a relationship, any relationship, is to have ambivalent feelings. The more he can accept that, the easier it is for him to also recognize and value his very real caring.

As Thérèse moves away from her indicting stance toward the world of others and looks at herself more squarely, she feels acutely that she is too sensitive, hypersensitive, that she feels "rejected at the drop of a hat!" I ask her, can she be hypersensitive? Is this allowable? No, she says, nobody will like me. It makes her feel worthless and disgusting. She finds herself trying to bury it, to be tolerant, agreeable, unruffled. But then she's living through a false self and always on the verge of explosion. I see it in our sessions, this poignant, childlike effort to be good at the expense of her feelings, while the poison pools beneath the surface, undiluted by mature thoughts.

So, look, you're hypersensitive, I say. You feel horribly rejected and want to fly at Bill, all teeth and nails, and rip him to shreds. Can she experience this without acting it out? Can she let him know what she's feeling, what she's going through, even the murderous part, without the implication of blame? She has to be able to accept this part of herself, her sensitivity and its murderous corollary, at least enough to be able to talk about it, to let people see it and her in all her supposed disgustingness, because it's the lack of acceptance, the shame, that puts the corollary into action, that causes her to denounce Bill and make him the problem. To reveal it, on the other hand, is to open herself to the possibility of caring and through that caring a deeper self-acceptance.

My patient Pat (Chapter 6), who believes she is too ugly and unlovable for any man to want, sits in a restaurant with Nick, whom she's been dating for several months. He flirts mildly with the waitress while ordering. She is flooded with the agony of rejection. She knows with certainty that he wants to dump her for the waitress. No death would be too painful for him. She turns cold and indicting for the rest of the weekend.

When Pat and I meet and I tell her what I think, she shakes her head and says, "I have to stop being so paranoid." It's a positive step for her. After a prolonged resistance, she is finally able to see what she is doing and want to stop it. But this is also a place where she gets stuck, because she wants to erase all traces of dysfunctional feeling; she can't accept any "badness" in herself. I urge Pat to recognize that she may not be able to stop being "paranoid" and that she doesn't have to indict herself for that. But she should at least know she's paranoid and struggle with it. You can hate him and want to dismember him, you can even tell him about it. But if you know the intensity comes from you, that it's largely your problem, it doesn't have to be destructive. It can even be a source of connection.

I imagine April seeing her best friend Roseanne with a new guy and thinking to herself, Wow, that's a great guy! And then maybe experiencing an envious, Hmm, *I* could go for that guy. And then maybe the depressive, victimized, What a lousy life I have; I'll never have a guy. And perhaps even, Maybe Roseanne will die and I'll inherit the guy! To have such thoughts is human, especially for someone who is without a mate, who fears her best friend may be on the verge of scoring and leaving her behind, who has suffered from emotional deprivation growing up. But such feelings don't have to define April, especially if she is aware that she has a tendency to envy and has been able to come to some acceptance of it. Yes, that's me, that's where I go, but it's not all there is to me, and I don't have to lose myself in it and let it control me. I know where it comes from; I can let it be. And even if such awareness eludes her, going to someone else and getting another perspective might help. Is it impossible to imagine her and Roseanne, at some later date, talking and laughing about the whole sequence of April's envious thoughts?

Ted, by contrast, who stole from his friend Sheldon and could never really speak about it, seemed to become so overwhelmed by his envy that he lost contact with every other aspect of himself. He seemed to succumb to a kind of psychosis where nothing existed of Sheldon but a Have, the Favored One, a man smug in his superiority and only pretending to care; while nothing existed of Ted himself but a small, neglected, disfavored child whose only recourse, whose only way to be a Have and to right the cruel imbalance, was to steal. It didn't have to end there. Anyone can lose himself and his connectedness and do bad things. Our paranoia or outraged entitlement gets the better of us, we denounce, we undermine, we betray. But usually there's a way back to connection through repair. Bad things have a way of becoming good things. Relationships can be strengthened when they've been through the fire and fixed. People get to know and understand and care about each other at a deeper level. They see each other's pain. They feel each other's love. But Ted could not take that route back, apparently because his shame was too great. When he behaved horribly, in his mind, it confirmed his worst feelings about himself; it blackened his soul. He couldn't repair, couldn't reach out, couldn't deal at all, because of the jaws of awfulness waiting to devour him. That was perhaps the greatest tragedy of the terrible events with Sheldon. Ted could not forgive himself.

Joyce, too, has a hard time forgiving herself, for not being a good-enough daughter, for not being a good-enough therapy patient, for not getting better fast enough. On this occasion she is talking about her unstable, infantile, explosive father, "Captain Selfish," as one of her friends once called him. She is speaking bitterly about how he has always treated "us," meaning her and her adored, unavailable mother. I tell her I hear in this "Mommy and I are one." She knows what I mean, her obsessive embrace with Mom that has so preoccupied her and kept her separate from the people who care about her. She looks downcast and says she doesn't know how to separate. I ask, Does she want to? The only way she can imagine it, she says, is with a feeling of bitter defeat, that she has lost every battle—for her mother's love, for her father's love, to save her mother from her father. How can she separate like this? Of course, bitter defeat is no separation at all; it's just embroilment by another name. But no matter, she has answered the question: She does not want to separate. At least not for now. And yet, obviously, in some way, she also does, and she has begun the process. For we never could have spoken like this before.

A FRIEND, a fellow psychologist, at the end of a long conversation about the role of forgiving and not forgiving in her life, says, "The hardest thing for me is forgiving myself. I think that forgiving others has been hard, really hard, I mean significant others, but forgiving myself, I find that to be the real challenge."

I asked her if there was anything in particular she couldn't forgive. "Not being the mother that I would have wanted, the ideal mother. It's so hard to accept that I have my definite limitations as a mother, that who I would have wanted to be is not who I am, and that there will be consequences for those limitations. And I'll have to live with the results of that when my kids grow up. I suspect if I live until ninety-two, I'll be working on that. It's not like there's an end-point in sight."

I told her I thought I heard something forgiving toward herself in what she was saying. She was surprised. I said, "Because you're not shooting yourself over the fact that you're not entirely cured of your self-hatreds. There's some self-acceptance in that. You know, I'm perfectionistic, I have a hard time forgiving myself about certain things. I hate myself and it's unfair, but that, too, is part of the struggle and it doesn't have to get in the way of my feeling that, overall, I have a good life."

"Right, right!" she said. "That's so true. I do feel some easing up on myself about that."

Not forgiving ourselves, not forgiving others, not forgiving, even when the whole world thinks we should, is a part of who we are. It is as natural to us as our defenses, our repression, our dissociation, our denial. No one is able to look at himself whole. No one is so evolved as to deal creatively with every loss and insult. No one is free from illusions about himself, positive and negative. No one is immune to the joys of victimhood and revenge. We all have this in us. We are all enmeshed to some degree in our inner dramas and the unimaginable passions and loyalties they represent, which hold sway over us in ways that not even we can know. If we can see some of this in ourselves, accept it, be concerned about it, talk about it, it is less likely to control or overwhelm us. We will have a better chance to stay connected, to expand our zone of connection, to dissolve whatever scar tissue we can from a life of hurt and conflict, and move on to the goodness of love.

ACKNOWLEDGMENTS

THIS BOOK HAS BEEN A LONG AND SOMETIMES ARDUOUS JOUR-
ney, and I cannot imagine having written it without the aid and comfort
of friends and colleagues. I am particularly grateful to Richard Billow, a
constant source of inspiration and encouragement, who will see his in-
fluence in every chapter; Beka Nanić, who read each chapter as it was being written and warmly supported my first good feelings about the
unfolding work; Katherine Coker for reading, and in some cases reread-
ing, the manuscript and for her generous feedback and thoughtful advice; Lewis Aron, Philip Bromberg, and Lucy Steig for their serious
consideration of the text and for encouraging me in this project; and,
not least of all, Didi Goldenhar, who provided invaluable editorial assis-
tance at the final hour.

For sharing their own experiences in the realm of forgiveness and
grudge, I owe a special thanks to Azim Khamisa, Fred Wright, Jenny
Cook, Phyllis Herfield, Dianne Lange, Robert Weinstein, Hettie Frank,
Jon Koslow, Emily Kelting, Warren Spielberg, Katherine Coker, Nita
Lutwak, Spyros Orfanos, Jeff Mermelstein, Annie Gow, Terry Baum,
and Ken d'Oronzio. Their thoughts, their openness, and their generosity immeasurably enriched the book.

I would also like to thank Fred Wright, Phyllis Wright, Warren
Spielberg, Jeff Mermelstein, Lee Solomon, and Sharon Bergner for read-

ing parts of the manuscript and offering valuable feedback and support, and to thank as well Wendy and Ken Stuart, Beka Nanić, Lucy Steig, and Leonard Barkin for their help with the title.

I want to thank, too, Amy Gross, who first suggested I write on forgiveness for *Mirabella* magazine; my agent, Kris Dahl (when Kris says sign, we sign), and her fine assistant, Sean Desmond; Betsy Lerner, who asked me to write a book on forgiveness and acquired it for Doubleday; as well as the rest of the Doubleday team, including my editors Jennifer Griffin and Amy Scheibe; Bill Thomas; Frances Jones; Ann T. Keene; Ashwini Jambotkar; Mauna Eichner; and Chris Litman, who managed all the hectic traffic in the final months.

In the past, before joining their ranks, when I noticed psychologist/authors acknowledging their patients on occasions like this, I wondered whether their patients' help could have been so meaningful. I no longer wonder. Without my patients, their efforts, their intelligence, their courage, this book could not have been possible, and I want to take this opportunity to thank them.

INDEX